the veresov

by Nigel Davies

EVERYMAN CHESS

Gloucester Publishers plc   www.everymanchess.com

First published in 2003 by Gloucester Publishers plc (formerly Everyman Publishers plc), Gloucester Mansions, 140A Shaftesbury Avenue, London WC2H 8HD

British Library Cataloguing-in-Publication Data
A catalogue record for this book is available from the British Library.

ISBN 1 85744 335 7

Distributed in North America by The Globe Pequot Press, P.O Box 480, 246 Goose Lane, Guilford, CT 06437-0480.

All other sales enquiries should be directed to Everyman Chess, Gloucester Publishers plc, Gloucester Mansions, 140A Shaftesbury Avenue, London WC2H 8HD
tel: 020 7539 7600 fax: 020 7379 4060
email: info@everymanchess.com
website: www.everymanchess.com

To Louise & Sam

EVERYMAN CHESS SERIES (formerly Cadogan Chess)
Chief advisor: Garry Kasparov
Commissioning editor: Byron Jacobs

Typeset and edited by First Rank Publishing, Brighton.
Cover design by Horatio Monteverde.
Production by Navigator Guides.
Printed and bound in Great Britain by Biddles Ltd.

CONTENTS

1 d4 ♘f6 2 ♘c3 d5 3 ♗g5

Other Variations

BIBILIOGRAPHY

Books

The Chameleon Chess Repertoire, Gufeld & Stetsko (Thinkers Press 1999)
Richter Veresov System, Adams (The Chess Player 1987)
Queen's Pawn: Veresov System, Bellin (Batsford 1983)
ECO D, 2nd Edition (Sahovski Informator 1977)
ECO Busted, Hays & Hall (Hays Publishing 1993)
Meeting 1 d4, Aagaard & Lund (Everyman Chess 2002)
Beating the Anti-King's Indians, Gallagher (Batsford 1996)

Periodicals, Magazines and Websites

Chess Informators 1-86
MegaBase 2003
TWIC 1-446
Chesspublishing.com web site
Tigerchess Yahoo Group

INTRODUCTION

The Veresov is a little played opening that is ideal for creative, aggressive players. As early as the second move White dares to be different by developing his knight to c3, and in so doing he contravenes the conventional wisdom about Queen's Pawn Openings which states that you must never obstruct your c-pawn. In fact White has a far more ambitious idea in mind; he wants to play for e2-e4.

The first Grandmaster to use this opening regularly in tournaments was Saviely Tartakower, but he was certainly not to be the last. Over the years many great players have enriched it with their games and ideas, including David Bronstein, Mikhail Tal, Boris Spassky, Bent Larsen, Lev Alburt and Kurt Richter. Yet it is Gavril Veresov who has contributed most to the theory of this opening, having played it week in and week out during his heyday in the 1950s and 60s. It is therefore fitting that it carries his name.

My first contact with the Veresov Opening came when I was a teenager and read a 1975 article in the magazine *Chess*. The author, Robert Bellin, wrote 'The Veresov is young and still molten, the crust of definite variations has yet to form. *You* can participate in the making of a new opening – if you try.' Being young and still molten myself, this sounded pretty good, and during my teenage years I played the Veresov regularly. It turned out that many other British amateurs had the same idea and this opening experienced an explosion of popularity in club and county games.

Since that time interest dwindled away with many of the Veresov specialists moving on to pastures new or disappearing from the chess scene altogether. Books have been written showing what are supposed to be effective answers for Black. Yet the Veresov is alive and well with the supposed 'antidotes' having been directed only at the traditional lines such as 3...♘bd7 4 f3 or 3...♘bd7 4 ♘f3. Having examined the evidence I believe that 3...♘bd7 is by no means as good as some books have made out, with 4 ♕d2!? (the ultra-violent approach), 4 ♘f3 (Veresov's own favourite) and 4 e3 (my personal recommendation) being quite dangerous for Black.

It's not just in the 3...♘bd7 lines that I've found myself disagreeing with the experts; it seems to me that just about every variation of the Veresov has been misanalysed and/or misassessed. This presents a wonderful opportunity for practical players to surprise and outfox their opponents. I'm not in the least bit surprised that the Veresov has recently attracted the attention of the Swedish GM Jonny Hector and the up-and-coming Russian superstar Alexander Morozevich. Morozevich in particular seems to revel in the complex and original positions that the Veresov offers.

Because of the uncharted nature of the Veresov I haven't attempted to pin down the 'theory' and 'main lines' on the basis of a handful of obscure games. Instead I've written this book as an exploratory guide, saying what I think is happening and what White's most promising plans are. Accordingly you will find a lot of my own suggestions and ideas which I've worked out in conjunction with *Fritz 8* as an analysis partner. Fritz has been very good at checking tactics and some of the sharp variations, though I have frequently had to lead it by the hand in positions where strategy predominates or a material imbalance exists.

In order to provide a complete repertoire I have suggested an option for White against moves which transpose into other openings. Thus in Chapter 8 you'll find my suggested method of dealing with 3...e6, which normally transposes to a French Defence. In Chapter 9 I've given some lines against 1 d4 d5 2 ♘c3 e6, 2...f5 and 2...c6, whilst in Chapter 10 I'll show you some things you can play against 1 d4 ♘f6 2 ♘c3 c5, 2...d6, 2...g6 and 2...e6. In these three chapters I've 'doctored' the early move order of games to show how they arise from a Veresov. My aim was to lend greater clarity to the material.

Learning a new opening should be a gradual process through which you get used to the positions before using them in serious games. The way I suggest you do this is by following the steps below:

1) *Familiarise* yourself with the basic pattern of play by playing through the games at speed. At this stage you should ignore the notes and sub-variations.

2) *Play* these lines in quick games at your local club or on the internet (www.freechess.org or www.chessclub.com).

3) *Look* up the lines that occurred in your games and cross-check your play against my own thoughts on these variations.

4) *Repeat* steps 2 and 3 for a month or two.

5) *Study* the book more carefully, working from cover to cover and making notes about any points of interest. Analyse the points of interest.

6) *Adopt* your new weapon in competitive games and matches.

7) *Analyse* your competitive games to establish what was happened and whether either side could improve.

I hope you enjoy this voyage through the uncharted waters of the Veresov Opening. I have certainly found this to be a fascinating subject to think and write about and after a 30 year hiatus I have started playing the Veresov again in a few games on the internet.

If you have any suggestions, comments or recommendations you might like to discuss them with me at the Tigerchess Yahoo Group. To enrol for this discussion group please go to my home page at http://www.tigerchess.com and enter your email address in the form provided. I look forward to meeting you and hearing about your Veresov triumphs!

Nigel Davies,
Southport,
July 2003

CHAPTER ONE

3...♘bd7 4 f3

1 d4 ♘f6 2 ♘c3 d5 3 ♗g5 ♘bd7 4 f3

The move 3...♘bd7 has been almost universally recommended as the most solid option for Black. He develops a piece, avoids the doubling of the f-pawns with 4 ♗xf6 and prepares ...c7-c5. On the other hand the knight is not as actively placed on d7 as it would be on c6. It also blocks in the light-squared bishop, which might be well placed on f5.

White's main line against 3...♘bd7 has traditionally been 4 f3 which has the clear aim of building a broad pawn centre with e2-e4. Yet this move has a somewhat extravagant look about it as White is doing very little for his development and is weakening dark squares such as e3. And in fact Black can exploit these factors by launching an energetic counter-attack in the centre.

Games 1-3 show Black's traditional strategy of ...c7-c6 followed by bringing the queen out to a5 or b6. The 6...e5!? of Rossetto-Gufeld already looked quite attractive for Black and 10...♗a3! will send White scurrying for earlier improvements. He should probably investigate the speculative 7 ♘f3, but I, for one, don't trust it for White. Nor am I too convinced by Morozevich's pawn sac in Game 2 (6...♕b6 7 ♘f3) and even the 6...♕a5 of Adam-Muller leaves me sceptical.

If I had to play 4 f3 then I would certainly meet 4...c6 with 5 ♕d2, transposing to Chapter 2.

Besides 4...c6, Black has another promising line in 4...c5, which is covered in Games 4-8. White's most popular reply to this has been 5 e4!?, after which I suggest that White meets 5...dxe4 with 6 d5!? (Kuijf-Hoeksma) rather than 6 fxe4 (Rajna-Vogt). This looks quite dangerous for Black, so he's probably well advised to play 5...cxd4 instead. I can't say that I'm particularly attracted by either of White's options in that position, 6 ♕xd4 e5 7 ♕a4 d4 looking preferable for Black (though complex) in Bellon Lopez-Keene, whilst 6 ♗xf6 looks distinctly dodgy after 6...♘xf6 (Ranniku-Bulinova; see the note to Black's 6th move). The 5 dxc5 of Wockenfuss-Timman is an attempt to cast doubt on 4...c5, but several authors have had a lot of fun showing the strength of Black's position after 5...♕a5. They're not wrong about this being quite good for Black, although the simple 5...e6 might be even better.

If Black has a more nervous disposition he might be disinclined to enter the complexities of 4...c6 or 4...c5, even though these seem favourable for him. However, the slow 4...e6 of Albburt-Kapengut and 4...h6 of Czerniak-Hamann do not seem as logical because White manages to erect his pawn centre. Nonetheless, these don't seem too bad for Black either.

Game 1
Rossetto-Gufeld
Camaguey 1974

1 d4 ♘f6 2 ♘c3 d5 3 ♗g5 ♘bd7 4 f3

A very logical move which has the clear aim of expanding in the centre with e2-e4. The drawback is that this costs some time, which Black can try to exploit by reacting energetically.

4...c6

Protecting the d-pawn and freeing a path for Black's queen to come out to b6 or a5. The alternatives are 4...c5, 4...e6 and 4...h6.

5 e4

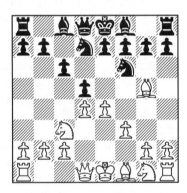

The sharpest continuation, but Black seems to obtain excellent counterplay. 5 ♕d2 transposes to the line 4 ♕d2 c6 5 f3, which is examined in the next chapter (De Souza Haro-Vescovi).

5...dxe4 6 fxe4

White has also tried the Blackmar-Diemer style 6 ♕d2, after which 6...♕a5 7 fxe4 e5 transposes to the note to White's 7th move in the Chapter 2 game, De Souza Haro-Vescovi. Black can also simply take the pawn – for example 6...exf3 7 ♘xf3 ♕a5 8 0-0-0?! e6 was the continuation of David-Ribeiro, Linares 1995, when White could find nothing

better than 9 a3 ♘d5 10 ♘e4, entering an endgame a pawn down. 8 ♗d3 is probably better, but White will be struggling to find compensation against an accurate defence.

6...e5!?

Black, in turn, plays the most trenchant continuation, counter-attacking on the central dark squares. But this is not the only move... For 6...♕b6 see Morozevich-Lazarev, whilst 6...♕a5 is examined in Adam-Muller.

7 dxe5

White has also tried swift development with 7 ♘f3, though this doesn't look like anything special after 7...exd4 (7...h6 8 ♗h4 ♕b6 9 ♕d2 exd4 10 ♘xd4 ♗b4 11 0-0-0 0-0 was quite promising for Black in the game Zhang Pengxiang-Shipov, Internet Chess Club 2002) 8 ♕xd4 (8 ♘xd4 ♗b4 9 ♘f5 0-0 10 ♗d3 ♘e5 11 ♗xf6 ♕xf6 12 0-0 ♗xf5 13 ♖xf5 ♕e7 was good for Black in Schiller-Ligterink, Reykjavik 1986) 8...♕b6 9 ♕d2 (9 ♕xb6 axb6 10 e5 ♘g4 11 ♗f4 was played in Berges-Delaunay, Angers 2001 and now 11...♖a5 renders e5 indefensible, rather than 11...♗b4 as played in the game) 9...♕xb2 10 ♖b1 ♕a3 11 e5 ♘d5 (11...♘g4) 12 ♘xd5 cxd5 13 ♗b5!? (White is attempting to tie Black down but the simple 13 ♕xd5 seems good; after 13...♗b4+ 14 ♔f2 ♗c5+ 15 ♔g3 White's king reaches a safe position and his pieces are very active) 13...♗c5 (13...a6 14 ♗xd7+ ♗xd7 15 ♖xb7 ♗e6 was the more solid option, with a fairly equal game) 14 ♕xd5 0-0!? (sacrificing a piece to get his king safe and obtain a dangerous passed a-pawn) 15 ♗xd7 ♗xd7 16 ♕xd7 ♕xa2 17 ♕d1 h6 18 ♗h4 a5 19 ♖a1 ♕b2 20 ♖b1 ♕a2 21 ♔e2?? (White should probably take a draw with 21 ♖a1) 21...g5 22 ♗f2 ♖ad8 0-1, Zhang Pengxiang-Benjamin, Cap d'Agde 2000. White's resignation seems somewhat overly prompt as after 22...♖ad8 23 ♘d2 (23 ♘d4 ♖fe8) 23...♗b4 24 ♖xb4 he can still fight on.

7...♕a5!?

This is the standard move, although Black

can also play 7...♞xe5. The game De Souza Haro-Tsuboi, Brasilia 2000 continued 8 ♕xd8+ ♚xd8 9 ♞f3 ♝d6 10 ♝e2 ♚c7 11 0-0-0 and now 11...♞fg4 (Davies) would have been slightly better for Black. In the game he played 11...♞fd7, which was sound enough but less incisive.

8 ♝xf6

Intended as an improvement for White, but I still don't trust his position. The stem game in this line was Alburt-Tal, USSR Ch., Baku 1972 which went 8 exf6 ♕xg5 9 fxg7 ♝xg7 10 ♕d2 (10 ♞f3 ♕e3+ 11 ♝e2 ♝xc3+ 12 bxc3 ♕xc3+ 13 ♞d2 ♞e5 14 0-0 ♝e6 15 ♞f3 ♜d8 16 ♕e1 ♞xf3+ 17 ♝xf3 ♕xe1 18 ♜fxe1 ♜d2 19 ♜e2 ♜xe2 20 ♝xe2 ♚e7 21 ♚f2 ♜g8 22 h4 ♚d6 brought about a horrible endgame for White in Elina-Chiburdanidze, USSR 1976) 10...♕xd2+ 11 ♚xd2 ♞c5 12 ♝d3 ♝e6 13 ♞f3 (13 ♞ge2 0-0-0 14 ♜hf1 seems more solid to me) 13...0-0-0 14 ♚e2 b5 (another good move was 14...♜he8) 15 a3 a5 16 h3 (16 ♜hd1 ♜he8 17 ♚f2 ♝g4 looks good for Black) 16...♜he8 17 ♜hd1 f5 18 e5 (18 exf5 ♝xf5+ 19 ♚f2 ♝xd3 20 cxd3 ♞xd3+ wins the b2-pawn) 18...♞d7 19 ♜e1 ♝xe5 (19...♞xe5 was equally good) 20 ♚f2 ♝f6 21 ♜e3 ♞c5 22 ♜ae1 ♚d7 (and not 22...f4? in view of 23 ♜xe6! ♞xe6 24 ♝f5 ♚d7 25 ♞e4, winning material) 23 ♞xb5 f4 24 ♜e5 (24 ♜xe6 ♞xd3+ 25 cxd3 ♜xe6 is no improvement) 24...♞xd3+ 25 cxd3 cxb5 26 ♜xb5 ♜b8 27

♞e5+ ♚d6 28 ♜xa5 ♝h4+ 0-1.

The alternatives all look rather good for Black, for example 8 ♞f3 ♞xe4 9 ♝d2 ♞xd2 10 ♕xd2 ♝b4 11 0-0-0 0-0 12 a3 ♝xc3 13 ♕xc3 ♕xc3 14 bxc3, which was soon drawn in Sahovic-W.Schmidt, Vrnjacka Banja 1981, but Black must surely have what chances are going because of his healthier pawn structure. Both 8 ♕d2 and 8 ♝d2 are met by 8...♞xe5 when Black's nicely centralised knight leaves White struggling for equality.

8...gxf6 9 e6!?

Trying to contest the initiative. After 9 exf6 Black's best may be the simple 9...♞xf6 (9...♕b6 10 ♜b1 ♝c5 11 ♞h3 ♞e5 12 ♕d2 ♝xh3 13 ♞a4 ♕b4 14 ♞xc5 ♕xc5 15 b4 ♕b6 16 ♕c3 turned out to be better for White in Kohout-Koenig, Bayern 1995; after 9...♝a3 White defends with 10 ♕c1 ♞xf6 11 ♞ge2, and 9...♝b4 is well met by 10 ♕d4) 10 ♕d4 ♝g7 11 0-0-0 0-0 12 ♕d2 (12 ♞ge2 ♝e6, while 12 ♕a4? ♕xa4 13 ♞xa4 ♞xe4 was just very bad for White in Philippe-Kennefick, Haifa Olympiad 1976) and now Gallagher suggests that 12...♞xe4!? should be considered as after 13 ♞xe4 ♕xa2 14 ♕f4 ♕a1+ 15 ♚d2 ♕xb2 Black's a-pawn is very dangerous. 12...♝e6 is simpler and gives good play for the pawn.

9...fxe6 10 ♝c4

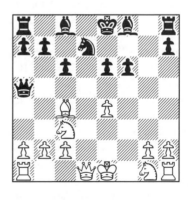

After 10 ♕g4?! Black's simplest reply is 10...♞e5 (10...♕g5 11 ♕xe6+ ♝e7 and

10...♘b6 have also been tried and seem fine, but the e5-square is tailor-made for Black's knight) 11 ♕h5+ ♔d8 and now the threat of ...♘d3+ makes White lose further time with his queen. Black's king, meanwhile, finds a nice post on c7.

10...♗b4?!

The move which appears in most of the books, but there may be two much stronger lines. At the Tigerchess Yahoo Group, Volker Jeschonnek pointed out that 10...♗a3! is very strong, a game of his from 1988 continuing 11 ♕b1 ♘c5 (11...♕g5 is also good) 12 ♗d3 (after 12 ♔f1 Jeschonnek gives 12...♕b4! 13 ♗b3 b6 which gives Black a winning attack) 12...♗xb2 13 ♕xb2 ♘a4 when Black won a pawn and later the game. It's also good to centralise Black's knight with 10...♘e5 11 ♕h5+ (11 ♗b3 ♗a3 12 ♕c1 ♕xc3+ gave Black a clearly advantageous endgame in Kostic-Todorovic, Nis 1995) 11...♔d7 12 0-0-0+ ♔c7 and White is threatened with both 13...♘xc4 and 13...♘d3+.

11 ♘ge2 ♘e5 12 ♗b3 ♖g8

As White gets compensation by sacrificing the g-pawn this might also not be Black's best. After 12...♕b6 13 a3 ♗xc3+ 14 ♘xc3 ♕e3+ 15 ♕e2 ♕xe2+ 16 ♘xe2 ♔e7 17 ♘f4 Black agreed a draw in what is probably a slightly better position in the game Gralka-Jagodzinski, Bydgoszcz 1978. Another possibility is 12...♗d7, after which Maksimovic-Chandler, Nis 1983 continued 13 ♕d2 c5 (the immediate 13...0-0-0 is also quite possible) 14 0-0-0 0-0-0 15 a3 ♗xc3 16 ♕xc3 ♕xc3 17 ♘xc3 ♖hg8 18 g3 b5!? and now 19 ♘xb5! ♗xb5 20 ♗xe6+ ♔c7 21 ♗xg8 held the balance.

13 a3! ♗xc3+

After 13...♗c5 White can play 14 ♘f4, when 14...♖g4 15 g3 is complex and double-edged.

14 ♘xc3 ♖xg2 15 ♕h5+ ♖g6 16 ♕h3!?

And not 16 ♕xh7 due to 16...♘f3+ 17 ♔f2 ♕g5 18 ♔xf3 ♖h6!.

16...♘g4 17 0-0-0!

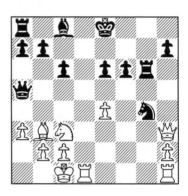

17...♘f2 18 ♕xh7 ♕g5+ 19 ♔b1 ♖g7 20 ♕h8+ ♖g8 21 ♕h7 ♖g7

21...♘xd1 22 ♖xd1 ♕g7 23 ♕h5+ ♕g6 24 ♕c5 is very risky for Black as his king is still in the centre.

22 ♕h8+ ♖g8 ½-½

Game 2
Morozevich-Lazarev
Alushta 1993

---

1 d4 ♘f6 2 ♘c3 d5 3 ♗g5 ♘bd7 4 f3 c6 5 e4 dxe4 6 fxe4 ♕b6!?

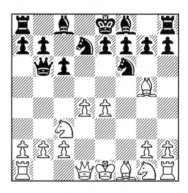

A murky alternative to the sharp 6...e5. Black hits the b2-pawn and prepares ...e7-e5.

7 ♘f3

This is no time to go passive. After 7 ♖b1 Black can play 7...e5! more effectively as 6...♕b6 is a far more useful move than 7

♖b1. White does have a couple of interesting alternatives at this point:

a) 7 e5 ♕xb2 8 ♗d2! (8 ♘a4 ♕b4+ 9 c3 ♕a5 10 ♗d3 ♘xe5! led to a win for Black in Ismail-Mikuev, Elista 1998) 8...♘d5 9 ♘xd5 cxd5 10 ♘f3 gives White compensation for the pawn (Davies).

b) 7 ♕d2 e5 8 ♘f3 exd4 9 ♘xd4 ♗b4 10 0-0-0 (10 ♘f5 0-0 11 ♗d3 ♖e8 also leaves White under pressure) 10...0-0 11 ♕e3 ♖e8 12 ♗d3 h6 13 ♗h4 ♘g4 14 ♕f4 ♕xd4 15 ♕xg4 ♘e5 16 ♕g3 ♗xc3 17 bxc3 ♕xc3 and Black soon won in Juglard-Kouatly, France 1991.

7...e5

Perhaps mindful of the identity of his opponent, Black decides against taking the pawn on b2 but, objectively speaking, White seems to have it all to prove: 7...♕xb2 8 ♗d2 e5 9 dxe5 (or 9 ♖b1 ♕a3 10 ♘xe5 ♘xe5 11 dxe5 ♘d7) 9...♘g4 10 ♖b1 ♕a3 11 e6 fxe6 does not leave White with a clear continuation of the attack and, meanwhile, Black has an extra pawn.

8 dxe5 ♘g4?

Still avoiding the capture on b2, which would transpose to the previous note after 8...♕xb2 9 ♗d2. Black's refusal to capture this pawn leaves White with an excellent home for his king on the queenside.

9 ♕d2 ♘dxe5 10 h3!

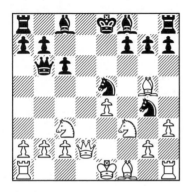

Forcing Black to exchange on f3, after which White obtains a useful pawn duo.

White already has a clear advantage.

10...♘xf3+ 11 gxf3 ♘e5 12 0-0-0

Threatening mate on d8.

12...♗e6 13 ♗e3 ♕a5?

Black had to try 13...♕c7, although after 14 f4 ♘c4 15 ♗xc4 ♗xc4 16 ♕d4 ♗a6 17 f5 he is tied up and very passive.

14 f4 ♘f3 15 ♕f2

Winning the knight. Black can only play for tricks, which are safely negotiated by the young Russian star.

15...♗b4 16 ♘b1 ♕xa2 17 ♕xf3 ♕a1 18 c3 ♗a5 19 ♗d3 ♗a2 20 ♕h5 0-0-0 21 ♕f5+ ♔b8 22 ♗xa7+ 1-0

After 22...♔xa7 23 ♕xa5+ ♔b8 24 ♗c2 Black is still a piece down and his queen is shut out of the game.

Game 3
Adam-Muller
Berlin 1989

---

1 d4 ♘f6 2 ♘c3 d5 3 ♗g5 ♘bd7 4 f3 c6 5 e4 dxe4 6 fxe4 ♕a5!?

Another alternative to 6...e5, hitting the bishop on g5 and threatening the e4-pawn. One of the main differences is that it does not prevent 7 e5 by White...

7 e5

This is White's critical reply, radically preventing ...e7-e5 and attacking the knight on f6. Two alternatives have been tried. 7 ♗d2 e5 8 d5 ♗c5 9 ♘h3 was played in Ranniku-

Chiburdanidze, Tbilisi 1974, and now 9...♕b4! (Fritz 8) wins a pawn for inadequate compensation. 7 ♕d2 is not very effective thanks to 7...e5!, which leads to the note to White's 7th move in de Souza Haro-Vescovi in Chapter 2.

7...♘e4

And not 7...♘xe5? because of 8 ♗xf6, winning a piece.

8 ♘f3

White continues developing at top speed, although Black has a fork trick which makes this line controversial. A couple of alternatives have been tried in this position, of which the second looks quite promising:

a) 8 ♗e3 ♘xc3 9 ♕d2 ♘b6 10 bxc3 ♗e6 11 ♗d3 (11 ♘f3 ♘c4 12 ♗xc4 ♗xc4 leaves White unable to castle) 11...♘c4 12 ♗xc4 ♗xc4 13 ♘e2 0-0-0 14 ♘c1 f6 was promising for Black in Klaman-Boleslavsky, USSR Ch., Leningrad 1947.

b) 8 ♗d2 ♘xd2 9 ♕xd2 leaves Black with the bishop pair but less space, and in fact looks rather promising for White. Miladinovic-Charbonneau, Montreal 2002, for example, continued 9...e6 10 ♘f3 ♗b4 (10...♗e7 11 ♗d3 c5 was played in Gasparian-Hefter, Fuerth 1999, and now I think that 12 d5 exd5 13 ♘xd5 looks very promising for White) 11 a3 c5 12 ♖b1 ♗xc3 13 bxc3 ♕xa3 14 ♗d3 and now 14...f5 should have been met by 15 0-0, threatening to trap Black's queen with 16 ♖a1. In the game White played 15 d5?! which could have been met by 15...♕a2!, forking b1 and d5.

8...♘xg5

Taking the opportunity to win a pawn and break up White's pawn centre, although, meanwhile, White gets a huge lead in development. The alternatives are as follows:

a) 8...♘xc3 9 bxc3 ♕xc3+ 10 ♗d2 gives White compensation for the pawn.

b) 8...♘b6 9 ♗d2 ♘xd2 10 ♕xd2 ♗f5 11 ♗d3 e6 12 0-0 g6 13 a3 ♘d7 14 b4 ♕c7 15 ♔h1 h6 16 ♘e4 0-0-0 17 ♕e2 ½-½, Bykhovsky-Ljavdansky, USSR Ch., Tallinn 1965.

c) 8...f6!? is also worth considering, though I think White gets good compensation for a pawn after 9 ♗d2 ♘xd2 10 ♕xd2 fxe5 11 0-0-0 etc.

9 ♘xg5 ♘xe5!

The point of Black's play, breaking up White's centre before he can consolidate. Meanwhile, however, White gets a huge lead in development...

10 dxe5 ♕xe5+ 11 ♘ce4 f6 12 ♗c4

Aiming at the sensitive f7-square.

12...fxg5 13 0-0 ♗e6?

Black hurries to exchange White's dangerous bishop but, in doing so, further weakens the light squares. 13...♗f5 is a much tougher nut to crack; Black blocks the f-file and is threatening to develop his pieces with 14...e6 or 14...g6, while 14 ♘xg5? is met by 14...♕e3+.

14 ♗xe6 ♕xe6 15 ♕f3

15 ♘xg5? ♕e3+ loses the knight.

15...h6 16 ♘d6+?!

Spectacular but quite unnecessary. Instead 16 ♘c5 is strong.

16...♔d7

The only move. Black loses his queen after either 16...exd6 17 ♖ae1 or 16...♕xd6 17 ♕f7+ ♔d8 18 ♖ad1.

17 ♘b5?!

Once again choosing the spectacular move. 17 ♘xb7 looks more effective as 17...♕c7 18 ♘c5 ♕d5 19 ♘e4 leaves Black rather hopelessly placed.

17...g4?

Losing immediately. 17...♖e8 18 ♖ae1 ♕g6 is far from clear.

18 ♖ad1+ ♔c8 19 ♕xf8+! ♖xf8 20 ♖xf8 mate

Game 4
Rajna-Vogt
Leipzig 1976

1 d4 ♘f6 2 ♘c3 d5 3 ♗g5 ♘bd7 4 f3 c5

Another interesting means of trying to exploit the dark side of 4 f3. Black immediately counter-attacks the d4-pawn.

5 e4!?

The sharpest response, stepping up the intensity of the battle for the centre. 5 dxc5 will be examined in Wockenfuss-Timman.

5...dxe4

For 5...cxd4 see Bellon Lopez-Keene.

6 fxe4

Although this has been White's most popular choice, the resulting positions look rather bad for him. I recommend that White sacrifices a pawn at this stage with 6 d5!?, which is covered in Kuijf-Hoeksema.

6...cxd4?!

This may well be okay for Black, but it appears that the main alternative is much stronger. In my opinion Black should play 6...♕a5 7 ♗xf6 (7 e5 ♘e4 is rather good for Black, a game Maksimovic-Janosevic, Bjelovar 1979 continuing 8 ♘f3 e6 9 d5 ♘xc3 10 bxc3 ♗e7 11 dxe6 ♘xe5 12 exf7+ ♘xf7 13 ♗d2 0-0 14 ♗c4 ♔h8 with much the better pawn structure) 7...exf6! (the most solid recapture – 7...♘xf6 8 e5 cxd4 9 ♕xd4 gave White excellent attacking chances in Juergens-Schrems, Germany 1990) 8 ♕h5?! (an ingenious way of preventing Black from capturing on d4 which has enjoyed the patronage of Alexander Morozevich, but Black has a massive improvement which puts this line out of business... 8 d5 would leave a gaping hole on e5, Barreto-Macagno, Mendoza 1985 leaving Black with an excellent

position after 8...a6 9 ♘f3 ♗d6 10 ♗e2 ♕c7) 8...g6 9 ♕d5 ♘b6! (Morozevich-Timoshenko, Alushta 1994 went 9...♗e7 10 ♗b5 0-0 11 ♗xd7 ♖d8 12 0-0-0 ♖xd7 ½-½, but the text is much stronger if followed up correctly) 10 ♗b5+? (White's best appears to be 10 ♕b3 cxd4 11 ♕b5+ ♕xb5 12 ♘xb5, after which 12...♗b4+ leaves him struggling for a draw) 10...♕xb5? (missing the opportunity to win White's queen with 10...♔e7! 11 ♕xc5+ ♔d8! etc.) 11 ♘xb5 ♘xd5 12 exd5 ♔d8 with an approximately equal endgame in Turner-Gross, Prague 1995. Does White have to play something as insipid as 8 ♘f3 here?

In Morejon Rodriguez-Penillas Mendez, Mondariz 1997 Black played 6...♕b6 and reached an excellent position after 7 ♗xf6 ♘xf6 8 ♗b5+ ♗d7 9 ♗xd7+ ♘xd7 10 ♘d5 ♕d8 11 dxc5 ♘xc5 12 ♕e2 a6 13 0-0-0 e6 14 ♘c3 ♕a5. While this may be of minor importance due to the apparent strength of 6...♕a5, it does reinforce the impression that 6 fxe4 leaves White fighting for equality.

7 ♕xd4

7...♕a5?!

After the game Vogt was highly critical of this move, but he might have been underestimating his defensive resources. Nevertheless it seems that Vogt's recommendation of 7...e5 8 ♕a4 ♗c5 is quite comfortable for Black (8...♗e7 may be less so after 9 ♗xf6!? ♗xf6 10 0-0-0 a6 11 ♘f3, threatening 12

♗b5, as in the game Muratov-Umansky, Moscow 1989), for example 9 0-0-0 0-0 10 ♘d5 (10 ♗b5 is answered by 10...♕b6, after which 11 ♗xd7 ♗xd7 12 ♖xd7 ♘xd7 13 ♕xd7 ♗xg1 leaves White the exchange down) 10...♗e7 11 ♘xf6+ (11 ♘xe7+ ♕xe7 12 ♘f3 ♕e6 also seems fine) 11...♗xf6 12 ♗e3 ♗g5 13 ♕a3 ♗xe3+ 14 ♕xe3 ♕a5 and Black was at least equal in Juergens-Schlaeger, Bundesliga 1990.

8 e5! e6

In his notes Vogt claimed that 8...♕xe5+ was poor in view of 9 ♕xe5 ♘xe5 10 ♘b5 but, on closer examination, this is not so clear. Black can defend with 10...♔d8, after which 11 ♗f4 (11 0-0-0+ ♗d7 was fine for Black in a game Svobodova-Gonzalez Garcia, Budapest 1995) 11...♘g6 12 ♗c7+ ♔d7 13 ♘f3 gives White what looks like good compensation for the pawn. Whether this can be defined as an advantage remains to be seen.

9 ♗b5 ♗b4

Here Vogt claimed that 9...♘d5 10 0-0-0 was also a clearly better for White, but this is probably nothing more than a slight edge in the endgame after 10...a6 11 ♗xd7+ ♗xd7 12 ♘xd5 exd5 13 ♕xd5 ♕xd5 14 ♖xd5. I think White's advantage in development and control of the d-file will slightly outweigh Black's bishop pair.

10 exf6 ♕xb5 11 fxg7 ♖g8 12 ♘f3

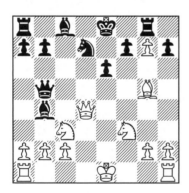

12...♕c5

A better try is 12...♕b6 when White must play 13 ♗h6 (the bishop is less potent here than on f6) to maintain the pressure. 13 ♕xb6 ♗xc3+ 14 bxc3 axb6 15 ♗h6 f6 followed by 16...♔f7 sees Black fighting back.

13 ♕xc5 ♘xc5 14 0-0-0 ♗d7 15 ♗f6

Putting Black in a horrible bind.

15...♗c6 16 ♘g5!? h6 17 ♘h7 ♘d7 18 ♖hf1 ♗xg2?!

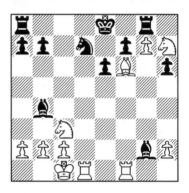

This should have lost on the spot. Vogt pointed out that Black had to play 18...♗e7, when 19 g3 ♘xf6 20 ♘xf6+ ♗xf6 21 ♖xf6 ♖xg7 22 ♖xh6 leaves him a pawn down but with some drawing chances.

19 ♖f4?

Missing an immediate win with 19 ♘b5! ♖c8 20 ♖f4 ♗c5 21 ♖c4 which threatens 22 ♖xc5 followed by 23 ♘d6 mate. And if White does not land a heavy blow soon, one starts to wonder about the position of his knight on h7...

19...♗c5 20 ♔b1 a6 21 ♖d3?!

A further slip after which White is struggling to draw. He should probably play 21 ♘e4, although this still looks promising for Black after 21...♗xe4 22 ♖xe4 ♗e7 due to White's badly placed knight and the passed centre pawns.

21...♗c6 22 ♘e4 ♗xe4 23 ♖xe4 ♗e7! 24 ♗d4 f6 25 ♖g3

And not 25 ♖xe6 because 25...♖xg7 26 ♘xf6+ ♘xf6 27 ♗xf6 ♖g1+ would result in mate.

25...♔f7 26 ♖eg4 e5 27 ♗c3 f5 28 ♖g6
♘f6 29 ♘xf6 ♗xf6 30 ♖xh6 ♖ae8

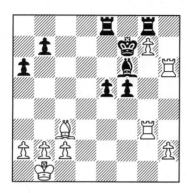

Black is now playing for the win.
30...♖xg7? would allow White to escape with
31 ♖xf6+! ♔xf6 32 ♗xe5+ ♔xe5 33 ♖xg7
with a drawish rook endgame.

**31 a4 ♖xg7 32 ♖xg7+ ♔xg7 33 ♖h3 f4
34 ♔c1 ♔g6 35 ♔d1 ♔f5 36 ♔e2 ♗g5
37 ♖h7 e4 38 h4**

In the event of 38 ♖xb7 there follows
38...f3+ 39 ♔f2 ♔g4 etc.

**38...♗e7 39 h5 f3+ 40 ♔f2 ♗c5+ 41
♔g3 ♗d6+ 42 ♔h4**

After 42 ♔f2 Black wins with 42...♗c5+
43 ♔g3 ♖g8+ 44 ♖g7 ♖xg7+ 45 ♗xg7 f2 46
♔g2 e3 47 ♔f1 ♔g4 etc.

**42...♗e5! 43 ♖xb7 ♗xc3 44 bxc3 e3 45
♔g3 e2 46 ♖f7+ ♔e6 0-1**

Game 5
H.Kuijf-Hoeksema
The Netherlands 1987

**1 d4 ♘f6 2 ♘c3 d5 3 ♗g5 ♘bd7 4 f3
c5!? 5 e4!?**

The most logical response, stepping up
the intensity of the battle for the centre. 5
dxc5 is featured in Wockenfuss-Timman.

5...dxe4

5...cxd4 is a popular alternative which is
examined within the game Bellon Lopez-
Keene.

6 d5!?

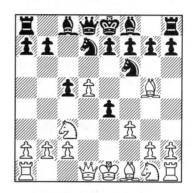

A move in the style of the Blackmar-
Diemer Gambit! White offers a pawn to
accelerate his development and drive a wedge
into Black's position. 6 dxc5 is well met by
6...♕a5.

6...exf3

Accepting the gambit. There are also a
couple of ways to decline White's offer:

a) 6...♕a5 7 ♕d2 (7 ♗xf6 exf6!) 7...a6
(7...exf3 8 ♘xf3 a6 9 0-0-0 b5 10 ♔b1 ♗b7
11 ♗xf6 ♘xf6 12 ♕e3 gave White good
compensation in Mertanen-Seppanen,
Finland 1992, and after 7...e3 8 ♗xe3 g6 9
0-0-0 ♗g7 10 ♗h6 0-0 11 h4 White's attack
looked the more dangerous in Johnsen-
Volodin, Prague 1996) 8 fxe4 b5 9 ♗xf6
♘xf6 10 e5 ♘g4 11 ♘f3 (11 ♕f4 is strongly
met by 11...♕b4! as in Ehrke-W.Hartmann,
Bad Neuenahr 1984) 11...g6 12 d6 ♗e6 was
approximately equal in Keller-Hartmann,
Krumbach 1981.

b) 6...e3 7 ♕d3!? (7 ♗xe3 ♘b6 8 ♗xc5
♘bxd5 was approximately equal in Stawski-
Allen, Gold Coast Open, Australia 1999)
7...g6 8 ♕xe3 ♗g7 9 0-0-0 0-0 10 h4 h5 11
g4 gave White a promising attack in
Duckworth-Stein, USA 1996.

c) 6...a6 seems well met by 7 ♕d2, intending 0-0-0.

7 ♘xf3

White can also play 7 ♕xf3, after which
7...g6 (7...h6 8 ♗h4 g5 9 ♗g3 a6 10 0-0-0
♗g7 11 d6 gave White a dangerous initiative

in Pasman-Lau, Skien 1979) 8 0-0-0 ♗g7 9 d6!? (I think this looks stronger than 9 ♗b5, e.g. 9...0-0 10 d6 ♘e5 11 dxe7 ♕xe7 12 ♘d5 ♘xd5 13 ♗xe7 – Keller-Till, Bayern 1999 – and now 13...♗h6+ 14 ♔b1 ♘xf3 15 ♗xf8 ♘d2+ would be at least equal) 9...0-0 10 dxe7 ♕xe7 11 ♘d5 gives a dangerous attack.

I also think that 7 ♕d2!? is worth considering as after 7...fxg2 8 ♕xg2 White has very rapid development and open lines.

7...g6

After 7...a6 I suggest that White plays 8 ♕e2!? intending 0-0-0, supporting the e4-square for his knight and preparing d5-d6 in some circumstances.

8 ♕d2

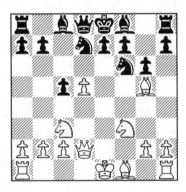

White's idea is simple: castle queenside and launch a devastating attack on the enemy king. Another interesting possibility is 8 a4 ♗g7 9 a5 which prevents Black's two main tries for counterplay with ...♘d7-b6 or ...a7-a6 and ...b7-b5. Heyken-Sosnicki, Pardubice 1996 continued 9...0-0 10 ♗c4 h6 11 ♗h4 ♘e8 12 ♕e2 g5 13 ♗g3 ♘d6 14 0-0 when it's not easy for Black to free his position.

8...♗g7 9 0-0-0

The immediate 9 ♗h6 is also possible.

9...0-0

9...h6 10 ♗f4 menaces d5-d6 and leaves Black temporarily unable to castle in view of the weakness of the h6-pawn.

10 ♗h6

It is always a key idea to eliminate Black's

dark-squared fianchettoed bishop as a prelude to a kingside pawn storm. Another possibility is 10 d6!? exd6 (10...e6!?) 11 ♕xd6 ♕b6 12 ♗b5 which left White with some pressure for the pawn in Mateuta-Istrate, Tusnad 1997.

10...♖e8 11 ♗xg7 ♔xg7 12 h4

Threatening to rip Black's kingside apart with 13 h5. Black's next move prevents this, but by doing so he creates a new weakness on g6.

12...h5 13 ♕g5 a6 14 ♗d3 b5 15 ♘e2 ♖h8

Black should have played 15...c4, after which White would continue his attack with 16 ♗f5 (the immediate 16 ♗xg6 does not work because of 16...fxg6 17 ♘f4 ♘f8) and after 16...♘b6 play 17 ♗e6 with strong threats.

16 ♘f4 ♖h6

The point of Black's previous move. Unfortunately he missed something...

17 ♗xg6! ♖xg6 18 ♕xg6+! 1-0

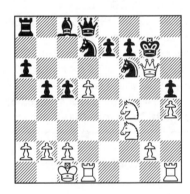

Black probably missed this when he played his 15th move. After 18...fxg6 19 ♘e6+ White wins material.

Game 6
Bellon Lopez-Keene
Dortmund 1980

1 ♘c3 d5 2 d4 ♘f6 3 ♗g5 ♘bd7 4 f3 c5 5 e4 cxd4

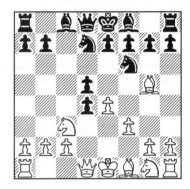

This is a major alternative to 5...dxe4, which was dealt with in previous games.

6 ♕xd4

And this is another parting of the ways. For 6 ♗xf6 see Ranniku-Bulinova.

6...e5 7 ♕a4

It's now too late to interpose the capture on f6. 7 ♗xf6 leaves White much worse after 7...exd4 8 ♗xd8 dxc3 9 ♗a5 cxb2 10 ♖b1 dxe4 thanks to his weak pawns.

7...d4

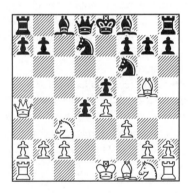

Black can also play 7...dxe4 but he would certainly have to be careful after 8 0-0-0!? (8 ♘xe4 ♗e7 9 ♗xf6 gxf6 brought about a complex position in Nieminen-Issakainen, Finland 1999) 8...♗e7 (8...exf3 9 ♘xf3, threatening 10 ♗b5, would be far too risky for Black) 9 ♗b5 a6 10 ♗xf6 ♗xf6 11 ♘xe4 ♗e7 12 ♘e2 ♖b8 13 ♗xd7+ ♗xd7 14 ♕b3 intending 15 ♘2c3 and 16 ♘d5.

8 ♘d5

The immediate 8 ♗xf6 is interesting, for example 8...♕xf6! (8...gxf6 9 ♘d5 ♗h6 10 ♕a3 left Black in trouble because of his pawn weaknesses in Steinberg-Stummer, Budapest 1993) 9 ♘d5 ♕d8 10 f4!? ♗c5 11 ♘f3 0-0 12 0-0-0 and now 12...exf4 (rather than 12...a6 13 fxe5 ♘xe5 14 ♘xd4 ♗g4, as played in Shteinberg-Anka, Balatonbereny 1993) 13 ♘xd4 ♘b6 is probably Black's best, when he has a clear advantage.

8...♗e7 9 ♘xe7

Securing the 'advantage' of the two bishops, although in this position they are not very effective. Once again White has tried capturing on f6, though once again with relatively little effect: Moreno Ruiz-Kolev, Vilanova 1993 went 9 ♗xf6 ♗xf6 10 ♕a3 (10 ♘e2 0-0 11 ♘c1 ♘b6 12 ♘xb6 ♕xb6 was better for Black in Alekseev-Akimov, Togliatty 2001, due to the potential pressure Black has on the c-file against the c2-pawn) 10...♗e7 11 ♘xe7 ♕xe7 12 ♕xe7+ ♔xe7 13 ♗c4 ♘b6 14 ♗b3 a5 and the pressure on the c-file left Black better in Moreno Ruiz-Kolev, Vilanova 1993.

9...♕xe7 10 ♘e2

White has also played 10 ♗d2 0-0 11 ♗b4 but this favours Black after 11...♘c5 12 ♕a3 b6 13 ♗xc5 bxc5 14 ♗d3 ♕c7 15 b3 ♗e6 (intending ...c5-c4), as in Zappas-Carvajal, Tel Aviv 1964.

10...h6 11 ♗d2 0-0 12 g4!?

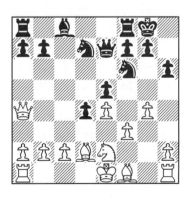

A risky but enterprising continuation which invites complications. After the sensible 12 ♘g3 Black is probably slightly better, for example H.Kuijf-Hoeksema, Holland 1996 continued 12...♘c5 13 ♕a3 ♗e6 14 ♗e2 ♖fc8 15 0-0 ♕d7 16 ♖fd1 ♕a4 with some pressure on the queenside.

12...♘b6?!

In his notes to the game GM Raymond Keene suggested 12...♘c5! 13 ♕a3 ♗xg4!? 14 fxg4 ♘fxe4, but this is far from clear after 15 ♗b4, for example 15...♘d3+ 16 cxd3 ♕h4+ 17 ♘g3 ♘xg3 18 ♗e7 with complex play.

13 ♕b4 ♕c7 14 ♘g3 ♘e8 15 c4 ♗e6 16 ♕a5 ♘d7 17 ♕a3 ♘d6!? 18 ♖c1?

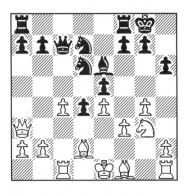

White should accept the exchange sacrifice offered by Black's previous move by playing 18 ♗b4! ♘c8 (not 18...♘xc4 19 ♖c1!) 19 ♗xf8 ♘xf8 although, admittedly, Black gets good compensation in the form of his passed d-pawn and the fact that his knight on f8 is en route for f4. Now Black gets his positional superiority at zero cost.

18...b6 19 h4 f6 20 ♘f5 ♘xf5 21 gxf5 ♗f7 22 b3 ♗h5 23 ♔f2 a5 24 ♗e2 ♘c5 25 ♖cg1 ♔h7 26 ♖g2 ♕b7 27 ♖hg1 ♖g8 28 ♖e1 ♖ad8 29 ♕c1? ♗xf3!

This neat tactic finishes matters quickly.

30 ♔xf3

Not 30 ♗xf3 in view of 30...♘d3+ etc.

30...♘xe4 31 ♗xh6 gxh6 32 ♖g6 ♖xg6 33 fxg6+ ♔g7 34 ♗d1 ♘c5+ 0-1

Game 7
Ranniku-Bulinova
USSR Women's Ch., Sochi 1971

1 ♘c3 d5 2 d4 ♘f6 3 ♗g5 ♘bd7 4 f3 c5 5 e4 cxd4 6 ♗xf6

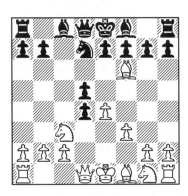

This zwischenzug aims to improve White's chances in comparison with 6 ♕xd4 e5 by denying Black the possibility of ...e7-e5.

6...gxf6?!

A controversial if not downright dubious decision. Black compromises his pawn structure for no particularly good reason and he should probably give preference to one of the alternatives:

a) 6...♘xf6 seems to be fine for Black after 7 ♕xd4 dxe4 8 ♗b5+ (after 8 ♕xd8+ ♔xd8 9 0-0-0+ ♔c7 10 ♗c4 e6 Black's king is safe and his bishop pair might become significant) 8...♗d7 9 0-0-0? (9 ♕e5 might be relatively best, after which Black played it safe with 9...♕b8 10 ♗xd7+ ♘xd7 11 ♕xe4 ♕e5 in G.Portisch-Szeberenyi, Hungary 2000, while 9...e6!? and 9...exf3 could be considered in this line) 9...♗xb5 10 ♘xb5 ♕xd4 11 ♖xd4 e5 (after 11...♖c8 12 ♘xa7 e5 White should play 13 ♘xc8 exd4 14 fxe4 ♘xe4 15 ♘f3 with approximate equality) 12 ♖c4 (12 ♘c7+ ♔e7 13 ♘d5+ is equal according to Alburt, presumably on the basis that the game is about to end in a draw by repetition, but I don't see why Black shouldn't take a pawn with 13...♔d6 14 ♖d1 exf3 etc.) 12...♖d8 13 fxe4 a6 14 ♘c7+ (14 ♘c3 b5 15 ♖c6 b4 16 ♘a4 ♘xe4 17 ♘f3 was Vogler-Muench, Germany 1996, and now 17...f6 18 ♖xa6 ♘c5 19 ♘xc5 ♗xc5 would have left Black with an edge because of his superior pawn structure) 14...♔d7 15 ♘f3 ♗d6 and White was struggling to rescue his errant knight in Vogler-Friedrich, Wiesbaden 1993.

b) 6...dxc3 7 ♗xc3 dxe4 8 fxe4 e6 also seems to be quite playable for Black, for example 9 ♘f3 (White has nothing special after other moves: 9 ♕f3 ♕h4+ 10 g3 ♕h6 was played in G.Portisch-Tunik, Budapest 1992, and 9 ♕h5 ♕b6 10 0-0-0 ♕c5 11 ♕g4 h5 appeared in Heyken-Chernyshov, Pardubice 1996, with good play for Black in both cases) 9...f6! 10 ♗c4 (10 ♕d2 is an alternative) 10...♕b6 11 ♘d4 ♘e5 12 ♗b5+ ♔f7 13 ♕e2 a6 14 ♗a4 ♗b4! 15 0-0 ♗c5 16 ♖ad1 ♖d8 17 ♕d2 ♘c4 18 ♕d3 ♖xd4! 19 ♗xd4 ♘xb2! 20 ♗e8+ (20 ♗xc5 ♕xc5+ 21 ♕d4 ♘xa4!) 20...♔xe8 21 ♗xc5 ♕xc5+ 22 ♕d4 ♘a4 and Black had a decisive material advantage in D.McDonald-Gallagher, Hastings 1991/92.

c) 6...exf6 7 ♘xd5 ♗c5 (Vogler-Doery, Wiesbaden 1990) might also be playable despite the weak d-pawn. Black has quick development and may be able to cause White some problems in view of the weaknesses on the dark squares.

7 ♕xd4 dxe4 8 0-0-0

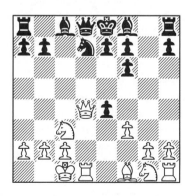

There is no particular hurry to recapture

the pawn. White's huge lead in development is becoming a serious problem.

8...♕b6

Hoping in vain for the exchange of queens. Treppner-Kyas, Bundesliga 1995 varied at this point with 8...a6, but then White still had massive pressure after 9 ♗c4 ♗h6+ 10 ♔b1 0-0 11 ♕xe4 e6 12 g4, threatening 13 ♗d3. I think that Black should develop his kingside with 8...♗g7, albeit with an unappealing position.

9 ♕xe4 ♘c5 10 ♕h4

Further hindering Black's development by preventing him from moving the e-pawn.

10...♗d7 11 ♗c4 ♘a4 12 ♘xa4 ♗xa4 13 ♘h3

Still pursuing his policy of fast development. 13 ♗xf7+ ♔xf7 14 ♕xa4 wins a pawn but allows Black to develop after 14...♗h6+.

13...♗b5 14 ♗b3 ♗g7 15 ♖he1 ♖d8

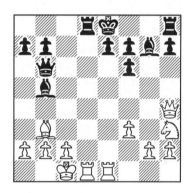

This loses, but it's hard to suggest a move for Black.

16 ♖xd8+ ♕xd8

After 16...♔xd8 17 ♗xf7 White threatens ♘h3-f4-e6.

17 ♕h5 1-0

White is hitting f5 and b5.

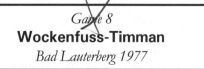

1 d4 ♘f6 2 ♘c3 d5 3 ♗g5 ♘bd7 4 f3 c5

5 dxc5!?

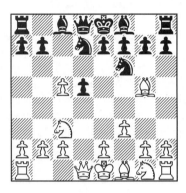

Less thematic than 5 e4 but not necessarily weaker. White wants to win a pawn.

5...♕a5

It could be that the simple 5...e6 is stronger, for example:

a) 6 b4 is met by 6...h6! 7 ♗h4 b6 8 c6 (8 e4 bxc5 9 exd5 cxb4 10 ♘e4 ♕a5 11 dxe6 fxe6 12 ♗d3 ♘d5 was complex but better for Black in Heyken-Chernikov, Ceske Budejovice 1995) 8...♘e5 9 a3 (after 9 b5 ♗b4 10 ♕d4 ♘c4 11 ♖b1 ♗c5 we see the point of driving White's bishop back to h4 – the e3 square is very weak) 9...♘xc6 10 e4 g5 11 ♗b5 ♗d7 12 exd5 ♘xd5 13 ♘xd5 gxh4 14 ♘e3 ♕f6 and Black had the initiative in Chiricuta-Kupreichik, Dresden 1969.

b) 6 e4 ♗xc5 7 exd5 (7 ♘h3 d4 8 ♘a4 ♕a5+ 9 c3 dxc3 10 ♘xc3 0-0 11 ♕a4 ♕xa4 12 ♘xa4 ♗d4 13 0-0-0 e5 left White struggling for equality in Heyken-Stripunsky, Ceske Budejovice 1995) 7...♕b6 8 ♘a4 (8 dxe6 ♗f2+ 9 ♔e2 ♗xg1 10 exd7+ ♗xd7 0-1 was Meijer-Vajda, Groningen 1997) 8...♕a5+ 9 c3 ♗xg1 10 ♖xg1 and now 10...b5 is a very risky way to win a piece, but the alternative 10...♘xd5 is much safer.

Perhaps the critical line is 6 b4 b6 7 e4.

6 ♗xf6 ♘xf6

6...exf6 7 a3 ♕xc5 8 ♕xd5 left Black with inadequate compensation for his pawn in Rossetto-Reshevsky, Mar del Plata 1966.

7 ♕d4

Black meets 7 e4 with 7...e6, once again emphasising rapid development.

7...e5!?

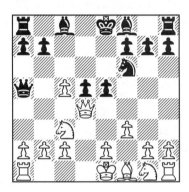

A very sharp move, giving up a pawn to gain more time for development and to prevent White from supporting his c5-pawn with b2-b4. A couple of alternatives have been tried:

a) 7...e6 8 b4 ♕d8 9 e4 ♗e7 10 ♗b5+ ♗d7 was played in Mestrovic-Janosevic, Sarajevo 1967, and now best is 11 ♗xd7+ (in the game White's 11 e5 was met by the nonchalant 11...0-0, after which 12 exf6 ♗xf6 13 ♕d2 ♗xb5 would have won back the piece with an immensely powerful pair of bishops) 11...♕xd7 12 ♖d1 and it's not easy for Black to find compensation for the pawn.

b) 7...♗d7 8 e3 (8 b4 ♕c7 9 ♘xd5 ♘xd5 10 ♕xd5 a5 gave Black very strong play in Rabinowitz-Shapiro, Philadelphia 1996) 8...♖c8 9 b4 ♕a3 10 ♖b1 b6 11 cxb6 axb6 12 ♔d2 e6 13 ♖b3 ♕a7 and Black had excellent compensation for the pawn in Espig-Vogt, Weimar 1968.

8 ♕xe5+ ♗e6 9 e4

White steps up the tension in the centre and threatens 10 ♗b5+ but his development isn't good enough for him to launch an attack. It might be better to play the quiet 9 e3, which gives White much more control of the dark squares. Khachian-Minasian, Yerevan 1994 continued 9...0-0-0 10 ♘ge2 ♗xc5 11 ♘d4 ♗d6 12 ♕g5 h6 13 ♕h4 g5 14 ♕f2

♗a3 15 ♘b3 and now in my view Black should have sacrificed his queen with 15...♗xb2, after which 16 ♘xa5 ♗xc3+ followed by 17...♗xa1 leaves him with good compensation for the queen. In the game he played 15...♕b4 and was worse after 16 bxa3 ♕xc3+ 17 ♕d2 ♕xd2+ 18 ♔xd2 followed by ♘b3-d4. Also good is 9...♗xc5 as in Przewoznik-Tomaszewski, Polish Ch. 1980, which saw Black recover his pawn after 10 ♗b5+ ♔f8 11 ♘ge2 a6 12 ♗d3 ♖e8 13 0-0 ♗d7 14 ♕g3 ♗xe3+ 15 ♔h1 g6 and now White's best is probably 16 ♘d1.

9...♗xc5!?

Another possibility is 9...0-0-0 but Timman's move is much crisper.

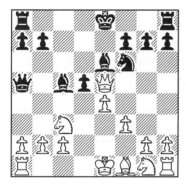

10 ♗b5+?!

This turns out badly but White's position looks unenviable in any case. The alternative is 10 0-0-0, when Gallagher gives some long and complex variations which look good for Black: 10...0-0 (in N.Cummings-Dive, New Zealand 1996 Black played the simpler 10...0-0-0 and after 11 ♗b5 a6 12 exd5 ♘xd5 13 ♘xd5 ♗xd5 14 c4 axb5 15 cxd5 ♕xa2 had strong threats such as 16...♖he8 and 16...b4) 11 exd5 ♗xd5 12 ♘xd5 (12 ♖xd5 ♘xd5 13 ♕xd5 ♖ad8 14 ♕b3 is answered by 14...♗xg1! 15 ♖xg1 ♕g5+ 16 ♔b1 ♕e3, winning on the spot) 12...♘xd5 13 ♖xd5 (13 ♕xd5 ♗e3+ 14 ♔b1 ♖ad8! etc.) 13...♕xa2 14 ♖xc5 ♕a1+ (after 14...♖fe8 White has 15 ♖a5) 15 ♔d2 ♖fe8 16 ♕g3 (Gallagher

doesn't mention 16 ♗d3 but Black's a-pawn will be dangerous after 16...♖xe5 17 ♖xe5 ♕xb2) 16...♕xf1 and Black has a continuing attack for the piece while White still can't develop his king's knight.

10...♔f8!

After 10...♔e7 Black's king is much more vulnerable and the bishop on e6 pinned.

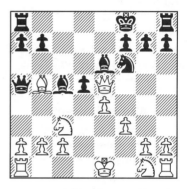

11 0-0-0

After 11 ♘ge2 a6 12 ♗d3 (or 12 ♗a4 dxe4) 12...dxe4 Black threatens 13...♗f2+. Black is also better after 11 exd5 ♘xd5 12 ♘ge2 a6 13 0-0-0 ♗e3+ 14 ♔b1 axb5 (and not 14...♘xc3+!? 15 ♘xc3 axb5 16 ♕xe3 b4 17 ♘e4 ♕xa2+ 18 ♔c1 because White's king runs away) 15 ♖xd5 ♗xd5 16 ♕xd5 b4 with an extra exchange.

11...♗e3+! 12 ♔b1 d4 13 ♕d6+

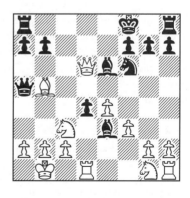

13 ♕c5+ is no better after 13...♔g8 14 ♘d5 ♗xd5 15 exd5 a6 etc.

13...♔g8 14 b4 ♕a3 15 ♘d5

White cannot play the alternative 15 ♖xd4 because of 15...♕c1 mate, and after 15 ♘ge2 there follows 15...dxc3! 16 ♘xc3 ♕xc3 17 ♕d8+ ♘e8 18 ♕xa8 ♕xb4+ 19 ♔a1 ♗d4+ 20 ♖xd4 ♕xd4+ 21 ♔b1 ♕b4+ and 22...♕xb5.

15...♘xd5 16 exd5 ♗f5 17 ♘e2

Neither of the lines 17 ♗d3 a5! nor 17 ♗c4 d3! 18 cxd3 ♗d4 19 ♖d2 ♕c3 would save White.

17...a5 18 ♘xd4 axb4 19 ♗c4 ♗xd4 20 ♖xd4 ♗xc2+! 21 ♔xc2 b3+ 0-1

Game 9

Alburt-Kapengut
USSR Ch., Baku 1972

1 d4 ♘f6 2 ♘c3 d5 3 ♗g5 ♘bd7 4 f3 e6

A solid move which steers the game along the lines of the French Defence. White has lost time with f2-f3 but Black's knight on d7 is poorly placed and takes away a square from the one on f6.

5 e4 ♗e7 6 ♕d2

Another possibility is 6 e5 ♘g8, e.g. 7 f4!? ♗xg5 8 fxg5 ♕xg5 9 ♘f3 ♕e3+ 10 ♗e2 (intending ♘b5) 10...a6 11 a4! ♘e7 12 ♖a3 ♕h6 13 0-0 ♘f5 14 ♖e1 0-0 15 ♗d3 which gave White attacking chances for the pawn in Lombard-Masic, Reggio Emilia 1971. A sensible way of playing it is 7 ♗xe7 ♘xe7 8 f4 with what is probably a slight edge for White

thanks to his space and better bishop.

6...c6 7 0-0-0 b5 8 e5 ♘g8 9 ♘h3 ♗b6 10 ♗d3 a5 11 f4 a4 12 ♖hf1 ♘c4 13 ♗xc4 bxc4 14 a3 ♕b6 15 ♘e2?!

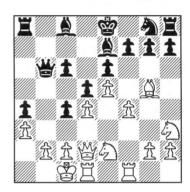

A stronger line of play is 15 ♗xe7 ♘xe7 16 ♘a2! when White can block the b-file with ♘a2-b4.

15...♖b8 16 ♕c3 h5 17 ♖de1 h4!

Threatening ...f7-f6.

18 f5?!

Attempting to take the initiative but this doesn't get enough compensation for the pawn. The simple 18 ♗xe7 is better.

18...exf5 19 ♘ef4 ♗e6 20 ♗xe7 ♘xe7 21 ♘g5 ♖h6

And not 21...♔d7? in view of 22 ♘xf7! ♗xf7 23 e6+ with a strong attack.

22 ♖d1 ♘c8 23 ♔b1 ♘a7 24 ♔a1 ♕d8 25 ♘gxe6 fxe6 26 ♘e2 ♘b5 27 ♕f3 ♕e7 28 ♔a2 ♔d7 29 ♖b1 ♖g6 30 h3 ♕g5 31 ♘f4 ♖h6 32 ♕e3 ♕e7 33 ♖fd1 ♖b7 34 ♕e1 ♕g5 35 ♕d2 ♕g3 36 ♘e2! ♕g6 37 ♘f4 ♕e8 38 ♕b4 ♕b8!?

This gives Black an attack, though it's not necessary to return the pawn. With 38...♕a8 Black maintains a big advantage.

39 ♕xa4 ♕f8 40 c3 ♖a7?

It would have been better to play 40...g5! 41 ♘e2 ♖a7 42 ♕b4 ♕a8, threatening 43...♖h8 followed by 44...♖b8.

41 ♕b4 ♕a8?!

Black finds it difficult to give up his dreams of mate. He should settle for

41...♕xb4! 42 cxb4 g5 (42...c3? 43 ♔b3 cxb2 44 a4! followed by ♘f4-d3-c5) 43 ♘e2 ♖h8 when Black has a slight edge in what is probably a drawish endgame.

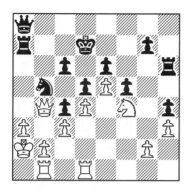

42 g4! g5

After 42...hxg3 there would follow 43 ♖g1 g5 44 ♖xg3! g4 (44...gxf4 45 ♖g7+ wins Black's queen) 45 hxg4 ♖h2 46 ♖g2 ♖xg2 47 ♘xg2 fxg4 48 ♘f4, threatening to bring the knight to f6 via h5.

43 gxf5!

And not 43 ♘h5 ♖a4 44 ♕c5 ♖a5 45 ♔a1 (45 ♕b4 c5! 46 dxc5 ♔c6 followed by 47...♖a4 wins the queen) 45...♔e8!, threatening 46...♘xa3.

43...gxf4 44 ♖g1 ♖h7 45 ♖g6!

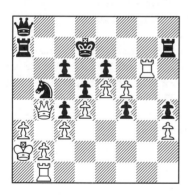

This last precise move secures the draw. After 45 f6 ♖a4 46 ♕c5 ♖a5 47 ♕b4 Black can once again trap White's queen with 47...c5 48 dxc5 ♔c6 etc.

45...♖a4 46 ♕c5 ♕a7 47 ♕f8 c5! 48 ♖c1! ♖xa3+ 49 bxa3 ♕xa3+ ½-½

Game 10
Czerniak-Hamann
Buenos Aires 1947

1 d4 ♘f6 2 ♘c3 d5 3 ♗g5 ♘bd7 4 f3 h6

5 ♗xf6!?

White gives up the bishop pair but gains time. 5 ♗h4 c5 is very similar to 4...c5 and possibly even better for Black than those lines because White's dark-squared bishop is further from the queenside. Play might continue 6 e4 (or 6 dxc5, when Black's best may be 6...e6 – as pointed out within the Wockenfuss-Timman game) 6...cxd4 7 ♗xf6 exf6?! (capturing with the knight or on c3 are quite playable with very similar play to that seen in the note to Black's sixth move in Ranniku-Bulinova) 8 ♕xd4 ♗c5 9 ♕xd5 ♗xg1 (9...♕b6 10 0-0-0 ♗xg1 11 ♗b5 ♗e3+ 12 ♔b1 0-0 13 ♗xd7 ♖d8 was suggested by Djukic and Illic, but 14 ♗xc8! ♖xd5 15 ♘xd5 looks good for White) 10 ♗c4 0-0 11 ♖xg1 and Black had inadequate compensation for his pawn in Maksimovic-Geller, Nis 1977.

A more interesting retreat of the bishop is 5 ♗f4 (threatening 6 ♘b5), when 5...c6 6 e4 e6 7 e5 ♘g8 left White ahead in development in Meijer-Fontaine, Brussels 2000. He should probably now play 8 ♗e3 (in the game he played the apparently less accurate 8 ♕d2) when 8...♘e7 9 f4 leaves White with a useful looking space advantage. It's not clear to me that Black has as much counterplay here as in the similar positions arising from the Classical French.

5...♘xf6 6 e4 dxe4?!

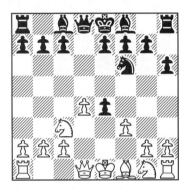

Unless Black can counter-attack White's pawn centre with either ...c7-c5 or ...e7-e5 he should not surrender the centre like this. A better continuation is 6...e6, e.g. 7 ♕d3 (7 e5 ♘d7 8 f4 c5 9 ♘f3 is also worth considering) 7...♗e7 8 0-0-0 0-0 9 f4 c5 10 dxc5!? ♗xc5 11 ♔b1?! (11 ♗e2 is safer) 11...♘g4 12 ♘h3 ♘e3 13 ♖e1 d4 14 ♘d1 ♕a5 15 ♗e2 ♖d8 16 g4 and now 16...e5 should be tried as 16...♗d7 17 g5 hxg5 18 ♘xg5 was very dangerous for Black in Sasu Ducsoara-Jovanovic, Banja Dvorovi 2000.

7 fxe4 c6 8 ♘f3 ♕a5 9 ♕d2 ♗e6 10 ♗d3

Steadily marshalling his forces behind the broad pawn centre.

10...g6 11 0-0 ♖d8 12 b4

Gaining time on the queen and ruling out a possible ...c6-c5.

12...♕c7

After 12...♕xb4 13 ♖ab1 ♕a5 14 ♖xb7 White wins his pawn back and has the initiative.

13 e5 ♘d7

Or 13...♘d5 14 ♘e4 and White is ready to eject Black's knight from d5 with 15 c4.

14 ♘e2 ♘b6 15 ♘f4 ♗g4?

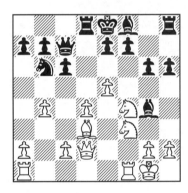

Given the strength of White's next move Black had to protect the bishop with 15...♕c8.

16 e6!

Shattering Black's defences.

16...♗xe6 17 ♘xe6 fxe6 18 ♘e5!

More accurate than the immediate capture on g6. White prevents his opponent's king from running away via d7.

18...♖d5

Black is forced to surrender material.

19 ♗xg6+ ♔d8 20 ♘f7+ ♔d7 21 ♘xh8 ♗g7 22 c3 ♗xh8 23 ♖f8 ♗f6 24 ♗e8+ ♔d6 25 ♕f4+ 1-0

After 25...e5 there follows 26 ♖xf6+ exf6 27 ♕xf6 mate.

Summary

The fact that 4 f3 has been White's main line has done much to damage the reputation of the Veresov. The play is tricky and intricate but if Black knows what he's doing his chances are rather promising.

After 4...c6 White could and should escape into Chapter 2 with 5 ♕d2, but 4...c5(!) deprives him of this option. I suppose that against a nervous opponent 4 f3 might be worth a try for its psychological value alone. But even Black's quiet options (4...e6 and 4...h6) don't look too bad.

1 d4 ♘f6 2 ♘c3 d5 3 ♗g5 ♘bd7 4 f3 *(D)* **c5**

    4...c6

        5 ♕d2 - *Game 12*

        5 e4 dxe4 6 fxe4 *(D)*

            6...e5 - *Game 1*; 6...♕b6 - *Game 2*; 6...♕a5 - *Game 3*

    4...e6 - *Game 9*

    4...h6 - *Game 10*

5 e4 *(D)*

    5 dxc5 - *Game 8*

5...dxe4

    5...cxd4

        6 ♕xd4 - *Game 6*; 6 ♗xf6 - *Game 7*

6 d5 - *Game 5*

    6 fxe4 - *Game 4*

4 f3

6 fxe4

5 e4

CHAPTER TWO

3...♘bd7:
4 ♕d2 and 4 ♕d3

1 d4 ♘f6 2 ♘c3 d5 3 ♗g5 ♘bd7

By moving his queen to d2 or d3 White prepares to castle queenside. Meanwhile he hasn't forgotten about playing for e2-e4, the usual follow up to 4 ♕d2 being f2-f3 and e2-e4. On d3 White's queen supports the e2-e4 advance directly and he might play this either with or without a preliminary ♘g1-f3. This means that the lines here can also be reached by transposition from 4 ♘f3.

In Game 11 Black meets White's 4 ♕d2 with 4...c5, which is well worth comparing with 4 f3 c5. As the position arising from the moves 4 f3 c6 5 ♕d2 can also be reached via 4 ♕d2 c6 5 f3 the choice between these two orders of moves is largely dependent on this comparison. I suspect that 4 ♕d2 is the more promising of the two, although my 'seat of the pants' judgement may not last the test of time.

Game 12 does in fact feature 4 ♕d2 c6 5 f3, but White plays the innocuous 7 ♘xe4. It looks more interesting to play 5 0-0-0!? or 6 0-0-0!?, although these can involve a sacrifice of White's a2-pawn. Khachian seems quite happy doing this and White does obtain attacking chances, but whether this is totally sound is another question entirely...

As usual 4...e6 is a sound reply and White can easily get into trouble if he doesn't react

energetically. In Game 13 (Smirnov-Yagupov) White was in trouble until his opponent lost the plot and finally produced an astonishing blunder. But 7 ♘f3 is a definite improvement for White.

4 ♕d3 makes a lot of sense, but White might be well advised to first play 4 ♘f3 and see Black's fourth move before deciding whether or not to commit his queen to this square. The reason is that this doesn't look very promising for White after either 4...h6 (Rossetto-Darga) or 4...e6 (Smyslov-Geller) but causes Black some problems after 4...g6 (Donev-Zlatilov) and 4...c6 (Alburt-Zilberstein, Miles-Watson and Ben Menachem-Boric).

Game 11
Reprintsev-Evelev
Geller Memorial, Moscow 1999

---

1 d4 ♘f6 2 ♘c3 d5 3 ♗g5 ♘bd7 4 ♕d2

An interesting move. Rather than play the immediate 4 f3 and get hit by a central counter-attack, White first develops his queen and prepares to castle long.

4...c5!?

A sharp response which steers the game into unknown territory. For 4...c6 see De Souza Haro-Vescovi, and for 4...e6 see Smirnov-Yagupov.

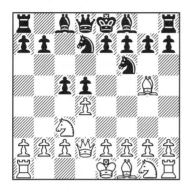

5 dxc5 e6 6 e4!?

It's worth noting that White has achieved this thematic breakthrough without having to prepare it with f2-f3.

6...dxe4 7 0-0-0

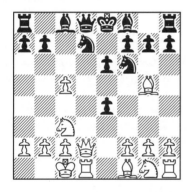

It was also worth considering 7 ♗b5!?, after which an independent possibility is 7...a6 (7...♗xc5 8 0-0-0 would lead us back to the game) 8 ♗xd7+ ♗xd7 9 0-0-0 ♗c6! 10 ♕f4 ♕b8 and White may have trouble equalising due to the strength of Black's light-squared bishop. Alternatively, after 9 ♗xf6 ♕xf6 10 0-0-0 Black can also play 10...♗c6, when 11 ♘xe4 ♕f5 12 ♘d6+?! ♗xd6 13 ♕xd6 loses material after 13...♕g5+ followed by capturing on g2.

7...♗xc5 8 ♗b5 0-0!

An excellent counter, temporarily parting with a piece for development.

9 ♗xf6 ♕xf6 10 ♘xe4

After 10 ♗xd7?! ♖d8 11 ♘xe4 ♕e5 12 ♘xc5 ♕xc5 Black recovers the piece with a slight edge. His bishop will be marginally stronger than White's knight.

10...♕e5! 11 ♕e2 ♘f6 12 ♘xc5 ♕xc5 13 ♘f3 b6

Black can also play 13...a6 14 ♗d3 ♗d7, which looks more or less equal.

14 ♕e5 ♘d5?!

This attempt to obtain dynamic play seems somewhat misguided. Black can equalise with either 14...♕xe5 15 ♘xe5 ♗b7 16 ♗c6 ♖ab8 17 ♖d4 ♖fc8 18 ♖hd1 ♔f8 or 14...♗b7 15 ♕xc5 bxc5 16 ♗e2 ♖fd8 followed by ...♔g8-f8-e7.

15 ♗d3 ♕xf2?!

With Black already behind in development it's very dangerous to grab pawns like this. He can still go solid with 15...♗b7 and meet 16 ♘g5 with 16...♘f6 etc.

16 ♖he1 ♕c5

Not 16...♕xg2?? 17 ♖g1 f6 18 ♕h5 etc.

17 ♗e4! ♗b7

Both 17...f6? 18 ♖xd5! exd5 19 ♕xd5+ and 17...♖d8? 18 ♗xd5 exd5 19 ♖xd5!! ♖xd5 20 ♕xd5! would win quickly for White, but Black could have considered 17...a6 and 17...h6.

18 ♘g5! ♔h8?

In a difficult position Black makes a mistake. Both 18...g6 and 18...h6 are refuted by 19 ♘xe6, but there's nothing clear after the cool 18...罝ac8.

19 ᐃxh7 罝fb8 20 ᐃxd5 ♔xh7

After 20...ᐃxd5 there follows 21 ♕h5 ♔g8 22 ᐃg5 ♕f2 23 罝f1 with a winning attack.

21 ♕e4+! f5 22 ♕h4+ 1-0

Black is mated after 22...♔g6 (or 22...♔g8 23 ᐃxe6+) 23 罝xe6+ etc.

Game 12

De Souza Haro-Vescovi

Sao Paulo Zonal 2001

---

1 d4 ᐃf6 2 ᐃc3 d5 3 ᐃg5 ᐃbd7 4 ♕d2 c6 5 f3

This position could also have arisen via 4 f3 c6 5 ♕d2. In Khachian-Vlad, Bucharest 1993, White tried 5 0-0-0!? which amounts to a gambit after 5...b5! 6 f3 ♕a5. The game reeled on with 7 e4 b4 8 ᐃb1 dxe4 (after 8...♕xa2 the idea is 9 e5 when Black's knight has to go back to g8) 9 ᐃc4 e6 and now White's best line may be 10 ᐃxf6!? ᐃxf6 11 ♕e2! exf3 12 ᐃxf3 with an improved version of the Blackmar-Diemer gambit as his king is safe and he can take pot-shots at Black's king on the e- and f-files. In the game he played 10 罝e1 and after 10...ᐃe7 11 h4 Black could have obtained a clear advantage with 11...c5!.

5...♕a5

Black can also interpose 5...h6, which is quite similar to 4 f3 h6. The differences are

that Black will now lose a tempo should he play ...c6-c5, and 6 ᐃf4 will not threaten 7 ᐃb5. Complex play resulted in Koneru-Pataki, Eger 2002 after 6 ᐃf4 ᐃh5 7 ᐃe3 e5 8 g4 ᐃhf6 9 ᐃf2 exd4 10 ᐃxd4 b5 11 0-0-0 b4 12 ᐃb1 ᐃe7, and 6 ᐃxf6 ᐃxf6 7 e4 e6 8 e5 ᐃd7 9 f4 c5 10 ᐃf3 brought about an unusual kind of French Defence in Maidla-Puranen, Vantaa 1993.

Consequently 6 ᐃh4 is more attractive now, e.g. 6...e6 7 0-0-0 b5 8 ♕e1:

a) 8...b4 9 ᐃb1 ♕a5 ended in a draw in Khachian-Milu, Bucharest 1995. I don't know what's happening in this position. Fritz likes Black, especially after a sacrifice of the a2-pawn, but computers tend to assess positions with a material imbalance quite poorly. Certainly Khachian was willing to repeat this in a later game so he evidently considers the position playable for White. And judging from his encounter with Vlad, he would probably sacrifice a pawn at this point with 10 e4 ♕xa2 11 e5 etc.

b) 8...♕a5 9 ♔b1 ᐃb6 10 e4 ᐃa4? (Khachian-Groszpeter, Cannes 1996) and White can win a pawn with 11 ᐃxd5!, so Black should play 10...ᐃb4 11 ᐃge2 ᐃc4 12 ᐃxf6 gxf6 13 罝d3 with a double-edged situation.

6 e4

I imagine that Khachian would play 6 0-0-0!? here with a murky position after 6...b5 7 ♕e1 b4 8 ᐃb1 ♕xa2 9 e4 etc.

6...dxe4

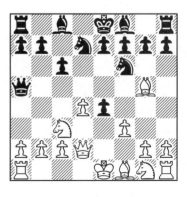

Here this is a good idea because Black can hit back in the centre with ...e7-e5. After the solid 6...e6 White can hope for an edge with 7 e5 ♘g8 8 ♗e3 thanks to his extra space.

7 ♘xe4

Playing for a draw. The thematic move is 7 fxe4 which can also arise after 4 f3 c6. Black should act in the centre with 7...e5!, e.g. 8 dxe5 ♘xe5 9 0-0-0 ♗e6 10 ♘f3 ♘fd7 11 a3 h6 12 ♗h4 ♗c5 13 ♘d4 0-0, Vooremaa-Bronstein, Tallinn 1981, and now 14 ♘xe6 (in the game 14 ♗e2 was played when 14...♖fe8 would have left Black with an edge) 14...fxe6 15 ♗e2 would have been fairly even.

8 ♗xf6 ♘xf6 9 dxe5 ♘g4 10 ♘f3 was played in Chernyshov-Rogic, Ohrid 2001 and now simply 10...♘xe5 is slightly better for Black in view of his two bishops and White's isolated e-pawn.

7...♕xd2+ 8 ♘xd2 e6

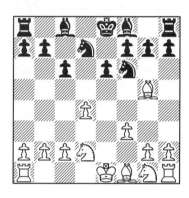

Black has a solid game and might even think about how to generate some winning chances. With this in mind he could consider 8...g6, when 9 ♗c4 ♗g7 10 ♘e2 0-0 11 0-0 c5 12 ♖fe1 a6 13 a4 b6 produced slightly less balanced play in Treppner-Dydyshko, Bundesliga 1994.

9 ♗d3 ♗e7 10 ♘e2 b6 11 0-0 ♗b7 12 c3 0-0 13 ♘e4 ♖fd8 14 ♖ad1

14 ♖fd1 looks slightly safer to me, freeing f1 for White's king.

14...♔f8 15 ♘xf6 ♘xf6 16 ♘g3?!

Almost imperceptibly White is giving his opponent chances. Here he should probably play 16 ♖fe1 with a likely draw.

16...c5 17 ♗xf6?!

White gets flustered and gives up his important dark-squared bishop but, in fairness, the position is no longer easy for him. After 17 dxc5 ♗xc5+ his king is forced into the corner; and 17 ♗e4 ♘xe4 18 ♗xe7+ ♔xe7 19 fxe4 cxd4 20 cxd4 ♖ac8 also leaves Black with some pressure.

17...gxf6 18 dxc5

White would like to initiate further exchanges with 18 ♗e4 but after 18...♗xe4 19 fxe4 cxd4 20 cxd4 ♖xd4! 21 ♖xd4 ♗c5 22 ♘e2 e5 he loses a pawn.

18...♗xc5+ 19 ♔h1 f5 20 ♗e2 ♔e7 21 ♖de1 f4! 22 ♘e4 ♗e3 23 ♖d1 f5

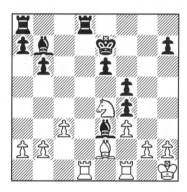

By now it has become clear that Black has a large advantage. His bishop on e3 is a thorn in White's flesh and his e-pawn is a candidate for promotion.

24 ♘g5 h6 25 ♘h3 ♖xd1

Black sees that after the exchange of rooks he can use his king to attack White's queen-side pawns. The immediate 25...e5 was also worth considering.

26 ♖xd1 ♖d8 27 ♖xd8 ♔xd8 28 g3 fxg3 29 hxg3 ♔e7 30 ♔g2 ♗c1 31 b3 ♗d2 32 c4 ♔d6 33 ♔f2 ♔c5

Another good move was 33...e5, e.g. 34 f4 (or 34 ♗d3 e4) 34...e4 35 g4 ♗c8 36 gxf5 ♗xf5 37 ♔g3 ♔c5 etc.

34 g4 fxg4 35 fxg4 ♗e4 36 ♗f3 ♗d3 37 ♘g1 ♗b1 38 ♗d1 ♗xa2 39 ♘f3 ♗f4 40 ♘e1 ♔d4 41 ♔f3 ♗d2 42 ♘c2+ ♔c3 43 ♘a3 a6 44 ♔e2 ♗c1 0-1

Game 13
Smirnov-Yagupov
Alushta 2002

---

1 d4 d5 2 ♘c3 ♘f6 3 ♗g5 ♘bd7 4 ♕d2 e6

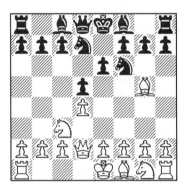

This sensible-looking move is a good answer.

5 0-0-0

In keeping with 4 ♕d2, White hoists the pirate flag. There are a number of alternatives, for example:

a) 5 e4!? dxe4 6 0-0-0 but in the game Sagalchik-Alburt, Parsipanny 2002 he found himself somewhat worse when he finally regained his pawn: 6...h6 7 ♗h4 ♗b4 8 ♘ge2 b6 9 a3 ♗e7 10 ♗xf6 ♘xf6 11 ♘g3 ♗b7 12 ♕e1 0-0 13 ♘gxe4 ♘xe4 14 ♘xe4 ♕d5 15 ♘c3 ♕g5+ and Black had a useful pair of bishops. Instead 6 f3 is interesting, with Loboda-Suetin, USSR Team Ch. 1975 seeing Black decline the sacrifice with 6...e3!? but having slightly the worse of it after 7 ♗xe3 ♗b4 8 a3 ♗xc3 9 bxc3 0-0 10 ♗d3 c5 11 ♘h3.

b) White can prepare e2-e4 with 5 f3 but after 5...c5 6 dxc5 ♗xc5 7 e4 dxe4 8 fxe4 h6 9 ♗e3 0-0 10 0-0-0 ♕a5 11 ♗d3 ♗b4 this

gave Black a good game in Smirnov-Zubarev, Alushta 2002.

c) 5 e3 seems inconsistent when combined with 4 ♕d2. It may be sound enough (especially if White castles short) but will certainly lack bite.

5...h6 6 ♗h4

I suggest that 6 ♗f4!? is worth considering, with the idea of 7 ♘b5.

6...c5 7 e3?!

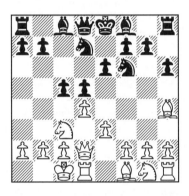

Abandoning the idea of e2-e4 in these lines seems like an admission of defeat. I suggest 7 ♘f3!? as being more promising – after 7...a6 White can play 8 e4! g5 (or 8...dxe4 9 ♘e5) 9 ♗g3 dxe4 10 ♘e5!? with the initiative.

7...a6 8 ♔b1 b5!

Black can get away with a delayed development as long as White cannot open up the position. Meanwhile he's taking a lot of space.

9 dxc5 ♗xc5 10 ♗d3 ♗b7 11 ♘f3 ♖c8

Black has a good game but 11...♗b4! looks even better. White will not find it easy to break the pin on his knight and it's very difficult for him to achieve the critical e2-e4 advance.

12 ♘e2

Evading 12...♗b4.

12...♗e7 13 ♗g3 ♘c5 14 ♘ed4 ♘fe4 15 ♕e1 ♘xg3 16 hxg3 ♗f6 17 ♘d2 ♕b6 18 ♘2b3 b4

Black should eliminate White's remaining

bishop with 18...♘xd3 with what must be an edge. Now things get very messy...

19 ♘xc5 ♖xc5 20 f4 a5 21 g4 a4 22 g5 hxg5??

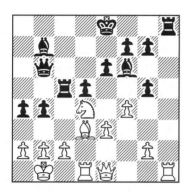

A truly horrific blunder by such a high rated player. It's difficult to imagine what was going through Black's mind. 22...♗e7 23 gxh6 gxh6 leaves a complex position in which both sides have chances.

23 ♖xh8+ 1-0

Game 14
Rossetto-Darga
Lugano Olympiad 1968

---

1 d4 ♘f6 2 ♘c3 d5 3 ♗g5 ♘bd7 4 ♕d3

Once again preparing to castle long, the queen also supporting the critical e2-e4 advance. There are some additional advantages of this move in that White's bishop might

drop back to d2 in some circumstances, while his queen may find useful employment along the third rank.

4...h6

GM Joe Gallagher has experimented with 4...c5!?, for example 5 ♘f3 cxd4 6 ♕xd4 e5 7 ♘xe5 ♗c5 8 ♕a4 ♕b6 9 0-0-0 d4 10 ♘c4 ♕e6 11 ♘b5 0-0 was P.Moore-Gallagher, Jersey 1984 and now 12 ♘xd4 ♗xd4 13 ♖xd4 and Black still has to demonstrate that he has enough for his pawns. In the game the greedy 12 ♘c7 ♕f5 13 ♗xf6 was played, giving Black excellent compensation for his small material investment after 13...b5! 14 ♘xb5 ♘xf6 etc.

5 e4 cxd4 6 ♕xd4 e5 7 ♕a4 d4 8 ♘d5 ♗e7 9 ♗xf6 ♗xf6 10 ♗b5 0-0 11 ♗xd7 ♗xd7 12 ♘xf6+ gxf6 13 ♕a3 ♖c8 14 0-0-0 ♖c6 gave Black an attack down the c-file in Richmond-Gallagher, Nottingham 1987.

5 ♗h4

White has also played 5 ♗f4 but then 5...c6 looks like a good reply there, too. 6 e4 leaves White with nothing after 6...dxe4 7 ♘xe4 ♘xe4 8 ♕xe4 ♘f6 9 ♕d3 ♕a5+ 10 ♗d2 ♕f5 etc. Thus Porper-Smirin, Tel Aviv 1991 continued 6 ♘f3 e6 and now White played the passive 7 a3 (7 e4 is admittedly well met by 7...♗b4) which allowed Black to assume the initiative after 7...b5 8 ♘e5 ♘xe5 9 ♗xe5 b4 10 axb4 ♗xb4 11 ♕g3 ♘e4 12 ♕xg7 ♖f8 13 ♗f4 ♕b6 etc.

5...c5!? was tried in Bellin-J.Nikolac, Eerbeek 1978, when I think White should have played the immediate 6 ♘b5, after which 6...c4 7 ♕d2 ♘e4 8 ♘c7+ ♕xc7 9 ♗xc7 ♘xd2 10 ♔xd2 ♘f6 11 f3 leads to an endgame in which his position looks preferable.

5...c6

The main alternative is 5...e6, which leads to a kind of Rubinstein French after 6 e4 dxe4 7 ♘xe4 ♗e7 8 ♘xf6+ (and not 8 0-0-0 ♘xe4 9 ♗xe7 ♘xf2 which won a pawn for Black in Lalev-Espig, Varna 1983), but one which is harmless for Black. Ansell-Whiteley, Newcastle-upon-Tyne 1995 continued

8...♗xf6 9 ♗xf6 ♘xf6 10 ♘f3 0-0 11 g3 b6 12 ♗g2 ♗b7 13 0-0 ♗e4 14 ♕e2 ♕d5 with complete equality.

Also playable is 5...b6 6 e4 dxe4 7 ♘xe4 ♗b7 (it's too late for 7...e6 because of 8 ♕f3! ♖b8 9 ♘xf6+ ♘xf6?! 10 ♗b5+ ♗d7 11 ♗xd7+ when Black has to play 11...♔xd7 or give up a pawn) 8 ♘xf6+ ♘xf6 9 ♗xf6 gxf6 10 0-0-0 e6 which was fine for Black in Khachian-Stripunsky, Pardubice 1996.

6 0-0-0?!

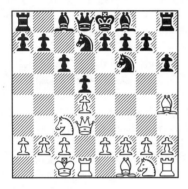

White's position is not very easy to play as two of his most natural moves leave him in trouble. Castling long turns out to be risky because of the speed of Black's counterplay on the queenside. He should be even more careful to avoid 6 e4??, which lost a piece after 6...♘xe4 7 ♘xe4 dxe4 8 ♕xe4 g5! 9 ♗g3 ♕a5+ 10 c3 f5! 11 ♕e2 f4 12 ♕h5+ ♔d8 13 ♗xf4 ♘f6 in Doljanin-Arsovic, Vrnjacka Banja 1999.

Relatively best is 6 ♘f3, e.g. 6...♕a5 7 ♘d2 e5 (Giannakoulopoulos-Dvoirys, Ano Liosia 2000 saw the preliminary 7...♕b6!?, but after 8 0-0-0 e5 9 dxe5 ♘xe5 10 ♕g3 ♘g6 11 ♗xf6 gxf6 12 e4 d4 13 ♘c4 ♕c5 White should have played 14 ♕d3 ♗g4 15 f3 with the better chances) 8 dxe5?! (I think White should take a look at 8 ♗xf6 ♘xf6 9 dxe5 ♘g4 10 ♕g3 with complex play) 8...♘xe5 9 ♕e3 ♘fg4 10 ♕d4 ♗c5 and White had serious problems in Ponomarev-Granda Zuniga, Kissimmee 1997.

6...e6 7 e4 ♕a5 8 ♘d2 ♗b4 was played in Panagiotopoulou-Kaza, Athens 2000 and now 9 e5 looks nice for White. After 6...g6 White must once again be careful to avoid 7 e4?!, e.g. 7...dxe4 8 ♘xe4 ♘xe4 9 ♕xe4 g5 10 ♗g3 ♕a5+ 11 c3 f5 12 ♕e6 f4 although, admittedly, White gets more compensation than with 6 e4. Karayannis-Tsichlis, Panormo 1998 continued 13 ♕g6+ ♔d8 14 h4 fxg3 15 hxg5 with some chances.

6...b5! 7 f3 b4 8 ♘b1

After 8 ♘a4 there follows 8...♕a5 9 ♕b3 ♗a6!, threatening 10...♗c4.

8...♕b6 9 e4 e6 10 e5 ♘h5 11 ♘h3 g5! 12 ♗f2 c5! 13 g4?

White should prevent Black's next with 13 dxc5, when 13...♗xc5 14 ♗xc5 ♘xc5 15 ♕d4 leaves White worse but still fighting.

13...c4 14 ♕e3 ♘f4!

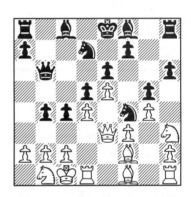

Not losing any time.

15 ♘xf4 gxf4 16 ♕xf4 ♗e7

Threatening 17...♗g5.

17 h4 ♕a5 18 ♗e1 ♕xa2 19 c3 b3 20 ♖h2 a5 21 ♖dd2 a4 22 g5 hxg5 23 hxg5 ♖xh2 24 ♕xh2 ♘f8 25 f4 ♕a1 26 f5 a3 0-1

1 d4 ♘f6 2 ♘c3 d5 3 ♗g5 ♘bd7 4 ♕d3 e6 5 e4

It does not make much sense delaying this move in favour of 5 ♘f3 but this position is significant because it can arise after 3...♘bd7 4 ♘f3 e6 5 ♕d3. One example is D.Trifunovic-Scherr, Frohnleiten 1999 which went 5...♗e7 6 0-0-0 ♘g4 7 ♗e3 ♘xe3 8 ♕xe3 c5 9 ♕d2 and now Black should have played 9...cxd4, when 10 ♘xd4 0-0 11 e4 can be met by 11...e5 12 ♘f3 (12 ♘f5?? ♗g5) 12...d4 with a territorial advantage. In the game he released the central tension with 9...c4, after which 10 e4 looked better for White.

5...dxe4

An interesting alternative is 5...♗b4!? 6 e5 h6, which steers play along the lines of the McCutcheon Variation of the French. Tests required!

6 ♘xe4 ♗e7 7 ♘xf6+

This looks like the only genuine attempt to eke something out of the position. After 7 ♗xf6 ♘xf6 8 0-0-0 ♘xe4 9 ♕xe4 ♕d5 Black had equalised in Myagmarsuren-J.Roose, Lugano 1968, and 7 ♘c3 0-0 8 ♘f3 c5 9 0-0-0 ♕a5 gave Black active counterplay in the game Ponomarev-Shipman, Los Angeles 2001.

7...♗xf6

The alternative is 7...♘xf6, which leads to much sharper play after 8 ♘f3 (8 0-0-0 ♕d5 forces White to exchange queens with 9 ♕b5+, which is quite harmless) 8...0-0 9 0-0-0!? (9 ♗e2 b6 10 0-0 is a quieter way of

playing it, trying to retain a modest space advantage) 9...c5 (9...b6 is quite possible here too) 10 dxc5 ♕a5 11 ♔b1. In Rodriguez Vargas-Cacho Reigadas, Spain 1993, White played 11 ♕b5 with the idea that 11...♕xa2 would be met by 12 ♗c4. But this looks quite good for Black after 12...a6 13 ♗xa2 axb5 etc.

8 ♗xf6 ♘xf6

Black does not find it easy to equalise after 8...♕xf6 9 ♘f3, for example 9...c5 10 0-0-0 cxd4 11 ♕xd4 ♕xd4 12 ♘xd4 a6 (12...♘f6 looks better as after 13 ♗b5+ Black can play the cold-blooded 13...♗d7 14 ♗xd7+ ♔xd7) 13 g3 b6 14 ♗g2 and Black was under pressure in Tolnai-Balogh, Budapest 2000. Hector-Koneru, Wijk aan Zee 2003 went 9...0-0 10 ♕e3 c5 11 0-0-0 b6 12 ♗b5 cxd4 13 ♖xd4 with an edge for White.

9 ♘f3 0-0 10 ♗e2 b6 11 0-0

11 0-0-0!? would be an altogether sharper interpretation of the position. Smyslov prefers to keep it simple and safe.

11...♗b7 12 ♖fd1 ♗e4 13 ♕b3 ♕b8!? 14 ♘d2 ♗d5 15 c4 ♗b7 16 ♘f1 ♖d8 17 ♘e3 ♗e4

After 17...c5 18 d5 White gets a passed pawn.

18 f3 ♗b7 19 d5!?

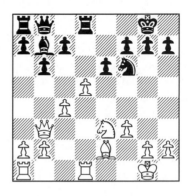

Perhaps White should continue to build with 19 ♖d2 followed by ♖ad1.

19...exd5 20 cxd5 c6 21 dxc6 ♗xc6 22 ♗c4 ♗e8 23 ♘d5 ♕e5 24 ♕c3 ½-½

On 24 ♖e1 Black intended 24...♕d4+ 25 ♔h1 b5 (25...♘xd5? 26 ♗xd5 – threatening 27 ♗xf7+ and 27 ♗xa8 – is unpleasant and the attempt to meet this with 26...♖xd5 is answered by 27 ♖ad1 ♗a4 28 ♕xd5, winning material) 26 ♘xf6+ ♕xf6 27 ♗d5 (27 ♗xb5?! is met by 27...♖ab8!) 27...♖ac8 with equality.

Game 16
Donev-Zlatilov
Elenite Open 1986

---

1 d4 ♘f6 2 ♘c3 d5 3 ♗g5 ♘bd7 4 ♕d3 g6

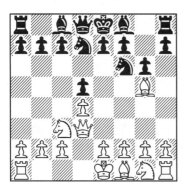

5 e4

A logical follow-up, though White has tried a number of alternatives:

a) 5 f3!? attempts to build a broad pawn centre but only after Black has 'wasted' time with ...g7-g6, and appears to be more promising than other f2-f3 lines as Black finds it difficult to counter-attack in the centre. Play might continue 5...♗g7 6 e4 dxe4 (6...c6 7 e5 ♘g8 8 h4 was also promising for White in Chernyshov-Szekely, Pardubice 2002) 7 fxe4 0-0 8 e5 ♘e8 9 h4 c5 10 ♘d5 f6 11 ♕b3 e6 (after 11...fxg5 there follows 12 ♘xe7+ ♔h8 13 ♘xg6+ hxg6 14 hxg5+) 12 ♘xf6+ ♘dxf6 13 0-0-0 ♕b6 14 exf6 ♘xf6 15 dxc5 ♕xc5 16 ♗c4 and White had a large advantage in Hector-Moberg, Sweden 2001.

b) 5 0-0-0 ♗g7 6 f3 (6 h4!? c6 7 f3 ♘h5 8

g4 ♘g3 9 ♖h2 was very messy in Laengl-G.Timoscenko, Seefeld 1999) is similar to 5 f3, but the extra developing move enjoyed by both sides may help Black's defence more than White's attack. Laengl-M.Ivanov, Bad Wörishofen 2000 continued 6...0-0 7 e4 dxe4 8 fxe4 c5 9 d5 (9 e5!? ♘g4 10 ♘d5 is certainly worth considering) 9...b5!? 10 ♘xb5 ♗a6 and Black had good counterplay.

c) 5 ♘f3 ♗g7 6 e4 transposes back to the main line.

5...dxe4 6 ♘xe4 ♗g7 7 ♘f3 0-0 8 0-0-0

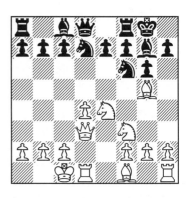

The sharp approach. White can also proceed quietly with 8 ♗e2, when a draw was agreed in Negulescu-G.Timoscenko, Cappelle la Grande 1993 after 8...c5 9 ♘xf6+ ♘xf6 10 dxc5 ♕a5+ 11 c3 ♕xc5 12 0-0 b6 13 ♕d4.

8...b6

Playing for solid development, although with White having castled long this may be rather too meek. A number of alternatives have been tried:

a) 8...c5!? is Black's sharpest response. In Poteas-Grivas, Nikea 2002 White played 9 ♘xf6+ ♘xf6 10 ♕a3, when 10...cxd4 11 ♖xd4 ♕b6 was probably best, with approximate equality. The critical line is 9 ♘xc5 ♘xc5 10 dxc5 ♕a5 11 ♕b5! ♕xa2 12 ♗c4 ♗d7! (both 12...♕a1+ 13 ♔d2 and 12...a6 13 ♕b4 a5 14 ♕b5 ♗d7 15 ♗xa2 ♗xb5 16 ♖he1 give White some pressure) 13 ♗xa2 ♗xb5 14 ♖he1 e6 15 ♘d4 ♗d7 was Zhang

Pengxiang-Pigusov, FIDE World Ch. Knock-Out, Moscow 2001, and now 16 ♘f5!? was best, after which 16...gxf5 17 ♗xf6 ♗xf6 18 ♖xd7 would have been equal according to Finkel. In the game White played 16 f3?! and got the worst of it after 16...♖fc8 17 ♗e3 ♗f8 18 ♗g5 ♗e7 19 ♘f5 gxf5 20 ♗xf6 ♗xf6 21 ♖xd7 ♖ab8.

b) 8...c6 9 ♔b1 (9 h4!?) 9...b5 expands on the queenside but it's difficult to see how Black intends to transform this into an actual attack. Khachian-Casella, Costa Mesa 2002 continued 10 h3 a5 11 g4 b4 12 ♘xf6+ ♘xf6 13 ♗xf6 ♗xf6 14 ♗g2 ♕c7 15 ♖he1 with a slight edge for White, with more space and a grip on the centre.

c) 8...♘xe4 9 ♕xe4 ♘f6 10 ♗xf6 (10 ♕h4!?) 10...♗xf6 11 ♗c4 c5 12 dxc5 ♕c7 13 ♕e3 ♗g4 14 h3 ♗xf3 15 ♕xf3 ♕xc5 equalised for Black in Freisler-Voloshin, Nymburk 1997.

d) 8...h6 9 ♗h4 (9 ♗xf6 ♘xf6 10 ♘xf6+ ♗xf6 11 ♕e3 ♗g7 12 ♗c4) 9...c6 10 ♗e2 ♕a5 11 ♔b1 ♘xe4 12 ♕xe4 ♘f6 13 ♗xf6 ♗xf6 14 ♗c4 ♗f5 was about equal in Ljubicic-Leventic, Pula 1994.

9 h4!?

Taking the bull by the horns. 9 ♗e2 ♗b7 10 ♘xf6+ ♘xf6 11 ♔b1 ♕d6 12 ♗h4 c5 was very comfortable for Black in Kaganovski-Kagan, Israel 1988.

9...♗b7 10 ♘xf6+ ♘xf6 11 ♗xf6 exf6

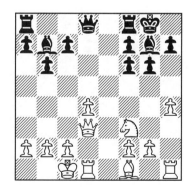

Making sure that a white knight can't

come to e5 or g5 but blocking in the bishop on g7 and giving White a queenside pawn majority. The cold-blooded 11...♗xf6 might be better but requires nerves of steel. Play could continue 12 h5 ♕d5 13 hxg6 hxg6 14 ♕e3 ♗g7, when 15 ♗d3!? (to prevent 15...♕e4) 15...♕xa2 16 c3 ♕a1+ 17 ♔b1 c5 18 ♘g5 is very complicated.

12 h5 ♕d6 13 hxg6 hxg6 14 ♕b3 a5 15 ♗c4 a4 16 ♕d3 ♕f4+ 17 ♔b1 ♗e4 18 ♕a3 ♕d6

Leading to an inferior endgame. Black's pawns are rather weak, a factor which White exploits with great ingenuity.

19 ♕xd6 cxd6 20 ♖he1 f5

It might be better to support the bishop with 20...d5 21 ♗d3 and only then 21...f5 as White's bishop is no longer on the critical a2-g8 diagonal.

21 ♘g5 ♗c6

After 21...♗xg2 there comes 22 f3! ♗f6 23 ♖d2 ♗xg5 24 ♖xg2 followed by ♖xg6+ when the bishop moves.

22 ♖e6!?

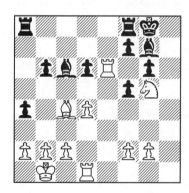

An interesting exchange sacrifice. Black has to accept as both d6 and g6 are under fire.

22...fxe6 23 ♗xe6+ ♔h8 24 ♖h1+ ♗h6 25 ♖xh6+ ♔g7 26 ♖h7+ ♔f6 27 f4

The point. Black's king is very poorly placed on f6.

27...♖ae8 28 ♖c7 ♗d5 29 ♔c1 ♗xg2

Not 29...♗xe6 in view of 30 ♘h7 mate.

30 d5 ♖e7 31 ♘h7+

White should take this opportunity to cash in as the careless 31 ♖c6?? meets with 31...♖xe6 32 ♘xe6 ♗xd5, completely turning the tables.

31...♖xh7 32 ♖xh7 g5 33 ♖h6+ ♔g7 34 ♖h5 g4 35 ♖g5+ ♔h6

36 c4

Around here White loses the plot. He should break up Black's kingside pawns with 36 ♗xf5, when 36...♗xd5 37 ♗xg4 ♗e4 38 ♖b5 ♖xf4 39 ♗d1 leaves him with excellent winning chances.

36...♗e4 37 b4 axb3 38 axb3 ♖f6 39 b4 ♗d3

This gives White some chances. Black can draw with 39...♖g6, for example 40 ♖xg6+ ♔xg6 41 ♔d2 g3 42 ♔e3 ♗d3 43 ♔f3 ♗xc4 44 ♔xg3 when neither side can make progress.

40 ♔d2 ♗xc4 41 ♗xf5 g3 42 ♔e3 ♗xd5 43 ♗h3 ♗c6?

After this Black encounters unexpectedly serious difficulties in the shape of White's passed f-pawn. Black should exchange bishops with 43...♗e6 when a draw is still likely.

44 ♖xg3 ♖g6 45 ♗g4 ♖g8 46 ♖h3+ ♔g6 47 ♗e6 ♖a8 48 f5+ ♔g7 49 ♖g3+ ♔f6 50 ♔f4 ♖a1 51 ♖g6+ ♔e7 52 ♖g7+ ♔f8 53 ♖f7+ ♔e8 54 ♖c7 ♗b5 55 f6 ♔f8 56 ♖c8+ ♗e8 57 f7 ♖f1+ 58 ♔e4 ♖xf7 59 ♗xf7 ♔xf7 60 ♔d5 ♔e7 61 ♖c7+ ♗d7 62 ♖a7 b5 63 ♖b7 1-0

Game 17
Alburt-Zilberstein
USSR Ch., Baku 1972

1 d4 ♘f6 2 ♘c3 d5 3 ♗g5 c6 4 ♕d3 ♘bd7 5 e4

With the moves ...h6 and ♗g5-h4 interposed this is simply bad, for reasons which were explained in the note to White's 6th move in Rossetto-Darga. Here it is quite playable. 5 ♘f3 is a good alternative and features in Miles-Watson (Game 18).

5...♘xe4

5...dxe4 6 ♘xe4 g6 7 ♘xf6+ ♘xf6 8 ♗xf6 exf6 was Mestrovic-S.Martinovic, Sarajevo 1973, and now 9 ♕e3+ ♗e7 10 ♗c4 looks slightly favourable for White.

6 ♘xe4 dxe4 7 ♕xe4 ♘f6

Black is willing to accept doubled pawns

after ♗xf6, but the positions which then arise are far from comfortable for the defender. He would do well to check out one of the alternatives:

a) 7...h6 8 ♗d2 ♘f6 9 ♕f4 (9 ♕d3 ♕d5 10 ♘e2 ♗f5 11 ♘f4 ♕e4+ gave Black complete equality in Mestrovic-Knezevic, Zagreb 1977) 9...g5 10 ♕e3 ♗f5 11 ♗d3 (11 0-0-0!?) 11...♗xd3 12 ♕xd3 ♕d5 13 ♘f3 ♕e4+ 14 ♕xe4 ♘xe4 brought about an equal endgame in Alburt-Furman, USSR Ch., Baku 1972.

b) 7...♕a5+ 8 ♗d2 ♕d5 (8...♕b6 9 0-0-0 ♘f6 10 ♕f4 ♗g4 11 f3 ♗d7 was also okay in Wockenfuss-Lombardy, Amsterdam 1985) 9 ♕e3 (exchanging queens on d5 gives White nothing – Goldin-Karpov, Moscow 1993 went 9 ♕xd5 cxd5 10 ♘f3 e6 11 ♗d3 ♗d6 12 0-0 b6 with equality) 9...♘f6 10 ♘f3 ♗f5 11 c4 ♕e4 12 ♘e5 ♖d8 13 ♕xe4 ♘xe4 (maybe 13...♗xe4 14 ♗e3 ♘d7 is more solid, when Segal-Van Riemsdijk, Sao Paulo 1978 continued 15 f3 ♗f5 16 ♗e2 e6 17 ♔f2 ♗e7 with a solid position for Black) 14 ♗e3 f6 (14...e6 can be met by 15 g4 ♗g6 16 ♗g2, when White has some pressure) 15 ♘f3 e6 16 0-0-0 ♔f7 17 ♘h4 ♘d6 18 c5 g5 19 ♘xf5 ♘xf5 20 ♗c4 and White's pressure on e6 was enough for an advantage in Khachian-Koniushkov, Moscow 1996.

c) 7...♕b6!? is an interesting move as Black intends to meet 8 0-0-0 with ...♕a5, forking g5 and a2. Negulescu-Kr.Georgiev, Cappelle la Grande 1992 continued 9 d5 ♘b6 10 dxc6 ♕xg5+ 11 f4 ♕f5 12 ♕xf5 ♗xf5 13 ♗b5 a6 14 cxb7+ axb5 15 bxa8♕+ ♘xa8 when Black's two minor pieces should outweigh the rook and pawn. 8 b3 might be White's best but there is no advantage.

8 ♗xf6 ♕a5+

After the immediate 8...gxf6 White should similarly play 9 ♗c4!. Instead 9 0-0-0 ♕d5! 10 ♕xd5 cxd5 was equal in Klaman-Ilivitzki, Tbilisi 1949.

9 c3 gxf6 10 ♗c4 ♗h6

Black has more commonly played 10...♗f5 after which 11 ♕f4 ♗g6 12 ♘f3 ♗g7 13 0-0 0-0 14 ♖fe1 e6 15 ♘h4 c5 was fine for Black in Alburt-Doda, Lublin 1972, while 11 ♕e2 should be met by the simple 11...e6 with equality. 11 ♕f3 is probably White's most dangerous move, Negulescu-Tomescu, Odorheiu Secuiesc 1993 continuing 11...♗d7 12 ♘e2 ♖g8 13 ♘g3 ♕g5 14 0-0 ♗g4 15 ♕d3 ♕g6 16 f4 and White was in the driving seat.

Another possibility is 10...♕f5 but then 11 ♕e3 ♕g6 12 ♕g3 ♗h6 13 ♘e2 0-0 14 ♗d3 ♕g5 15 f4 ♕g4 16 0-0 led to a similar advantage for White in Mestrovic-Krogius, Hastings 1970/71.

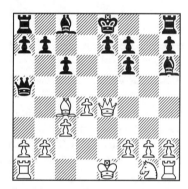

11 ♘e2 ♕f5 12 ♕xf5 ♗xf5 13 0-0 ♗d7

This looks like a necessary precaution. After 13...e6 there follows 14 ♘g3 ♗g6 15 f4 when Black is obliged to play 15...f5, entombing the bishop on g6.

14 ♖ae1 ♖c8?!

Aiming for ...c6-c5 but Black should probably settle for defensive moves for the time being. 14...e6 is better, although I still prefer White.

15 ♘g3 ♔f8 16 ♖e4 e6 17 ♖h4 ♗g5 18 ♖h5 ♗f4 19 ♘e4 f5 20 ♘f6!? ♔e7 21 ♘xh7

An enterprising if risky pawn grab. It's not easy for White to extricate this knight but then neither can Black easily trap it.

21...♖cg8

Perhaps Black should take this opportunity to develop counterplay elsewhere; 21...c5 looks logical.

22 ♖e1 ♖g6 23 h4 ♖hg8?!

Black should maintain the pin.

24 g3 f6?

After this further slip White's advantage crystalises. 24...♖h8 is preferable.

25 ♖xf5 ♗d2 26 ♖e2 ♗c1 27 ♖f3 ♖h6 28 ♖c2

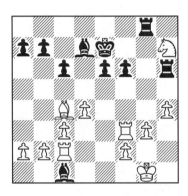

28 ♗d3 is probably even stronger, but the text stays a good pawn up.

28...♖xh7 29 ♖xc1 ♖xh4 30 ♖e1 ♖h6 31 ♖f4 ♖gh8 32 ♔g2 ♔d6 33 b4 f5 34 ♔f3 b6 35 ♔e3 ♖h2 36 ♖g1 ♖8h6 37 g4 ♖6h3+ 38 ♖f3 fxg4 39 ♖xg4 ♖xf3+ 40 ♔xf3 ♖h3+ 41 ♖g3 ♖h1 42 ♔e4 ♖e1+ 43 ♔d3 c5 44 ♔d2 ♖e4 45 ♔d3 ♖e1 46 dxc5+ bxc5 47 b5 e5 48 ♖g6+ ♔c7 49 ♖a6 ♔b8 50 a4 ♗f5+ 51 ♔d2 ♖b1 52 ♖f6 ♖b2+ 53 ♔e3 ♖c2 54 ♖xf5 ♖xc3+ 55 ♗d3 c4 56 ♖xe5 ♖xd3+ 57 ♔e4 ♖a3 58 ♔d5 ♖f3 59 ♖e2 ♔c7 60 ♔xc4 ♔b6 61 ♖e6+ ♔b7 62 ♖e7+ ♔b6 63 a5+ ♔xa5 64 ♖xa7+ ♔b6 65 ♖a2 ♖f4+ 66 ♔d5 ♖f8 67 ♖b2 ♖d8+ 68 ♔e6 ♖f8 69 ♔e5 ♖e8+ 70 ♔f6 ♖f8+ 71 ♔g6 ♖g8+ 72 ♔f7 ♖g4 1-0

Game 18
Miles-W.Watson
British Ch., Torquay 1982

---

1 d4 ♘f6 2 ♘c3 d5 3 ♗g5 ♘bd7 4 ♘f3

c6!? 5 ♕d3!

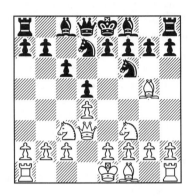

5...♕a5

Certainly a consistent follow up but this is not the only move:

a) 5...g6 6 e4 dxe4 (6...h6 7 ♗f4 dxe4 8 ♘xe4 ♘xe4 9 ♕xe4 ♘f6 10 ♕d3 ♕a5+ 11 ♕d2 ♕xd2+ 12 ♗xd2 was equal in Bellin-Lanka, Amsterdam 1994) 7 ♘xe4 ♗g7 8 0-0-0!? (White can also keep pieces on with 8 ♘g3, when Borge-Tzermiadianos, Arnhem 1989 went 8...♘f8 9 ♕d2 ♘e6 10 ♗h6! ♗xh6 11 ♕xh6 ♘xd4? 12 0-0-0 ♕a5 13 ♖xd4 ♕xa2 14 ♗c4 ♕a1+ 15 ♔d2 with inadequate compensation for Black, while L.Karlsson-Jonsson, Sweden 1994 saw the solid 8 c3 but White had nothing after 8...♕b6 9 ♘xf6+ ♘xf6 10 ♕c2 ♗f5 11 ♕b3 ♗e6 etc.) 8...0-0 9 h4?! (White should probably settle for the quiet 9 ♖e1 ♕a5 10 ♔b1 ♘xe4 11 ♕xe4 ♖e8 12 ♗c4, which was a bit more comfortable for White in Bellin-Toth, Torino 1983) 9...♘xe4 10 ♕xe4 ♘f6 11 ♗xf6 (11 ♕e3 ♗e6 12 ♔b1 c5 gave Black strong counterplay in Martinez-Magem Badals, Alicante 1989) 11...♗xf6 12 h5 ♕d5 13 ♕xd5 cxd5 and Black's bishops gave him the better of it in Alburt-Savon, USSR 1970.

b) 5...b5 6 a3 a5 discourages White from castling long, but leaves Black's queenside pawns weak. Donev-Weindl, Bad Ragaz 1993 continued 7 e4 b4 8 axb4 ♗a6 9 b5 cxb5 10 ♘xd5 ♘xd5 11 exd5 b4 12 ♕xa6 ♖xa6 13 ♗xa6 with more than enough for the queen.

c) 5...♕b6 pushes White into castling long, but he probably wants to do that anyway. After 6 0-0-0 e6 7 e4 ♗b4 8 ♘d2 ♕a5 9 e5 ♗xc3 10 ♕xc3 ♕xc3 11 bxc3 ♘g4 12 ♗h4 White had an edge in Van Mil-Bosch, Wijk aan Zee 1995.

d) 5...e6 is a solid move which hasn't been tried much. Comas-De la Villa, Palencia 1999 continued 6 e4 dxe4 7 ♘xe4 ♗e7 8 ♘xf6+ ♗xf6 and now 9 h4 looks promising (rather than the anemic 9 ♗xf6, as played in the game).

For 5...h6 see the next main game.

6 ♗d2

One of the ideas behind Black's last move is that 6 0-0-0 can be met by 6...♘e4!? 7 ♘xe4 dxe4 8 ♕xe4 ♕xa2 when White has problems with his king. Besides the move played in the game White has two alternative ways of handling the position:

a) The exotic 6 ♘d2 e6 7 h4 was played in Shirazi-Lazic, Le Touquet 1998, after which Black should probably play 7...♕b6 8 0-0-0 e5 with a good game for Black. Instead 7...♗d6 8 e4 ♘xe4 9 ♘cxe4 dxe4 10 ♕xe4 was quite promising for White.

b) 6 a3 e6 7 ♖b1 was played in Schweber-Bravo, Ville de Parque 1998, but this is hardly going to harm Black if he plays sensibly with 7...♗d6, for example.

6...♕b6

The solid 6...e6 is possible here although it looks rather passive for Black after 7 e4 dxe4

8 ♘xe4. Black has also played 6...♕c7, when 7 e4 dxe4 8 ♘xe4 ♘xe4 9 ♕xe4 ♘f6 10 ♕e3 ♗f5 11 0-0-0 e6 12 ♘h4 ♗g6 13 ♕h3 was played in Van Mil-Markus, Antwerp 1995. Black met the threat of 14 ♘xg6 with 13...♖g8 but stood slightly worse after 14 ♘xg6 hxg6 15 ♗e2 0-0-0 16 c3. Here the e3-square seems best for the queen, as 10 ♕d3 saw Black generate counterplay in Neukirch-Csulits, Gera 1962 after 10...g6 11 0-0-0 ♗f5 etc.

7 0-0-0 e5?!

After White's reply this starts to look suspicious as it looks as if Black has opened the centre prematurely. A solid move is 7...e6, transposing to Opocensky-Schubert, Prague 1919 after 8 e4 dxe4 9 ♘xe4. This game went 9...a5 10 ♘e5 ♘xe4 11 ♘xd7 ♗xd7 12 ♕xe4 ♗e7 13 ♗e3 ♕d8 14 g4 with attacking chances for White.

8 e4!

Not 8 dxe5? ♘g4.

8...exd4 9 ♘xd4

In his notes Miles also suggested 9 ♘a4!?, and after 9...♘c5! (both 9...♕c7 10 exd5 and 9...♕b5 10 ♕xd4! are good for White) 10 ♘xb6 ♘xd3+ 11 ♗xd3 axb6 12 exd5 ♘xd5 13 ♖he1+ claimed an edge for White.

9...♘c5

After 9...♘e5 Miles suggested that 10 ♕g3 ♕xd4 11 ♗f4 ♘xe4 12 ♘xe4 ♕xe4 13 ♗xe5 would give White adequate compensation for the pawn but it seems to me that he is struggling to do so after 13...♕g4 (or 13...♕g6).

10 ♕g3 ♘cxe4 11 ♘xe4 ♘xe4

In this position 11...♕xd4 gives White more for his pawn than in the previous note after 12 ♘xf6+ ♕xf6 13 ♗c3 etc.

12 ♕e5+ ♗e7 13 ♗e3! f6

The attempt to bail out with 13...♕d8 14 ♕xg7 ♗f6 15 ♕h6 ♗g5 leaves Black with the worse endgame after 16 ♗xg5 ♕xg5+ 17 ♕xg5 ♘xg5 due to his split pawns.

14 ♕h5+ g6 15 ♕h6 ♗f8 16 ♕h4 c5?!

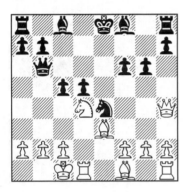

Further weakening his structure by leaving d5 unprotected. Black's best is 16...♕d8, when 17 f3 ♘d6 18 ♖e1 ♔f7 leaves White with adequate compensation for the pawn but not more.

17 ♘b3! ♗e6 18 f3 ♘g5 19 ♕e1! d4?

Accidentally opening the floodgates for White's pieces. After 19...0-0-0 20 ♕c3!

White wins back his pawn with a large advantage. Black had to try 19...♖c8, meeting 20 ♗xg5 fxg5 21 ♕e5 with 21...♔f7 22 ♕xh8 ♗g7 23 ♕xh7 ♖h8 24 ♕xh8 ♗xh8 when Black has attacking chances on the queenside.

20 ♗xg5! fxg5 21 ♕e5 ♖g8 22 ♖e1! ♖g7

Or 22...♔f7 23 ♕xe6+ ♕xe6 24 ♖xe6 ♔xe6 25 ♗c4+, winning the rook on g8.

23 ♕xe6+ ♖e7 24 ♗c4 ♖xe6 25 ♖xe6+ ♕xe6 26 ♗xe6 ♔e7 27 ♗d5 1-0

Game 19
Ben Menachem-Boric
European Cup, Eupen 1997

---

1 d4 ♘f6 2 ♘c3 d5 3 ♗g5 ♘bd7 4 ♘f3 c6 5 ♕d3 h6 6 ♗d2

After 6 ♗h4 Black can play 6...♕a5 under better circumstances than in Miles-Watson as White can no longer play his bishop to d2. After 7 e3 Black has a good reply in 7...♘e4, so White should try 7 ♘d2!?, when 7...e5?! leads to interesting complications after 8 ♗xf6! ♘xf6 (8...gxf6? 9 ♘b3 ♕c7 10 e4! leaves Black with problems over his pawn structure and where to put his king) 9 dxe5 ♘g4 10 h3 (10 f4? is powerfully met by 10...♗c5) 10...♘xe5 11 ♕e3 f6! (11...d4 12 ♕xd4 ♗e6 13 ♘b3 ♗xb3 14 cxb3 was good for White in Karayannis-Pavlovic, Nikolaos Open 1997) 12 f4 ♗c5 13 ♕g3 ♘f7 14

♕xg7 ♗e3 15 ♕xf6 ♕b4 16 0-0-0 ♖g8 and White is threatened with 17...♗d4. 6...e6 7 e4 ♕a5 is also possible, as in Schinzel-Suetin, Lublin 1976.

The attempt to save time with 6 ♗xf6 leaves White with less than nothing after 6...♘xf6 7 e4 dxe4 8 ♘xe4 ♘xe4 9 ♕xe4 ♕d5 etc., but 6 ♗f4 is worth considering. Krsnik-Starcevic, Bela Crkva 1983 went 6...e6 7 e4 ♗b4 8 e5 ♘e4 9 ♘d2 ♘xc3 10 bxc3 ♗e7 11 ♕g3 with attacking prospects for White.

6...b5

Trying to prevent White from expanding with 7 e4 (Black would reply with 7...b4) whilst gaining space on the queenside to make it less habitable for White's king. White gets a good game after 6...♕b6 7 0-0-0 e6 8 e4 (Schumacher-Staller, Bad Ragaz 1991), but chances are fairly balanced after 6...g6 7 e4 dxe4 8 ♘xe4 ♗g7, as in I.Zaitsev-Makarichev, Moscow 1986.

7 a3 ♗b7 8 e4 dxe4 9 ♘xe4 e6 10 ♘e5

In his notes to the game Boris Avrukh gave 10 ♘xf6+ ♕xf6 (10...♘xf6 11 c4 bxc4 12 ♕xc4 ♕b6 13 b4 is slightly better for White because of his pressure on the c-file) 11 c4 c5!? 12 cxb5 ♗xf3 13 ♕xf3 ♕xf3 14 gxf3 cxd4 15 ♗d3 with a complex endgame in which chances are about equal.

10...♘xe5 11 dxe5 ♕xd3?!

The endgame is marginally better for White thanks to his extra space and the potential vulnerability of Black's queenside pawns. Avrukh gave 11...♘xe4 12 ♕xe4 ♕b6 as equal.

12 ♗xd3 ♘xe4 13 ♗xe4 0-0-0 14 ♗e3 c5 15 ♗xb7+ ♔xb7 16 ♔e2 ♗e7 17 c4! a6 ½-½

A rather dubious move which would leave Black under serious pressure had his opponent not agreed to a draw. Black should play 17...bxc4 18 ♖hc1 ♖d5, when 19 f4 g5! gives him some much needed counterplay. After 17...a6?! White should continue 18 ♖hc1 ♖c8 19 a4 with a definite pull.

Summary

4 ♕d2 seems like a dangerous move in the hands of rabid attackers such as Reprintsev and Khachian. I'm not sure I'd recommend it to everyone; White should be able to unleash unexpected tactical blows and not worry too much about his a2-pawn disappearing when his king is castled queenside.

Putting the queen on d3 is a good idea, but White should wait a move with 4 ♘f3 before committing himself. 5 ♕d3 is quite a good line after 4...c6 or 4...g6, but against 4...e6 it is better to play 5 e4, while 4...h6 should be answered with 5 ♗f4!?.

1 d4 ♘f6 2 ♘c3 d5 3 ♗g5 ♘bd7 4 ♕d3 *(D)*

    4 ♕d2 *(D)*

        4...c5 - *Game 11*; 4...c6 5 f3 - *Game 12*; 4...e6 - *Game 13*

4...c6

    4...h6 - *Game 14*; 4...e6 - *Game 15*; 4...g6 - *Game 16*

5 ♘f3 *(D)*

    5 e4 - *Game 17*

5...♕a5 - *Game 18*

    5...h6 - *Game 19*

4 ♕d3

4 ♕d2

5 ♘f3

CHAPTER THREE

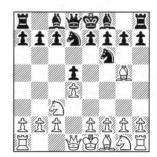

3...♘bd7:
4 ♘f3, 4 e3 and Others

1 d4 ♘f6 2 ♘c3 d5 3 ♗g5 ♘bd7

Veresov himself used to meet 3...♘bd7 with either 4 ♘f3 or 4 e3 and, in my opinion, he was right to do so. White has some initiative with these moves, whereas after the 'main line' 4 f3 he appears to be fighting for survival.

One of the most frequently recommended replies to 4 ♘f3 is 4...g6, but White can choose between 5 e3 (as in Miles-Andersson) or 5 ♕d3 (transposing to Donev-Zlatilov from Chapter 2) with chances of a pull in either case. The other recommended set-up is to play ...e7-e6 either before or after ...h7-h6, when the gambit line (reached via 4 ♘f3 e6 5 e4 h6 6 ♗h4 or 4 ♘f3 h6 5 ♗h4 e6 6 e4) seems playable for White after 6...g5 7 ♗g3 ♘xe4 8 ♘xe4 dxe4 9 ♘d2 (Otero-Camacho), but very dubious after 9 ♘e5 (Reynolds-Nunn).

White has ways of avoiding this after either move order by Black. After 4 ♘f3 e6 5 e4 h6 he can play 6 ♗xf6 ♘xf6 7 ♕e2, as in Yermolinsky-Kaidanov, and he might also consider 7 ♕d3!?. After 4 ♘f3 h6 he can vary from the traditional 5 ♗h4 with 5 ♗f4, and in Kupreichik-Gutman it wasn't at all clear that White's ambitious play was so bad.

White can add a few twists to the play with the quiet 4 e3, one of the main points

being that he has the option of going for a Stonewall formation with a later f2-f4. After the standard 4...g6 White delayed this a little in Ermenkov-Grivas, but in Brandner-Miniboeck he plunges straight in with 5 f4. White can also answer 4...c6 with 5 f4 but after 4...e6 I consider it a bit premature. Here I suggest 5 ♕f3!? as a move that offers White interesting possibilities.

> ### Game 20
> ## Miles-Andersson
> *London Phillips & Drew 1982*

1 d4 ♘f6 2 ♘c3 d5 3 ♗g5 ♘bd7 4 ♘f3 g6

After 4...c6 White can play 5 ♕d3, transposing to positions from Chapter 2.

5 e3

A quiet developing move, but one which calls for accurate play from Black. The interesting 5 ♕d3!? is dealt with under the 4 ♕d3 lines in Chapter 3.

5...♗g7 6 ♗d3

Aiming to open the game up with e3-e4. White can also play 6 ♗e2 at this point, but this essentially commits White to a plan based on ♘f3-e5 and f2-f4, which can be thwarted by Black. A case can be made here for the immediate 6...c6!?, but in E.Sokolov-

Lautier, Bad Zwesten 1999 the game went 6...0-0 7 0-0 (the immediate 7 ♘e5!? is worth considering, before Black protects his d-pawn). Now after 7...b6 8 ♘e5 ♗b7 White should support his prize knight with 9 f4!?, while 7...♘e4?! is dubious in view of 8 ♘xe4 dxe4 9 ♘d2 f5 10 f3! etc. Instead Lautier played 7...c6!, an excellent idea, defending the d-pawn and taking the sting out of White's main plan: ♘f3-e5 followed by f2-f4. The point is that 8 ♘e5 can be answered by 8...♘xe5 9 dxe5 ♘d7. The game continued 8 h3 b6 9 ♗f4 ♗b7 10 ♖e1 c5 11 ♘e5 a6 (after 11...e6?! White can probe Black's position with 12 ♘b5) 12 a4 ♖c8 13 ♗f3 e6 14 ♕e2 ♕e7 and Black was at least equal, the main problem for White being his lack of effective pawn levers.

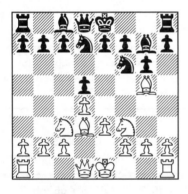

6...0-0 7 0-0 c5

Challenging the centre before White plays e3-e4. In Miles-King, Amsterdam 1982, Black played 7...b6 but found himself under pressure after 8 e4 dxe4 9 ♘xe4 ♗b7 10 ♕e2 h6 11 ♗f4 ♘xe4 12 ♗xe4 ♗xe4 13 ♕xe4 ♘f6 14 ♕e2!, intending ♖ad1 and ♖fe1 with more space and central pressure.

Black can also interpose 7...h6 before playing ...c7-c5. In Miles-Portisch, London 1982, Black managed to keep the balance after 8 ♗f4 c5 9 ♖e1 b6 10 ♘e5 ♗b7 11 ♕f3 ♘h5 12 ♗b5 ♘xe5 13 ♗xe5 ♗xe5 14 dxe5 ♕c7 15 ♘xd5 ♕xe5 16 ♘f6+ ♘xf6 17 ♕xb7 ♕xb2 18 ♕xe7 ♘d5 19 ♕b7 ♕xb5 20

♕xd5 ♖ad8 etc. 8 ♗h4 is also possible and would probably transpose to Miles-Christiansen in the note below.

8 ♖e1

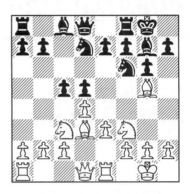

Continuing the build-up for e3-e4. In this particular position White should not play 8 ♘e5?! because of 8...cxd4 9 exd4 ♘xe5 10 dxe5 ♘g4. Peters-Browne, USA Ch. 1981 continued 11 ♗e2 d4! 12 ♘b5 (12 ♗xg4?! dxc3 13 ♕xd8 ♖xd8 14 ♗xc8 cxb2 ruins White's structure) 12...♘xe5 13 ♘xd4 ♕b6! 14 c3 (14 ♗xe7 ♖e8 15 ♗a3 ♖d8 16 c3 ♘c6 recovers the pawn with some initiative) 14...♕xb2 15 ♗xe7 ♖e8 16 ♗b4! a5! and now White should have played 17 ♖b1! (17 ♕b3? ♕xb3 18 axb3 ♗g4! was good for Black in the game) with drawing chances after 17...♕xa2 18 ♖a1 ♕d5 (18...♕b2 is only a draw) 19 ♘b5 ♕xd1 20 ♗xd1 (20 ♖fxd1? ♘c6! is even better) 20...♗d7 21 ♘c7 axb4 22 ♖xa8 ♖xa8 23 ♘xa8 bxc3 although, as Gallagher points out, Black has all the chances.

8...b6

Black can also play 8...h6 here. Miles-Christiansen, London 1982 continued 9 ♗h4 b6 (9...e6) 10 e4 (10 ♘e5!? is also worth considering as after 10...♘xe5 11 dxe5 ♘g4 White has 12 ♗e2 ♘xe5 13 ♕xd5) 10...dxe4 11 ♘xe4 cxd4 (11...♗b7 12 ♘xf6+ ♗xf6 13 dxc5 will give White an edge in the shape of Black's isolated c-pawn) 12 ♘xd4 ♗b7 13 c3 ♖c8 14 ♕e2 ♘c5!? 15 ♘xf6+ exf6 16 ♗c4 when White's healthier pawn majority was the main factor in the position.

9 e4

Black's last move made 9 ♘e5 possible, leading to complex play after 9...♗b7 (9...♘xe5 10 dxe5 ♘g4 is met by 11 ♗e2 ♘xe5 12 ♕xd5) 10 f4 ♘e8!? (10...♖c8!? 11 ♕f3 ♘e8 12 ♖ad1 a6 13 a3 f6 14 ♘xd7 ♕xd7 15 ♗h4 ♘d6 16 g4 b5 17 ♔h1!? also led to a tense and interesting position in Tihonov-Neverov, Minsk Open 1996) 11 ♗h4 ♘xe5 12 fxe5 (12 dxe5 f6!?) 12...♘c7 13 ♗e2 ♕d7 14 ♗g4 ♘e6, Meshkov-Sergienko, St Petersburg 1999. Then 15 ♘e2?! f5 16 exf6 exf6 17 ♘f4 f5 favoured Black, so White should have played 15 e4!, when 15...cxd4 16 ♘xd5 ♖fe8 (16...♗xd5 17 exd5 ♕xd5 18 ♗f3 ♕c5 19 ♗xa8, while 16...♗xe5 meets with 17 ♗xe7 ♖fe8 18 ♘f6+ ♗xf6 19 ♗xf6 with dangerous weaknesses on the dark squares around Black's king) 17 ♕xd4!? ♘xd4 18 ♗xd7 ♖ed8 19 ♘xe7+ ♔f8 20 e6!? with a strong initiative.

9...dxe4 10 ♘xe4

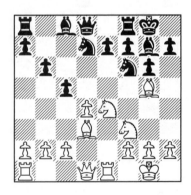

10...cxd4

Miles-Speelman, London 1982 varied with 10...♗b7 11 ♘xf6+ (11 c3 cxd4 12 ♘xd4 goes back into the main line) after which Black mutilated his own pawn structure with 11...exf6 in order to gain some time. The game continued 12 ♗h4!? (Miles sacrifices a pawn for the initiative but this is not mandatory – 12 ♗f4!? and 12 ♗e3 are also worth

considering and the latter move looks like a slight edge for White to me) 12...♗xf3 13 ♕xf3 cxd4 14 ♖ad1 ♖c8 15 ♗a6 ♖xc2!? 16 ♖xd4 ♘e5 17 ♕d1 ♕c7 18 f4 and now Black played the imaginative 18...♘g4! 19 ♕xg4 f5 with the game leading to equality after 20 ♕d1 ♕c5 21 ♗f2 ♖xf2 22 ♖c4 ♖d2+ 23 ♖xc5 ♖xd1.

11 ♘xd4 ♗b7 12 c3 ♖c8

In the game Black has difficulty finding a decent square for his queen, inspiring a search for alternatives:

a) 12...♕c7 13 ♕e2 ♖fe8 14 ♖ad1 a6 15 ♘xf6+ ♘xf6 16 ♘f3 e6 17 ♕e5 ♕xe5 18 ♘xe5 b5 kept the balance for Black in Miles-Olafsson, Lucerne Olympiad 1982.

b) 12...♘e5 13 ♘xf6+ exf6 14 ♗f4 ♘d3 15 ♕xd3 ♕d5 16 ♕f3 ♕d7 (16...♕xf3 17 ♘xf3 ♗xf3 18 gxf3 is good for White because his pawn majority can yield a passed pawn whilst Black's cannot) 17 ♕g3 and White had an edge thanks to his superior pawn structure in Hoi-King, Jurmala 1985.

c) 12...h6 13 ♘xf6+ (13 ♗h4 is more testing) 13...♘xf6 14 ♗h4 ♕d5 15 ♗f1 g5 16 ♗g3 ♘e4 17 ♘b5 ♕c6 18 ♘d4 ♕d5 was fine for Black in Berg-Gschnitzer, Bundesliga 1988-89.

d) 12...♘xe4 13 ♗xe4 ♗xe4 14 ♖xe4 ♘f6 15 ♖e1 ♕d5 16 ♘f3 ♕b7 was only minimally better for White in Plaskett-Hazai, Maribor 1985.

e) 12...♘c5 can be answered by 13 ♘xc5! bxc5 14 ♘b3 ♕d5 (Gallagher suggested that the modest 14...♕c7 may be Black's best) 15 ♕f3! ♕xf3 (not 15...c4? 16 ♗xc4, or 15...♕d7? 16 ♘xc5) 16 gxf3 ♗xf3 17 ♖xe7 and the rook on the seventh plus Black's pawn weaknesses leave him with problems according to analysis by Gallagher. Instead after 13 ♗xf6 exf6 14 ♘xc5 bxc5 15 ♘b3 ♕b6 16 ♕e2 f5 Black's bishop pair compensated for his structural weaknesses in Veresov-Shagalovich, Byelorussian Ch. 1957.

13 ♕e2 ♘e5

Black also seems to be under pressure af-

ter other moves. 13...♕c7 14 ♘xf6+ ♗xf6 15
♗xf6 exf6 leaves him with the usual problem
of having the kingside pawn majority crip-
pled, while 13...♖e8 14 ♖ad1 is uncomfortable.

14 ♗c2 ♘c4 15 ♖ad1 ♕c7

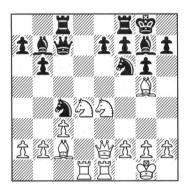

After 15...♘xb2 Miles simply mentions 16
♘e6 but this is far from clear after 16...♕e8.
White can win Black's queen with 17 ♘xg7
♔xg7 18 ♘xf6 (18 ♖d4!? looks much more
dangerous for Black) 18...exf6 19 ♗h6+
♔xh6 20 ♕d2+ ♔g7 21 ♖xe8 ♖fxe8 but
Black has quite adequate compensation.

16 ♘b5! ♕b8 17 ♗xf6! ♗xf6

17...exf6 18 ♗b3 is much better for White
– he has the better pawn structure and his
knights are about to jump into the d6-square.

**18 ♘xf6+ exf6 19 ♗b3 ♘e5 20 f4 ♘c6
21 ♘d6 ♖c7 22 ♕e8!**

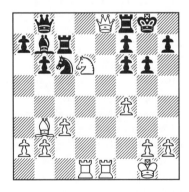

Miles conducts this part of the game with

great precision and power. 22 ♘e8 is far
from clear after 22...♖e7!.

**22...♖xe8 23 ♖xe8+ ♕xe8 24 ♘xe8 ♖e7
25 ♘d6!**

The spectacular 25 ♖d7!? allows Black to
defend with 25...f5.

25...♗a8 26 ♘xf7! ♔g7

Not 26...♖xf7 27 ♖d7.

**27 ♘d8 ♘xd8 28 ♖xd8 ♗c6 29 ♔f2 h5
30 ♖d6 ♖c7 31 ♖e6 ♗b7 32 g3 ♗c8 33
♖d6 ♗d7 34 ♗d5 ♔g4 35 a3 ♖e7 36
♗c4 ♖c7 37 ♗f1 ♔f7 38 h3 ♔e7 39 ♖d4
♗e6 40 ♗d3 ♗xh3 41 ♗xg6 ♔g4 42
♖d5 ♔e6 43 ♗e4?**

According to Miles, 43 ♖d8! would have
been more precise.

43...♖c8 44 ♔e3 ♔e7 45 f5?

And here White starts to lose the plot by
moving his pawns away from the dark
squares.

45...♖g8 46 ♖d2 ♗h3 47 ♖h2??

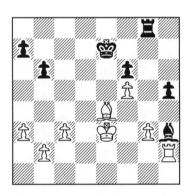

Returning the pawn! 47 ♔f3 keeps
White's winning chances alive.

47...♖xg3+ 48 ♔f2 h4

It seems that Miles had missed this simple
move. He was probably counting on
48...♖g4??, when White wins with 49 ♗f3
♖h4 50 ♔g3.

**49 ♖h1 ♔d6 50 ♖d1+ ♔e5 51 ♖d4 ♗g4
52 a4 a5 53 ♗h1 ♗xf5 54 ♖xh4 ♖h3 55
♖xh3 ♗xh3 56 ♗c6 ♔d6 57 ♗e4 ♗d7
58 ♗c2 ♔e5 59 ♔e3 ♗g4 60 ♗b3 ♗f5
61 ♗d1 ♗b1 62 ♗b3 f5 63 ♗d1 f4+ 64**

♔f3 ♗e4+ 65 ♔f2 ♔d5 66 ♗b3+ ♔c5
67 ♔e2 ♗c6 ½-½

Game 21
Otero-Camacho
Cuba (1st matchgame) 1997

**1 d4 ♘f6 2 ♘c3 d5 3 ♗g5 ♘bd7 4 ♘f3
h6**

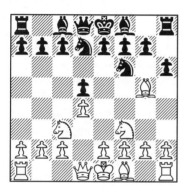

After 4...e6 5 e4 h6 White has an interesting alternative in 6 ♗xf6, as in Yermolinsky-Kaidanov.

5 ♗h4

White can also try 5 ♗f4 (Kupreichik-Gutman).

5...e6

Leaving White to decide how to develop his pieces. For 5...c5 see Mestrovic-Deze.

6 e4!?

The sharpest and most logical move in the position, although probably insufficient to give White an advantage. The quiet 6 e3 may be objectively better but does not pose Black particular problems after 6...♗e7 7 ♘e5 ♘xe5 8 dxe5 ♘d7 9 ♗g3 ♗b4 10 ♕g4 ♗xc3+ 11 bxc3 ♕g5, which led to complex play in Hort-Szmetan, Biel 1982. Black had a good game in O.Rodriguez-Christiansen, Indonesia 1982 after 7 ♗d3 c5 8 0-0 0-0 9 ♘e5 ♘xe5 10 dxe5 ♘d7 11 ♗xe7 ♕xe7 12 f4 f6 13 exf6 ♘xf6 14 ♕f3 ♗d7 15 e4 c4 16 e5 ♕c5+ 17 ♔h1 cxd3 18 exf6 ♖xf6 19 cxd3 ♖af8 20 g3 e5.

6...g5!

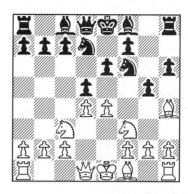

This is probably good for Black but some players might be afraid to go down this route due to the sharp nature of the ensuing positions. Accordingly Black has also played a number of more solid alternatives:

a) 6...♗e7 7 exd5 exd5 8 ♗d3 0-0 9 0-0 c6 10 ♖e1 ♖e8 was equal in Saigin-Averbakh, Moscow 1963, but White engineered attacking chances in Seul-Schlick, Wittlich 1985: 7 e5!? ♘e4 8 ♗xe7 ♕xe7 (another possibility is 8...♘xc3!? 9 ♗xd8 ♘xd1, which Averbakh might have rejected because the position looked too drawish after 10 ♖xd1 ♔xd8) 9 ♘xe4 dxe4 10 ♘d2 ♕b4 (10...f5!? is interesting) 11 c3 ♕xb2 12 ♘xe4 0-0 13 ♗d3 etc.

b) 6...dxe4 7 ♘xe4 ♗e7 is super-solid and 8 ♘xf6+ ♗xf6 9 ♗xf6 ♕xf6 10 ♕d2 0-0 11 0-0-0 e5 was a complete equaliser in Hoi-Larsen, Copenhagen 1985.

c) 6...♗b4 turns out to be difficult for Black after 7 exd5 exd5 8 ♕e2+ ♕e7 (8...♗e7 9 0-0-0 0-0 10 ♘e5, intending 11 f4 and 12 g4, looks dangerous) 9 ♕xe7+ ♔xe7 (9...♗xe7 10 ♘b5 ♗d8 11 ♗g3 is strong for White) 10 0-0-0 g5 11 ♗g3 according to my analysis.

7 ♗g3 ♘xe4

There's no reason to avoid this move as White will find it difficult to justify his play. Less good is 7...dxe4 8 ♘d2 (after 8 ♘e5 ♗b4 White will find it difficult to generate enough compensation) 8...♗b4 (after 8...♗g7

White can play 9 ♕e2, preparing to castle long and recapture on e4) and now 9 ♕e2, when 9...♘xc3 10 bxc3 c5 11 ♘c4 0-0 12 h4 starts prising open a lot of dark squares (my analysis).

The game Alburt-Lutikov, USSR 1970 varied with 7...♗b4 8 exd5 ♘xd5 9 ♕d3 c5 10 ♘d2 ♗xc3 11 bxc3 ♕a5 12 h4 g4, and now I think that 13 ♘c4 (rather than 13 ♗d6 b6 14 ♘b3 ♕xc3+ 15 ♕xc3 ♘xc3 16 dxc5) 13...♕xc3+ 14 ♕xc3 ♘xc3 15 dxc5 would have been nice for White and his two bishops.

8 ♘xe4 dxe4 9 ♘d2

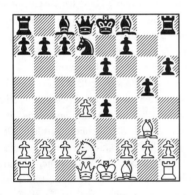

For 9 ♘e5 see Reynolds-Nunn.

9...♗g7

The critical line. The alternatives give White excellent attacking chances, for example:

a) 9...♘f6 10 ♗e5 ♗d6 11 h4?! (rather than pouring gasoline onto the flames White should try the simple 11 ♗xf6 ♕xf6 12 ♘xe4 with a useful space advantage) 11...gxh4 12 ♕e2 ♗d7 13 ♖xh4 ♗c6 14 ♕e3? ♕d5! 15 ♕h3 ♗xe5 16 dxe5 ♕g5 17 ♖xe4, Shagalovich-Zinn, Berlin 1967, and now Black should play 17...0-0-0! threatening 18...♕xd2+. In the game he played 17...♘f4? and stood worse after 18 ♕c3! ♘xg2+ 19 ♗xg2 ♕xg2 20 ♖d4.

b) 9...f5 is quite weakening, for example 10 ♗c4 ♘f6 (after 10...f4 11 ♕h5+ ♔e7 12 ♗xf4 gxf4 13 ♘xe4 White gets compensa-

tion for the piece) 11 ♗e5 ♗g7 (11...♗d6 12 ♕e2 ♗xe5 13 dxe5 ♘g4 14 f3 e3 15 fxg4 ♕xd2+ 16 ♕xd2 exd2+ 17 ♔xd2 fxg4 18 ♖hf1 was better for White despite his pawn deficit in van Mil-Geenen, Virton 1988) 12 f3 e3 (12...exf3! is probably Black's best) 13 ♘b3 0-0 14 ♕d3 ♘d5 (14...f4 is strongly answered by 15 0-0-0, threatening 16 g3) 15 0-0-0 ♘b6 16 ♗xg7 ♔xg7 17 ♘a5! ♘d5 18 ♗xd5 ♕xd5 19 ♘c4! b5 20 ♘e5 ♕xa2 21 ♕xe3 and White had a clear advantage in Veresov-Radashkovich, USSR 1969 as his control of the dark squares more than compensated for the pawn. Had Black taken a second pawn with 21...♕a1+ 22 ♔d2 ♕xb2, White would have played 23 ♖b1 ♕a2 24 ♖xb5 with his rook coming to c5 and the h2-h4 lever in the air. Alternatively, Shagalovich-Sakharov, USSR 1969 went 10 h4 f4 11 ♕h5+ ♔e7 12 hxg5 fxg3 13 0-0-0 ♕e8 14 ♕h4 ♔d8 15 ♘xe4 ♗e7 and now Bellin's 16 ♕xg3 gives White two pawns plus a strong initiative for the piece.

10 h4!

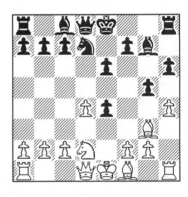

Offering a second pawn in order to accelerate his initiative. It's difficult for White to justify his play after 10 c3, for example 10...f5 11 h4 g4 12 ♗c4 ♘b6 (12...♘f6 13 ♕e2 0-0 14 h5 ♘d5 15 0-0-0 c6 16 f3 b5 17 ♗b3 was also very difficult to assess in Ignatiev-Rogovoi, Russia 1998. White is hoping to worm his way into the holes around Black's king but he is a pawn down) 13 ♗b3 0-0 14

♕e2 a5 (the immediate 14...f4!? is also interesting as White would be obliged to sacrifice a piece with 15 ♗xf4) 15 a3 ♕e7 16 0-0-0 ♖a6 17 ♘xe4 fxe4 18 ♕xe4 left White with inadequate compensation for the piece in Hoi-Larsen, Denmark 1989, though the position isn't easy for Black as shown by the fact that Hoi managed to win.

10...♗xd4 11 c3

Less good is 11 ♘xe4 ♗xb2 12 hxg5 (12 ♖b1 ♘f6! 13 ♕xd8+ ♔xd8 left Black material up in the endgame in Neukirch-Uhlmann, DDR 1972) 12...hxg5 13 ♖xh8+ ♗xh8 14 c3 ♗g7! 15 ♕b3 (15 ♕h5? ♘f6! 16 ♕xg5 ♘xe4 17 ♕xg7 ♕d2 mate) 15...f5! and White had little compensation for the sacrificed pawns in Mestrovic-Vukic, Yugoslav Ch. 1974.

11...♗e5!

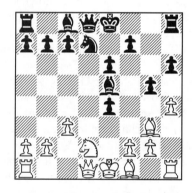

This, in turn, looks like Black's best defence. If Black plays 11...♗g7 White gets a strong initiative for the pawn with 12 hxg5 hxg5 13 ♖xh8+ ♗xh8 14 ♕h5 followed by 0-0-0.

The other move to have been tried is 11...gxh4?, but then there follows 12 ♖xh4! ♗f6 (relatively best is 12...♗g7 but then 13 ♘xe4 ♕e7 14 ♕h5 ♘f6 15 ♘xf6+ ♗xf6 16 ♖f4 e5 17 ♖xf6 ♕xf6 18 ♗xe5 gave White more than enough for the exchange in Tischbierek-Uhlmann, Leipzig 1983) 13 ♕h5! ♗g5 14 ♘xe4 ♖g8 15 ♖g4 a6 (15...♕e7 is met by 16 f4) 16 ♖d1 (16 f4 is more brutish

but equally effective) 16...e5 17 ♗h4 ♕e7 18 ♗c4 ♘f6 19 ♖xg5! hxg5 (or 19...♖xg5 20 ♕xh6 etc.) 20 ♗xf7+ ♔f8 21 ♘xf6 1-0, Veresov-Zheliandinov, USSR 1969.

11...e3 has been suggested by the likes of Alburt and Yudovich but apparently never tried. White's position looks promising after 12 cxd4 exd2+ 13 ♕xd2 with very good play on the dark squares.

12 ♗xe5

Preferable to 12 ♘xe4 ♗xg3 13 fxg3 gxh4 14 ♖xh4 ♕e7 15 ♕d2 (after 15 ♕d4 White is driven back with 15...e5 16 ♕d2 ♘f6!?) 15...f5! 16 ♘g5 (16 ♘f2 ♘f6 17 ♖xh6 ♖xh6 18 ♕xh6 ♗d7, when Black intends to castle long and ultimately use the passed e-pawn) 16...♘f6 17 0-0-0 ♗d7 18 ♘f3 0-0-0 19 ♖xh6 ♘e4 20 ♕e3 ♖xh6 21 ♕xh6 (after 21 ♕xa7 Black defends with 21...c5 22 ♗a6 ♗c6 etc.) 21...♘xg3 and Black emerged with a good extra pawn in Galkin-Volzhin, Perm 1997.

12...♘xe5 13 ♕a4+

After 13 hxg5 there follows 13...e3 (13...♕xg5 14 ♘xe4 ♕f4 15 ♕d4 is good for White) 14 ♘e4 (not 14 fxe3 ♕xg5) 14...exf2+ 15 ♔xf2 ♕xd1 16 ♖xd1 ♔e7 17 ♗e2 h5 18 ♖xh5 with a likely draw in the endgame.

13...♗d7 14 ♕xe4

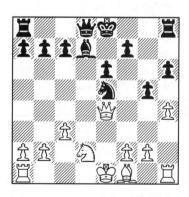

In the third game of their match Otero varied with 14 ♕d4!? but failed to trouble Black unduly. The game went 14...♘g6 15 h5 e5 16 ♕xe4 ♗c6 17 ♗b5!? ♘e7 (17...♗xb5

18 hxg6 is very dangerous for Black) 18 ♕xe5 0-0 19 0-0-0 ♕d5! 20 ♕xe7 ♗xb5 21 ♘b3 ♕f5 22 ♘d4 ♕f4+ 23 ♔b1 ♖fe8 24 ♕c5 ♗d7 25 g3 ♕e5 and Black had equalised. Another possibility is 15 ♕g7!?, when Camacho analzyed 15...♕e7! 16 h5 ♕f8 17 ♕d4 e5! 18 ♕xe4 ♗c6 19 ♗b5! ♘e7 20 ♕xe5 0-0-0 21 ♗xc6 ♘xc6 22 ♕f5+ ♔b8 23 0-0-0 ♕g7 as being equal, but White might also consider 20 ♗xc6+ ♘xc6 21 ♕f5. Both 15 hxg5?! ♕xg5 16 ♘xe4 ♕e5 and 15 ♘xe4?! ♗c6! leave White struggling to find enough for the pawn.

14...♘c6 15 ♘f3

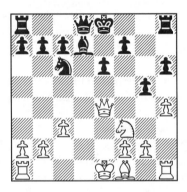

15...gxh4

Black can also equalise with 15...♕f6, the likely sequel being 16 hxg5 hxg5 17 ♖xh8+ ♕xh8 18 ♘xg5 ♕f6 etc.

16 ♘e5!?

White doesn't have enough for the pawn after 16 0-0-0?! ♕e7, intending ...0-0-0.

16...♘xe5 17 ♕xe5 ♖g8 18 ♖d1 ♕e7 19 ♕xc7 ♗c6 20 ♕xe7+ ♔xe7 ½-½

Game 22
Reynolds-Nunn
London 1987

---

1 d4 ♘f6 2 ♘c3 d5 3 ♗g5 ♘bd7 4 ♘f3 e6 5 e4 h6 6 ♗h4 g5 7 ♗g3 ♘xe4 8 ♘xe4 dxe4 9 ♘e5

A sharp gambit continuation, though one which leaves White struggling to find ade-quate compensation. Black can simplify the position and leave White struggling to recapture the e4-pawn. For 9 ♘d2 see Galkin-Volzhin.

9...♗g7

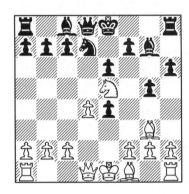

Black should be careful to avoid 9...♘xe5 10 ♗xe5 f6? (10...♖g8 is mandatory) because 11 ♕h5+ ♔e7 12 ♕g6! fxe5 13 dxe5 brings with it the deadly threat of 14 ♕f6+. However, Black does have interesting alternatives here:

a) 9...h5 10 h4 g4 11 ♕e2 (or 11 ♗c4 ♘xe5 12 dxe5 ♕xd1+ 13 ♖xd1 ♗h6, which left White with the task of regaining the e4-pawn in Schmittdiel-Mainka, Dortmund 1988) 11...♘xe5 12 dxe5 ♕d4! (stubbornly hanging onto the pawn makes it difficult for White to justify his play, whereas 12...♗h6 13 ♖d1 ♕e7 14 ♕xe4 favoured White in Aronian-Nalbandian, Yerevan 1996) 13 c3 ♕a4 and White still needs to get that e4-pawn back!

b) 9...♖g8 10 ♕e2 ♘xe5 11 ♗xe5 (11 dxe5 ♕d4) 11...f6 12 ♗g3 ♕xd4 13 ♕h5+ ♔e7 also put the onus on White to prove his compensation in Spal-Soukal, Czech Republic 1995.

10 h4

White is also struggling for equality after 10 ♕e2. Then 10...♕e7 11 0-0-0 ♘xe5 12 dxe5 ♗d7 13 ♕xe4 0-0-0 14 ♗a6 c6 15 ♖d6! led to a spectacular win for White in Muratov-Lipman, USSR 1980, the concluding moves being 15...♗e8 16 ♖hd1 ♖xd6 17 exd6 ♕d7 18 ♕b4 bxa6 19 ♖d3 a5 20 ♕xa5 f5 21 ♖b3 1-0. However, Black has the far superior 10...♘xe5! 11 dxe5 ♕d5 12 ♖d1 ♕a5+ (even 12...♕xa2 13 ♕d2 0-0 is not unthinkable) 13 c3 ♗d7 14 ♕xe4 0-0-0, intending 15...♗c6.

10...♘xe5

10...♕e7 is also playable but not quite as incisive.

11 ♗xe5

After 11 dxe5 ♕xd1+ 12 ♖xd1 ♗d7 Black keeps the extra pawn.

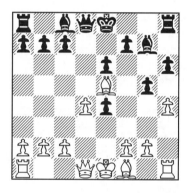

11...♗xe5

An interesting alternative is 11...f6!?, when Shagalovich-Shamkovich, Grozny Team Ch. 1969 continued 12 ♗g3 0-0! (after 12...♔f8 13 hxg5 hxg5 14 ♖xh8+ ♗xh8 15 ♕h5 ♗g7 16 0-0-0 White had enough compensation in Spal-Pachman, Ceske Budejovice 1992) 13 hxg5 fxg5! (opening lines for the counterattack; 13...hxg5 14 ♕h5 is unpleasant) 14 c3 ♗d7 15 ♗c4 ♕f6 16 ♕e2 ♕f5. Now Black obtained a strong attack after 17 ♗xc7?! ♖ac8 18 ♗g3? (18 ♗d6 ♖fd8 19 0-0 ♗c6 20 ♗g3 ♗d5 21 ♗xd5 exd5 is nice for Black but still a game) 18...♖xc4! 19 ♕xc4 e3 20 ♕e2? (White should bail out with 20 0-0 ♗b5 21 ♕c5, exchanging as many pieces as possible) 20...exf2+ 21 ♗xf2 (21 ♕xf2 is strongly met by 21...♗d5!) 21...♗b5 22 ♕d2 (after 22 ♕e3 Black opens more lines with 22...e5!) 22...♕e4+ 23 ♗e3 (23 ♕e3 ♕xg2 is

also good for Black but offers more resistance than the text) 23...♕h4+! 0-1. According to Shamkovich White should have played 17 0-0, after which 17...b5! 18 ♗b3 b4 19 ♗c2 ♗c6 would bring about a double-edged position with chances for both sides. Another possibility is 17 0-0-0.

12 dxe5 ♗d7 13 ♕g4

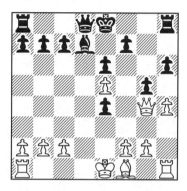

Bellin's recommendation for White to 'hang on', although this is hardly a mandate for 9 ♘e5. In Mestrovic-Bobotsov, Sarajevo 1971 White played 13 ♕d2 but found himself struggling after 13...gxh4 14 ♕b4 ♗c6 15 ♗b5 ♕d5 16 ♗xc6+ bxc6 17 ♖xh4 e3 18 fxe3 0-0-0 etc. In the event of 13 ♕d4 Black replies 13...♗c6! 14 ♕xd8+ ♖xd8 15 hxg5 ♖d5 and after 16 gxh6 (16 ♖xh6 ♖xh6 17 gxh6 ♖xe5 18 ♗e2 ♔f8 also leaves the h6-pawn weak) 16...♖xe5 he will round up h6 with 17...♖g5 and 18...♖g6.

13...♕e7

Black can also play 13...♗c6 14 hxg5 ♕d4, Muratov-Kiselev, Moscow 1988 continuing 15 c3 ♕xe5 16 0-0-0 ♔e7 17 ♖xh6 ♖xh6 18 gxh6 ♖h8 with the h6-pawn being in big trouble.

14 0-0-0

In Hector-Simon, Naestved 1988 White varied with 14 ♕xe4 but he was still struggling after 14...♗c6! 15 ♕d4 (the ingenious 15 ♗b5 backfires after 15...♗xb5 16 ♕xb7 ♕b4+ 17 c3 ♕xb2, threatening mate on e2 and the rook on a1) 15...♖d8 16 ♕c3 gxh4 etc.

14...0-0-0 15 ♕xe4 ♗c6 16 ♖xd8+ ♖xd8 17 ♕e3 gxh4! 18 ♕xa7?!

Capturing the other rook's pawn would also be wrong: 18 ♕xh6? is answered by 18...♕c5 19 ♕f4 (or 19 ♕xh4 ♕xe5) 19...♕d5 20 b3 h3! etc. White's best is 18 f4!, when 18...♕b4 19 ♖xh4 ♕a4 20 a3 ♗e4 gives White good drawing chances after 21 ♗d3 (21 ♕c3 ♖g8, threatening 22...♖g3!, with some pressure for Black) 21...♗xd3 22 cxd3 ♕c6+ 23 ♔b1 ♕xg2 24 ♖xh6 etc.

18...♕g5+ 19 ♕e3 ♖d4! 20 ♕xg5

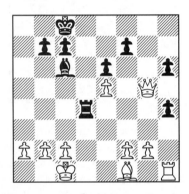

The only move. In response to 20 c3 Black has 20...♖e4, while after 20 ♗d3 there is 20...♗xg2 followed by ...h3 etc.

20...hxg5 21 f3 ♖d5 22 f4 gxf4 23 ♖xh4 f3! 24 ♖h5?

This certainly makes it easier for Black, although White might be losing in any case. White had to try 24 gxf3 ♖xe5 25 ♗g2 (25 ♗d3 ♗xf3 26 ♖f4 ♗h5 is probably winning because of the connected passed pawns), which is nevertheless quite unpleasant after 25...♖e2 26 ♖g4 ♔d7.

24...♖d8! 25 ♖h2

Neither 25 ♖g5 ♖h8, 25 g3 ♖g8, nor 25 g4 ♖d4 26 ♖g5 f2 followed by 27...♖e4 would help.

25...♖g8 26 g3

After 26 gxf3 ♖g1 27 ♖f2 ♗b5 White loses a piece.

26...♖xg3 27 ♔d2 ♖g1 28 ♔e1

Or 28 ♖f2 ♖g5 etc.

28...♗b5 29 ♖f2 ♗e2 30 c4 c5 31 a3 b6 32 b4 ♔c7 0-1

Game 23
Yermolinsky-Kaidanov
New York 1993

---

1 d4 d5 2 ♘c3 ♘f6 3 ♗g5 ♘bd7 4 ♘f3 e6

Black can avoid the line played in this game (6 ♗xf6!?) by playing 4...h6 5 ♗h4, and only then 5...e6. But in this case he must also reckon with 5 ♗f4.

5 e4 h6 6 ♗xf6!?

White has this option if Black plays 4...e6 and 5...h6. We have already seen 6 ♗h4 in Galkin-Volzhin and Reynolds-Nunn.

6...♘xf6! 7 ♕e2!

An excellent innovation from Yermo, which really deserved a better fate. Here are the alternatives:

a) 7 ♗d3 is strongly met by 7...♗b4! 8 exd5 (8 e5 ♘e4 is good for Black) 8...♘xd5! (8...exd5 9 0-0 0-0 was slightly better for Black in Rossetto-Gligoric, Havana 1967 but the text is even stronger) 9 ♕d2 c6! 10 ♘e5 (10 a3 is met by 10...♕a5) 10...♕b6! (and not the immediate 10...♕a5? because of 11 ♘c4, when 11...♗xc3 12 ♘xa5 ♗xd2+ 13 ♔xd2 actually looks better for White) 11 ♖c1 (11 0-0 ♕a5 wins a pawn in this position, the fact that White has castled leaving the knight on d2 unprotected) 11...♕xd4! 12 ♘xf7 ♘xc3! 13 ♘xh8 ♕e5+! 14 ♔f1 ♘xa2 15 c3 ♘xc1 16 ♕xc1 (16 ♗g6+ ♔e7 is no better) 16...♗c5, with a good extra pawn for Black in Arkell-Thipsay, Calicut 1987.

b) 7 e5 ♘e4 is very comfortable for Black.

c) 7 ♕d3!? in my view deserves consideration. Like 7 ♕e2, it prevents 7...♗b4? due to 8 ♕b5+. It also prepares queenside castling, leaves e2 open for White's bishop and may afford White the option of using his queen on the third rank.

7...♗e7

The point of Yermo's last move is that 7...♗b4? can be answered by 8 ♕b5+, picking up the bishop. White maintains a slight advantage after 7...dxe4 8 ♘xe4 ♘xe4 9 ♕xe4 ♕d5 10 ♗d3, or 7...a6 8 exd5 (here 8 0-0-0?! is answered by 8...dxe4 9 ♘xe4 ♘xe4 10 ♕xe4 ♕d5, hitting the a2-pawn) 8...♘xd5 9 ♘e4 etc.

8 e5 ♘d7 9 0-0-0 a6 10 h4 c5 11 g4?!

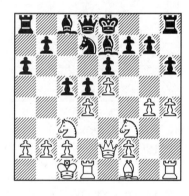

Lurching forward on the kingside might not be the correct plan. White should probably focus on the centre with 11 dxc5 ♗xc5! 12 ♘d4! b5 13 f4 ♕c7.

11...b5?!

Ftacnik recommended 11...c4, and it does seem quite good for Black after 12 ♕e3 b5 13 ♘e2 b4 with ideas such as ...♕a5 or ...c4-c3.

12 ♗g2?

White should still opt for 12 dxc5 before

Black's attack becomes too strong.

12...b4 13 ♘xd5

Played with the courage of despair. After 13 ♘b1 ♕a5 or 13 ♘a4 c4 14 ♘d2 ♖b8 (intending 15...♕a5) White comes under a strong attack.

13...exd5 14 dxc5 ♘xc5 15 ♘d4 ♗b7 16 f4

White's compensation is also inadequate after 16 ♘f5 g6 (or 16...0-0 17 ♗xd5 ♗xd5 18 ♖xd5 ♕c7) 17 ♘xe7 ♕xe7 etc.

16...♘e6 17 ♘xe6 fxe6 18 g5 hxg5 19 hxg5 ♖xh1 20 ♖xh1 ♕b6 21 ♕h5+ ♔d7 22 ♕f7 ♕e3+ 0-1

After 23 ♔b1 ♖f8 24 ♕xg7 ♕xf4 Black wins easily, 25 ♖h7? being answered by 25...♕f1+!.

Game 24
Mestrovic-Deze
Yugoslavia 1969

---

1 d4 ♘f6 2 ♘c3 d5 3 ♗g5 ♘bd7 4 ♘f3 h6 5 ♗h4 c5!? 6 dxc5!?

Only with this greedy capture can Black's idea be tested. The solid move is 6 e3.

6...e6

After 6...♕a5 White obtains an edge with 7 ♗xf6! ♘xf6 8 e4 (8 ♕d4 is also worth considering) 8...e6 (it looks as if White is better after 8...dxe4 9 ♘e5 a6 10 ♕d4, intending 11 b4 or 11 0-0-0, while 8...♘xe4?? loses on the spot to 9 ♗b5+) 9 ♗b5+ ♗d7

10 ♗xd7+ ♘xd7 11 exd5 ♗xc5 12 dxe6 fxe6 13 0-0 0-0-0 14 ♕e2 and White had an edge in Hort-Ostermeyer, Dortmund 1982.

7 b4!?

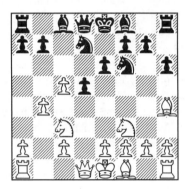

7...b6

This certainly succeeds in undermining White's advanced pawns but it involves Black in the sacrifice of a piece. A less costly way of attempting to do this is with 7...a5, after which Ribli-Planinc, Sombor 1970 continued 8 a3 g5 9 ♗g3 ♗g7 10 ♖b1 (10 ♘b5!? ♘e4 11 ♘fd4 could be an improvement) 10...axb4 11 axb4 ♘e4 12 ♘xe4 dxe4 13 ♘d4 ♘xc5!, recovering the pawn with a good game.

8 c6 ♗xb4! 9 cxd7+ ♗xd7 10 ♕d4 ♕e7

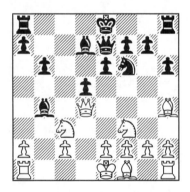

11 ♗xf6?!

Unpinning the knight on c3 with 11 ♔d1 runs into 11...♖c8 12 ♘b1 ♗a4 with a powerful attack for the sacrificed piece. On the other hand it's well worth examining 11 ♖b1!? without the preliminary exchange on f6, the point being that 11...♗a5 12 ♖b3 e5? makes 13 ♘xe5 possible. Tests required!

11...gxf6 12 ♖b1

In the event of the alternative 12 ♘d2 there follows 12...♖c8 13 ♘cb1 ♖xc2 14 e3 ♖c1+ 15 ♔e2 0-0 when White is horribly tied up.

12...♗a5 13 ♖b3

After 13 ♔d1 Deze gave 13...♖c8! 14 ♖b3 ♖c4 15 ♕d3 (or 15 ♕e3 d4 16 ♘xd4 ♕d6 winning back the piece with a huge advantage) 15...♕c5 16 ♘b1 ♔e7! but White may be able to continue with 17 e3 ♖c8 18 ♖b2 etc.

13...e5 14 ♕xd5 0-0 15 e3?!

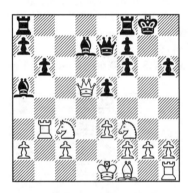

This looks like desperation on White's part – he parts with a whole rook in order to try to regain the initiative. He should play 15 ♘d2 ♗e6 16 ♕d3 though even then Black's attack looks very strong because White finds it so difficult to develop. A possible line of play is 16...♖ac8 17 ♘cb1 ♗xb3 18 axb3 ♖fd8 19 ♕g3+ ♔h7 20 c3 ♗xc3 21 ♘xc3 ♕a3 etc.

15...♗e6 16 ♕e4 ♗xb3 17 axb3

After 17 ♗d3 there follows 17...♗xc3+ 18 ♔f1 f5! 19 ♕xf5 e4 20 ♗xe4 ♗c4+ 21 ♔g1 ♖fd8 etc.

17...♗xc3+ 18 ♔e2 f5 19 ♕xf5 ♖fd8 20 ♕e4 ♕d6 21 ♕d3 ♕c5 22 ♕c4 ♕xc4+ 23 bxc4 e4 24 ♘d4 a5 25 f3 a4 0-1

Game 25
Kupreichik-Gutman
USSR 1976

1 d4 ♘f6 2 ♘c3 d5 3 ♗g5 ♘bd7 4 ♘f3 h6 5 ♗f4!?

An unstereotyped move. White threatens 6 ♘b5, though there are a number of ways for Black to meet this idea.

5...a6

Black can also defend the b5-square with 5...c6, when White should play 6 ♕d3, preparing e2-e4 and 0-0-0. This transposes to the note to White's 6th move in the game Ben Menachem-Boric in Chapter 2. Aiming for nothing more than quiet development with 6 e3 will not trouble Black. A good way to meet this is with 6...♘h5 (6...e6 is also quite solid) 7 ♗e5 ♘xe5 8 ♘xe5 ♘f6 9 ♗d3 e6 10 0-0 ♗d6 11 f4 ♕e7 12 ♔h1 ♗d7 13 e4 dxe4 14 ♘xe4 ♘xe4 15 ♗xe4 0-0-0 which was fine for Black in Bairachny-Tolnai, Zalakaros 1996.

The immediate 5...c5 can lead to interesting complications after 6 dxc5 ♘xc5 7 e4 ♘cxe4 8 ♘b5 e5!? (8...♘d6 9 ♘xd6+ exd6 10 ♗b5+ ♗d7 11 ♗xd7+ ♕xd7 12 0-0 ♗e7 13 ♘d4 0-0 14 ♕d3 gave White compensation for the pawn in Bairachny-J.Horvath, Budapest 1996) 9 ♗xe5 ♗c5 10 ♘c7+ ♔f8 11 ♘xa8 ♘xf2 etc. Black can also prepare this lever with 5...e6 6 ♕d2 (after 6 ♘b5

Black has 6...♗b4+ 7 c3 ♗a5) 6...a6 7 a3 c5 8 e3 b5, which gave him quite a good game in Galinsky-Grabinsky, Alushta 2002.

6 e4!?

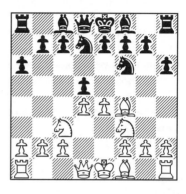

An ambitious idea from Kupreichik. It is also possible to prepare this thrust with 6 ♕d3, when 6...e6 (or 6...c5 7 e4) 7 e4 dxe4 (7...♗b4!?) 8 ♘xe4 ♘xe4 9 ♕xe4 ♘f6 10 ♕d3 ♗d6 11 ♘e5 was slightly better for White in Biyiasas-Vranesic, Toronto 1972. Quiet development with 6 e3 leaves White's knight on c3 somewhat misplaced. In L.Karlsson-Dive, Wrexham 1994 Black had a good game after 6...e6 7 ♗e2 ♗e7 8 0-0 c5 9 h3 0-0 10 ♘e5 ♘xe5 11 dxe5 ♘d7 12 ♗g3 b5 13 f4 b4 14 ♘b1 f5 thanks to the extra space on the queenside space and White's lack of kingside counterplay.

6...dxe4 7 ♘d2 e3 8 fxe3 g6 9 ♗e2 ♗g7 10 e4 0-0 11 e5?!

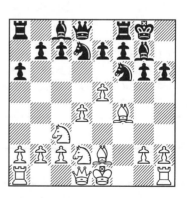

White's pawn centre briefly looks quite impressive but over the next few moves Black effectively undermines it. Here it seems better to play instead the line 11 0-0 c5 12 d5 with a complex position which needs some tests.

11...♞e8 12 ♞de4 c5! 13 dxc5 ♞c7 14 ♞a4?!

Probably overlooking or underestimating Black's 16th. Both 14 ♕d2 and 14 ♕c1 look better.

14...♞e6 15 ♗g3 ♕a5+ 16 c3 b5! 17 cxb6 ♞xb6 18 ♞xb6

After 18 ♞ac5 Black has 18...♖d8 with a continuing initiative.

18...♕xb6 19 ♕c2 ♗b7 20 ♗f3 ♖ab8 21 0-0-0?!

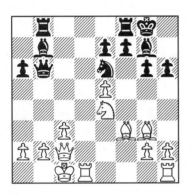

An incredibly risky decision, castling straight into open files.

21...♖fc8

Black's open files on the queenside give him more than enough compensation for the pawn.

22 ♔b1 ♕a5 23 ♔a1 ♖c4 24 ♞d2 ♞d4 25 ♕c1 ♖a4 26 a3 ♗xf3 27 gxf3 ♞e2! 28 ♞c4 ♖xc4 29 ♕e3 ♖xc3 30 ♕xe2 ♖xa3+ 31 ♔b1 ♖a1+ 0-1

Game 26
Ermenkov-Grivas
Sofia 1986

---

1 d4 d5 2 ♞c3 ♞f6 3 ♗g5 ♞bd7 4 e3!?

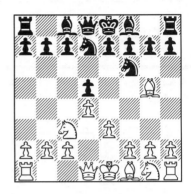

This looks rather harmless but there are some subtle effects compared with 4 ♞f3. For one thing White keeps open the option of advancing his f-pawn; in some positions he might also bring his queen out to f3...

4...g6

After 4...e6 I suggest 5 ♕f3!? which prepares queenside castling but also supports a pawn storm with a later g2-g4. Meanwhile White's queen is relatively safe from harassment because the e6-pawn restricts the activity of Black's light-squared bishop. A sample variation is 5...♗e7 6 0-0-0 0-0 7 g4 c5 8 h4 with what I think is quite a promising position for White. Tests are required! For 4...c6 see Bricard-Todorov.

5 ♗d3

For the immediate 5 f4 see the next game. It's not clear why Ermenkov delays this advance for so long; perhaps he wanted Black to castle first.

5...♗g7 6 ♕d2!?

White can still transpose to Miles-Andersson with 6 ♞f3. The text lends the game an independent flavour.

6...0-0 7 f4 c5!

Grivas felt that 7...c6?! would have been poor in view of 8 0-0-0 when White has dangerous attacking chances. While I'm not sure that Black is without resources in this position, the idea of castling long is certainly worth noting.

8 ♞f3 b6 9 ♞e5 ♗b7 10 ♖d1!

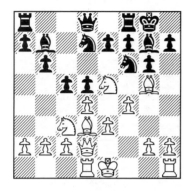

According to Grivas 10 0-0? is punished by 10...♘e4! 11 ♗xe4 dxe4 12 ♘xd7 ♕xd7 13 ♘e2 cxd4 14 exd4 (or 14 ♘xd4 e5) 14...♗a6. Certainly White's position has no great appeal here.

10...♘e8!?

In this position 10...♘e4 fails to 11 ♗xe4 dxe4 12 ♘xd7 ♕xd7 13 dxc5 etc. Gallagher mentions the possibility of 10...cxd4 11 exd4 ♘e4 but this seems better for White after 12 ♘xe4 dxe4 13 ♗b5 (rather than Gallagher's 13 ♗c4, which is well met by 13...♘xe5 followed by 14...♕c7) 13...♘xe5 14 fxe5 ♕c7 15 0-0 with more space and the better pawn structure.

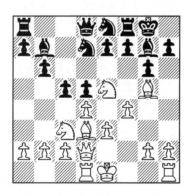

11 0-0

The attempt to win the d5-pawn with 11 ♘xd7 ♕xd7 12 dxc5 bxc5 13 ♗b5 falls flat after 13...♕c7! 14 ♘xd5 (or 14 ♗xe8 ♖fxe8 15 ♘xd5 ♗xd5 16 ♕xd5 ♖ad8) 14...♗xd5

15 ♕xd5 ♕a5+ 16 c3 ♘c7 17 ♕xc5 ♘xb5 18 ♗xe7 ♖fe8, when the piece is worth far more than the three (weak) pawns.

11...♘d6 12 ♗h4 ♖c8! 13 ♘b5 ♘xb5 14 ♗xb5 ♘xe5 15 fxe5 c4!?

Almost always a controversial decision because it presents White with an e3-e4 pawn lever.

16 c3 ♗c6 17 ♗xc6 ♖xc6 18 e4! f6

After 18...dxe4? 19 ♕e2 White wins the e4-pawn.

19 exf6 ♗xf6 20 ♕e1! ♗xh4! 21 ♕xh4

White can also interpose 21 ♖xf8+ ♕xf8 before playing 22 ♕xh4 but then Black can hang on with 22...dxe4! 23 ♕xe4 ♖f6 24 ♕d5+ ♕f7 25 ♕a8+ ♔g7 26 ♕xa7 ♕e6 with adequate counterplay.

21...♖cf6 22 ♖xf6 ♖xf6 23 exd5

After 23 ♖e1 Black has 23...e6!, gaining time with the threat of 24...♖f1+.

23...♕xd5 24 ♕g3 ♕d6! 25 ♕e3 ♔f7! 26 ♖e1 ♕e6 27 ♕g3

In the pawn endgame Black can draw by eliminating his e-pawn: 27 ♕xe6+ ♖xe6 28 ♖xe6 ♔xe6 29 ♔f2 ♔d5 30 ♔e3 e5! with equality.

27...♕f5 28 h3 ♕f4 29 ♔h2 h5

Another possibility was 29...g5.

30 h4 ♕f2! 31 ♖e4 ♕f5

Better than 31...♕xb2 32 ♕c7 ♕a3 33 ♕xc4+ when White retains some chances.

32 ♕e3 ♖e6 33 ♖xe6 ♕xe6 34 ♕f4+

Or 34 ♕xe6+ ♔xe6 35 ♔g3 ♔f5 36 ♔f3

b5 etc.

34...♔g7 ½-½

Game 27
Brandner-Miniboeck
St Poelten 2002

1 d4 ♘f6 2 ♘c3 d5 3 ♗g5 ♘bd7 4 e3

The immediate 4 f4 looks premature to me. Gueneau-Lane, Parthenay 1992 went 4...e6 5 a3 c5 6 e3 ♕a5! 7 ♘f3?! (White should unpin with 7 ♕d2 but then 7...cxd4 8 exd4 ♗b4 looks better for Black, while 7 ♗d3 doesn't help White after 7...c4 8 ♗e2 ♘e4 etc.) 7...♘e4 8 dxc5 ♗xc5 9 ♗d3 ♘xc3 10 ♕d2 ♕b6 11 ♕xc3 f6 12 0-0 ♗xe3+ 13 ♔h1 0-0 14 ♗h4 ♗xf4 0-1.

4...g6 5 f4!?

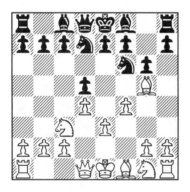

With Black having played ...♘bd7 and ...g7-g6 this becomes very interesting. Had he been able to play ...c7-c5 and ...♘b8-c6 he would put far more pressure on White's centre. And had he not played ...g7-g6 he could put pressure on the knight on c3 as in the note above.

5...♗g7

5...c6 transposes to Bricard-Todorov.

6 ♘f3 0-0 7 ♗d3

White might also consider the modest 7 ♗e2 which reduces Black's opportunities for counterplay by leaving d4 better protected.

7...b6

Black should play the more active 7...c5

but after 8 0-0 ♕b6 White can calmly play 9 ♖b1.

8 0-0 ♗b7 9 f5

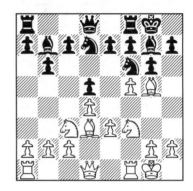

The standard move is 9 ♘e5 but White approaches the situation far more imaginatively. Breaking open lines on the kingside like this illustrates a further disadvantage of Black's 3...♘bd7. The light-squared bishop no longer covers f5.

9...c5 10 fxg6

White could also think about delaying this exchange as after 10 ♕e1!? c4 11 ♗e2 gxf5 he has attacking chances against Black's weakened kingside.

10...hxg6

It's probably better to play 10...fxg6, leaving Black's king somewhat better protected.

11 ♕e1 ♘e4 12 ♕h4 f6?

The decisive error. Black had to play 12...♘df6 when White would probably bring his queen's knight over, starting with 13 ♘e2.

13 ♘xe4 dxe4 14 ♗xe4

14 ♗c4+ was even better as after 14...♖f7 15 ♘d2 White wins the exchange for zero compensation.

14...♗xe4 15 ♕xe4 ♕e8

Black prefers to decline the piece and stay a pawn down in a hopeless position. Admittedly it's very dangerous to take as after 15...fxg5 16 ♕e6+ ♔h8 17 ♘xg5 ♘f6 White has the nasty 18 ♖f3 with powerful threats.

16 ♗f4 e6 17 ♗d6 f5 18 ♕h4 ♖f7 19 ♕g3

After 19 ♘g5 Black can delay resignation with 19...♗f6.

19...♖f6 20 ♘g5 ♗h6 21 ♗f4 ♔g7 22 ♖ae1 ♖c8 23 c3 ♕g8 24 e4 ♖e8 25 ♘h3 cxd4 26 cxd4 ♗xf4 27 ♘xf4 1-0

Besides 28 ♘h5+ White threatens 28 e5.

Game 28
Bricard-Todorov
St Affrique Open 2000

---

1 d4 d5 2 ♘c3

The move order was actually 2 ♗g5 c6 3 ♘c3 ♘d7 4 e3 ♘gf6 5 f4. I've used a Veresov move order for the sake of clarity.

2...♘f6 3 ♗g5 ♘bd7 4 e3 c6

This position can also arise via 3...c6 4 e3 ♘bd7.

5 f4

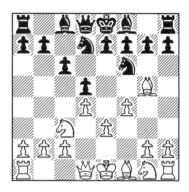

Once again this becomes interesting, this time the justification being the somewhat passive ...c7-c6. This pawn will lose a tempo in advancing to c5. White can also develop some pieces before switching to the ♘f3-e5 and f2-f4 plan, for example Vyzhmanavin-Bronstein, Moscow Ch. 1981 went 5 ♘f3 e6 6 ♗d3 ♗e7 7 0-0 0-0 8 ♘e5 ♘xe5 9 dxe5 ♘d7 10 ♗xe7 ♕xe7 11 f4 f6 12 ♕h5! g6 13 exf6 ♕xf6?! (13...♘xf6 14 ♕h4 e5 was better with complex play) 14 ♕h6 and White had a slight edge.

5...g6

Black doesn't generate much counterplay after this move so he would do well to consider the alternatives:

a) After 5...♕a5 6 ♗d3 e6 I suggest that White gambits a pawn with 7 ♘f3 (7 a3 c5 was awkward for White in Ratolistka-Altschul, Kosice 1961 as 8 ♘f3 could be answered by 8...c4 9 ♗e2 ♘e4) 7...♗b4 8 0-0 ♗xc3 9 bxc3 ♕xc3 10 ♖b1!? (10 ♘e5?! c5 favoured Black in Stulik-Hannak, Olomouc 1944) 10...♘e4 11 ♖b3 ♕a5 12 ♗xe4 dxe4 13 ♘d2.

b) 5...b5 6 ♗d3 ♘b6 was played in Atanasov-Sydor, Ruse 1984 and now 7 b3 makes sense, simply depriving Black's knight of the c4-square. In the game White played 7 ♘f3 after which 7...♘c4 8 ♕c1 ♕b6 9 0-0 e6 10 f5 ♗e7 11 e4 e5 led to a complex game.

c) 5...♕b6 6 ♖b1 e6 7 ♗d3 c5 8 ♘f3 cxd4 9 exd4 a6 10 0-0 ♗e7 11 ♔h1 gave White good attacking chances in Wade-Shah, Hampstead 1998.

d) 5...h6 6 ♗h4 g5!? (sacrificing a pawn for a dangerous initiative; 6...♕a5 7 ♗d3 ♘e4 8 ♗xe4 dxe4 9 ♕d2 ♕h5 10 ♗f2 ♘f6 11 ♘ge2 ♕g6 12 ♖g1 ♗g4 13 0-0-0 e6 14 h3 left White with the superior pawn structure in R.Pert-Taksrud, Copenhagen 2002) 7 fxg5 (I think that White should decline the offer with 7 ♗g3, when there are some weaknesses in Black's camp) 7...hxg5 8 ♗xg5 e5 9 ♘f3 ♕b6 10 ♖b1 ♘h7 11 ♗h4 e4 12 ♘d2 ♘df6 13 ♗e2 ♗h6 and Black had plenty for the pawn in Francisco-Leite, Odivelas 2001.

6 ♗d3 ♝g7 7 ♘f3

White can also consider 7 ♕d2!? with the idea of meeting 7...0-0 with 8 0-0-0 and then launching some sort of attack on the kingside. The passive nature of ...c7-c6 makes such things possible.

7...0-0 8 0-0 c5

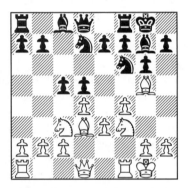

8...b6 9 ♕d2 (White would do better to play 9 ♘e5 at once or even 9 f5!? – in either case the position looks promising for him) 9...♝b7 10 ♖ae1 c5 11 ♘e5 a6 12 f5 ♘e4 13 ♗xe4 dxe4 14 ♘xd7 ♕xd7 was Wade-D'Costa, British League, Birmingham 2001, and now 15 f6 (rather than 15 fxg6 as played in the game) looks promising after 15...exf6 16 ♗xf6 ♝xf6?! 17 ♖xf6, attacking b6.

9 ♕e1 h6 10 ♗h4 b6 11 ♘e5 ♝b7 12 ♖d1 ♕c7

Black should probably try the move 12...e6 in order to cover the f5-square. But even then I don't like his position after 13 g4, for instance. White's next move is very strong and inflicts permanent damage on Black's kingside.

13 f5! g5

After 13...♘xe5 14 dxe5 ♕xe5 White can trap his opponent's queen with 15 ♗g3.

14 ♗g3 ♘h5 15 ♘xd7 ♘xg3 16 ♕xg3 ♕xd7 17 dxc5 bxc5 18 h4?

A good move at the wrong time. White should first win the d5-pawn with 18 ♗b5 ♕c8 19 ♘xd5 ♝xd5 20 ♖xd5 and only after 20...♝xb2 play 21 h4.

18...♝f6?

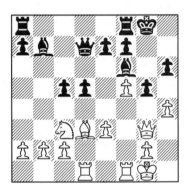

Giving White a second bite of the cherry. Black should play 18...♝xc3 19 bxc3 ♕d6 20 ♕g4 ♕f6, holding his position together.

19 ♗b5 ♕c8 20 ♘xd5 ♝xd5 21 ♖xd5 ♖b8 22 hxg5 hxg5 23 ♗d7 ♕a6 24 b3 ♔g7 25 a4 ♕e2 26 ♖xc5 ♖h8 27 ♗b5 ♕h5 28 ♗d3 g4?

A forlorn attempt to attack which just loses another pawn.

29 ♖c4 1-0

29...♕h1+ 30 ♔f2 ♝h4 31 ♖xh1 ♝xg3+ 32 ♔xg3 ♖xh1 33 ♖c7 will soon leave White with three connected passed pawns on the queenside.

Summary

The gambit lines with 4 ♘f3 e6 5 e4 h6 6 ♗h4 are just about playable for White, but only if he plays 9 ♘d2. He also has the option of avoiding this with either 4 ♘f3 h6 5 ♗f4 or 4 ♘f3 e6 5 e4 h6 6 ♗xf6, both of which offer White some interesting possibilities.

My own favourite move is 4 e3, which steers play into some unexplored backwaters in which White's prospects appear to be quite promising. The 'Stonewall' formation looks rather good once Black's knight is committed to the passive d7-square, and 4...e6 5 ♕f3 deserves to be tested.

1 d4 ♘f6 2 ♘c3 d5 3 ♗g5 ♘bd7 4 ♘f3 *(D)*

> 4 e3 *(D)* g6
>> 4...c6 5 f4 - *Game 28*
>
> 5 f4 - *Game 27*; 5 ♗d3 - *Game 26*

4...e6

> 4...h6
>> 5 ♗f4 - *Game 25*; 5 ♗h4 c5 - *Game 24*
>
> 4...g6 - *Game 20*

5 e4 h6 6 ♗h4

> 6 ♗xf6 - *Game 23*

6...g5 7 ♗g3 ♘xe4 8 ♘xe4 dxe4 *(D)*

> 9 ♘d2 - *Game 21*; 9 ♘e5 - *Game 22*

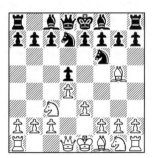

4 ♘f3   *4 e3*   *8...dxe4*

CHAPTER FOUR

3...c5

1 d4 ♘f6 2 ♘c3 d5 3 ♗g5 c5

3...c5 is a fighting move which brings about a Chigorin with colours reversed (1 d4 d5 2 c4 ♘c6 and now 3 ♘f3 ♗g4). The Chigorin itself has a somewhat dubious reputation which may or may not be deserved. In any case we are getting this position with an extra tempo, and that makes a difference in an open and potentially sharp position.

White certainly can't consider any attempts to build up with f2-f3, he has to attack Black's centre. The traditional way to do this is via 4 ♗xf6, when 4...gxf6 is Black's most important move, as in Games 29-31. In Veresov-Shustef, White plays the razor-sharp 5 e4, and after 5...dxe4 6 dxc5 ♕a5 White might be well advised to play 7 ♕d5 rather than Veresov's 7 ♕h5. Although White won this game in glorious style it was hardly convincing when subject to scrutiny by Fritz. In addition to the problems after 6...♕a5 White must also be prepared to face 6...f5. Thus far this has looked distinctly unappealing for White, Miladinovic-Smagin being an excellent advert for Black's position.

White is probably better off playing the deceptively quiet 5 e3, as in Mihaijlovskij-Gershon. In fact this has the dangerous idea of bringing White's queen to h5, castling queenside and later launching a pawn storm with f2-f4 and perhaps g2-g4. Although White lost the game in question his play could certainly be improved – I quite like 6 ♕xd4, for example.

The search for improvements for White has led him to consider delaying ♗xf6 and instead continue development with 4 e3 (Games 32-34). After 4...♘c6 White can still play 5 ♗xf6, leading back to Mihaijlovskij-Gershon whilst removing the possibility of ...h7-h5. In Hort-Van der Wiel White's 5 ♘f3 also looked interesting after 5...♗g4 6 dxc5, but the big question is whether White has anything after quiet moves like ...e7-e6, as in Mestrovic-Zivkovic and Speelman-Saltaev. On the evidence of these games this doesn't look like much for White, although there is a tiny drop of poison.

Last but not least we come to Sagalchik-Ariel, in which White brought about a reversed Albin Counter Gambit with 4 e4 and the play followed a wild path. If you think this is your kind of game then go for it – just don't blame me for the consequences!

Game 29
Veresov-Shustef
USSR 1974

---

1 d4 ♘f6 2 ♘c3 d5 3 ♗g5 c5 4 ♗xf6

Taking the earliest opportunity to weaken Black's pawn structure. As we'll see in later games White can also delay this capture.

4...gxf6

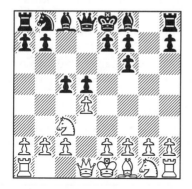

The alternative recapture may also be playable, despite the obvious weakening of Black's d-pawn. After 4...exf6 White plays 5 e3, intending to build up pressure against the d5-pawn, usually with ♘ge2, g2-g3 and ♗g2. Play might continue 5...♗e6 6 ♘ge2 ♘c6 7 g3 cxd4 (7...♛b6 8 ♗g2 cxd4 9 exd4 ♖d8 10 0-0 ♗b4 11 ♘a4 was nice for White in Kuebart-Balanel, Miedzyzdroje 1952) 8 exd4 ♗d6 (8...♗b4 9 ♗g2 ♛d7 10 0-0 0-0 11 ♘b1 ♗g4 12 c3 ♗a5 13 ♛d2 ♗h3 14 ♘a3 with a pleasant position for White in Rossetto-Alvarez, Quilmes 1980) 9 ♗g2 ♘e7 10 0-0 a6 11 ♘c1 (11 ♛d2 seems better, envisaging 12 ♘d4 or 12 ♘d1 followed by ♘e3) 11...h5 12 ♖e1 ♔f8 13 ♘d3 ♖c8 14 ♘e2 g5, and complex play had resulted in Smyslov-Bobotsov, Sochi 1963.

After 5...♘c6 White can try 6 dxc5!? ♗e6 7 ♛h5 intending to castle long with the initiative. Black has also tried 5...c4, but after 6 ♘ge2 ♗b4 7 g3 b5 8 ♗g2 ♗b7 9 a3 ♗a5 10 0-0 ♛d7 11 b4 ♗c7 12 a4 bxa4 13 ♘xa4 the outpost on c5 and the weak pawn on d5 gave White a clear advantage in Shaw-A.Hunt, Isle of Man 1993.

5 e4

Blasting the position wide open in order to try to exploit his lead in development. For

the quieter 5 e3 see Mihajlovskij-Gershon.

5...dxe4 6 dxc5

6 d5!? is an attempt to play a strange looking Albin Counter Gambit with colours reversed, although White's compensation appears to be rather nebulous. Play might continue 6...f5 7 ♛h5 ♗g7 8 ♗b5+ (8 ♘ge2 ♛b6 9 0-0-0 ♛h6+ 10 ♛xh6 ♗xh6+ 11 ♔b1 ♘d7 left White with woefully insufficient compensation for the pawn in Hebden-V.Milov, Isle of Man 1995) 8...♔f8 9 ♘h3 ♛d6 10 ♗e2 ♛h6 11 ♘g5 ♛xh5 12 ♗xh5 ♘d7 13 ♖d1 (13 ♘xf7 ♘f6 wins material) 13...♗xc3+ 14 bxc3 ♘f6 15 ♗e2 ♖g8 16 ♘h3 ♖xg2, when Black went on to win in Mestrovic-Sermek, Tucepi 1996.

6...♛a5

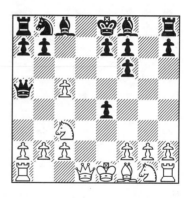

For 6...f5 see Miladinovic-Smagin.

7 ♛h5

This prepares long castling, defends c5 and probes the weak f7-pawn. But is it White's best? According to Gligoric, White should play 7 ♛d4 with an even game but then 7...♘c6 8 ♗b5 ♛xb5 9 ♘xb5 ♘xd4 10 ♘xd4 ♗d7 gives Black the better endgame according to Gufeld and Stetsko. A superior version of this is 7 ♛d5, when Goldin-Aseev, Podolsk 1990 continued 7...a6 (7...♘c6 8 ♗b5 ♗d7 9 0-0-0 is unpleasant for Black) 8 0-0-0 ♘c6 9 ♛xe4 f5 10 ♛e3 ♗e6 11 a3 ♗g7 12 ♘ge2 ♘e5 13 ♘d4 ♘g4 14 ♛e2 ♗xd4 15 ♖xd4 ♛xc5 16 ♛d2 ♖c8, which was about equal. Goldin-Khalifman,

USSR 1984 went instead 9 ♗c4 ♗e6 10 ♕xe4 f5 11 ♕e2 ♗xc4 12 ♕xc4 e6 13 ♘a4 ♕b5 14 ♕b3 ♘d4 15 ♕xb5+ axb5 and now White should have played 16 c3 ♘c6 17 ♘b6 ♖xa2 18 ♔b1 followed by 19 b4 with equality.

7...♗g7

After the passive 7...e6 White generated a powerful attack in Veresov-Smoljaninov, USSR 1963 with 8 0-0-0 f5 9 ♗b5+ (9 ♘h3, intending 10 ♘g5, also looks strong) 9...♘c6 10 g4! a6 11 ♗xc6+ bxc6 12 gxf5 exf5 13 ♘ge2 ♕xc5 14 ♘d4 ♖b8 15 ♖he1 ♗e7 16 ♘xe4! fxe4 17 ♖xe4. Black should avoid 7...f5 8 0-0-0 ♕xc5 in view of 9 ♘xe4! etc.

8 ♗b5+

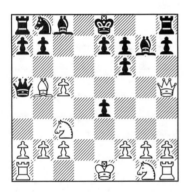

White concentrates on completing his development as soon as possible while leaving open the option of castling short. The other natural move is 8 0-0-0!?, e.g. 8...0-0 9 ♗c4 ♘c6 (9...♘d7 10 ♗d5 ♘xc5 11 ♘xe4 ♗e6 12 ♘c3 f5 13 ♘ge2 was double-edged in Haubt-Mevel, Bundesliga, Germany 1981) 10 ♗d5 (10 ♗b3 ♘e5 11 ♕h4 ♕xc5 12 ♘xe4 ♕c7 13 ♘e2 ♘g6 14 ♕g3 ♕xg3 15 hxg3 ♗f5 was also fairly even in Vaisman-Pytel, Wroclaw 1972) 10...♘e5 11 f4!? ♘g6 (11...exf3 12 gxf3 opens the g-file) 12 f5 ♘f4 13 ♕h4 ♘xd5 14 ♖xd5 e6 15 ♖d2 exf5 16 ♘ge2 and in Hoi-Bang, Copenhagen 1991 White had compensation for his pawn(s) in the form of the beautiful f4-square.

8...♘c6

Black can also play 8...♗d7 as the supposed refutation with 9 ♕g4!? is quite playable for Black after 9...♔f8 (9...♖g8 10 ♗xd7+ ♘xd7 11 ♘ge2 ♕xc5 12 ♕xe4 0-0-0 is also okay, as in Schneider-Odendahl, Germany 1993) 10 ♗xd7 f5! 11 ♕xf5 ♗xc3+ 12 ♔f1 ♘xd7 13 ♕xd7 ♕a6+ 14 ♘e2 ♗xb2, Heitland-Wessendorf, Dortmund 1987. This leaves an argument for 9 ♗xd7+ followed by 10 0-0-0, when Black would lose the f7-pawn if he castled long.

9 ♘ge2 0-0

9...a6 10 ♗xc6+ bxc6 11 0-0 (11 0-0-0!? looks like an extra tempo compared with the analogous 9...0-0 10 ♗xc6 line) 11...♖b8 (11...f5 12 ♖ad1 is given as slightly better for White by Kapengut and Boleslavsky, but the position looks complex and unclear to me) 12 ♘xe4 ♖xb2 13 ♘d4 0-0 14 ♖ae1 ♕c7 15 ♘g3 e6 16 ♕h4 followed by 17 ♘h5 gave White a dangerous attack in Radashkovich-Mart, Israel 1974.

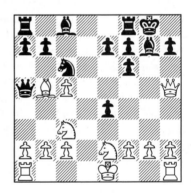

10 ♗xc6

In such a sharp and little explored position it's difficult to know which line is best. Although this move works beautifully in the game, it does seem that Black was doing well when you take a closer look.

a) 10 0-0-0 allows 10...♘e5, when the knight helps in the defence of Black's kingside. Nevertheless this is far from clear, for example 11 ♕h4 a6 12 ♗a4 ♗g4 13 ♗b3 ♗xe2 14 ♘xe2 ♕xc5 15 ♕xe4 ♕xf2 left

White with a tremendously active game for his pawn in Veresov-Lomaja, USSR 1967. The game continued 16 ♘d4 e6 17 ♖hf1 ♗h6+ 18 ♔b1 ♕e3 19 ♕xb7 a5, and now – instead of 20 a4 – 20 ♖fe1 ♕f2 21 ♖e2 would have been best, with a possible edge in this sharp position. 11 f3!? a6 12 ♗a4 ♕xc5 13 ♔b1 exf3 ½-½, Bellin-Schellhorn, Hamburg 1980 doesn't tell us much except that both players could have been worried.

b) With 10 a3 White intends to hold the c5-pawn by capturing on c6 and then playing b2-b4, although this might not be sharp enough to be in tune with the position. After 10...f5 11 0-0 ♕c7 12 b4 ♗e6 13 ♖ad1 ♖ad8 14 ♗a4 a5 Black had a very active game in Mestrovic-Gligoric, Hastings 1970/71.

c) 10 0-0 f5 11 ♕g5 e6 was played in Schneider-Mehler, Bundesliga Germany 1983. Then the simple 12 a3 was interesting, trying to maintain the c5-pawn. In the game White played 12 f3 exf3 13 ♖xf3 but his 'attack' was unconvincing after 13...♕d8 14 ♕h5 ♘e5 15 ♖h3 h6 16 ♖g3 ♔h7 etc.

10...bxc6 11 0-0-0

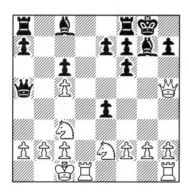

Probably necessary, as 11 0-0 f5 leaves White with little compensation.

11...♗e6

Too slow? In my view Black should be attacking b2 as quickly as possible. The position after 11...f5 12 g4!? ♕xc5 13 gxf5 ♕xf5 14 ♕h4 has been evaluated as 'unclear' by Boleslavsky and Kapengut. Here 12...♖b8 is

critical in my opinion, as Black wants to play 13...♕b4.

12 ♘d4 f5 13 g4 ♖ab8

After 13...♗xa2 White can simply get on with it by playing 14 gxf5 ♗c4 15 ♖hg1 as 15...♔h8 leads to mate after 16 ♖xg7 ♔xg7 17 f6+ exf6 18 ♖g1+ ♔h8 19 ♕h6 etc.

14 gxf5 ♖xb2

What does White do after 14...♕b4 here? It seems to me that 15 ♘b3 is forced (15 ♖hg1 ♕xb2+ 16 ♔d2 ♖bd8), after which 15...♗xb3 16 axb3 ♗xc3 17 bxc3 ♕xc3 18 ♕g4+ ♔h8 19 ♕xe4 ♖xb3 20 ♕d4+ might escape with a draw in the rook endgame.

15 fxe6 ♕xc3 16 ♖hg1 ♖xa2?

In my view it's only here that Black makes the decisive mistake. He still seems to be okay after 16...♖xc2+ 17 ♘xc2 ♕b2+ 18 ♔d2 ♕c3+.

17 ♖xg7+ ♔xg7 18 ♕e5+ 1-0

Black will either lose his queen (if he allows ♘f5 with check) or get mated.

Game 30
Miladinovic-Smagin
Montreal 2000

---

1 d4 d5 2 ♘c3 ♘f6 3 ♗g5 c5 4 ♗xf6 gxf6 5 e4 dxe4 6 dxc5 f5

A serious alternative to the more popular 6...♕a5. If Black manages to complete his development unscathed he'll have an extra pawn and the two bishops.

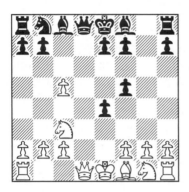

7 ♗b5+

This fails to cause Black much trouble and we soon reach a position in which White has zero compensation. Therefore White should probably look for improvements at this point:

a) 7 ♕h5 is a standard move in these lines but then 7...e6 (7...♗g7 8 ♗b5+ ♘c6 9 ♘ge2 is given as 'unclear' by V.Kovacevic) 8 g4 ♗xc5 9 gxf5 ♕d4 10 ♕h4 (after 10 ♕e2?! exf5 11 ♘b5 ♕e5 Black has a massive position) 10...e3 11 ♕xd4 ♗xd4 12 fxe3 ♗xc3+! 13 bxc3 exf5 brought about complete equality in Mestrovic-Popov, Banjaluka 1974. Popov gave the line 8 ♖d1 ♕f6! 9 ♗b5+ ♗d7 10 ♗xd7+ ♘xd7 11 ♘b5 0-0-0! 12 ♘xa7+ ♔b8 13 ♘b5 ♗xc5, when Black is clearly better.

b) 7 g4!? is an attempt to break up Black's pawn centre but seems well answered by 7...♕a5 8 ♕d4! ♖g8 9 b4!, when Florian claimed a clear advantage for White. The exact opposite seems to be the case after 9...♘c6! 10 ♗b5 ♕xb5 11 ♘xb5 ♘xd4 etc. Alternatively 7...♕xd1+ 8 ♖xd1 fxg4 9 ♘d5! is obviously good for White, but Black can consider 7...♘d7 8 gxf5 ♗g7 with a lead in development and a strong dark-squared bishop. 7...♗g7 8 ♕xd8+ ♔xd8 9 0-0-0+ ♗d7 10 ♘ge2 fxg4 11 ♘xe4 was about even in Bellin-Duncan, Gausdal 1996.

c) 7 ♕xd8+ attempts to cause problems by displacing Black's king but in fact looks

rather good for Black according to Gufeld and Stetsko after 7...♔xd8 8 0-0-0+ ♗d7 9 ♗c4 e6 10 b4 (10 g4?! fxg4 11 ♘xe4 ♔e7! 12 f3 ♗c6 favoured Black in Floreen-Alburt, New York 1993) 10...a5 11 a3 b6 12 ♘a4 bxc5 13 ♘xc5 ♗xc5 14 bxc5 ♔c7 followed by 15...♘a6. Lipski-Lorenc, Wisla 1998 went 8...♘d7 9 g4, and now 9...fxg4 10 ♘xe4 f5 11 ♘g5 ♗h6 12 h4 ♔c7 looks good for Black.

7...♗d7 8 ♘ge2

After 8 ♗xd7+ ♘xd7 9 ♕d5 e6 10 ♕xb7 ♖b8 11 ♕xa7 ♗xc5 12 ♕a4 ♖g8 Black's pieces start to generate demonic activity.

8...♘c6 9 ♕d2 e6 10 0-0 ♖g8!

10...♗xc5? runs into 11 ♘xe4! fxe4 12 ♕c3, forking c5 and h8, though even this might be only equal.

11 ♖ad1 ♗xc5 12 ♘a4

This position is distinctly unappealing for White. Both 12 ♘g3 ♖g6 and 12 ♕h6 ♕g5 repulse White's pressure.

12...♗b4 13 c3 ♗f8 14 b4 ♘e5

This leads to massive exchanges and an easy win for Black. All by move 14!

15 ♗xd7+ ♕xd7 16 ♕xd7+ ♘xd7 17 f3 ♘f6

17...exf3 18 ♖xf3 ♘f6 is also good.

18 ♘d4 ♖d8 19 ♖fe1 exf3 20 ♘xf3 ♖xd1 21 ♖xd1 ♘d5 22 ♘d4 a6! 23 ♘xf5 b5 24 ♘c5 ♖g5!

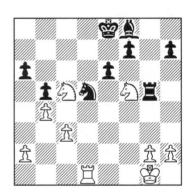

Ejecting the knight.

25 ♘d4 ♘xc3 26 ♖d3 ♗xc5 27 bxc5 ♖xc5 28 ♘b3 ♖c7 29 ♖d6 ♖a7 30 a3

♘b1 31 ♘c5 ♘xa3 32 ♘xa6 ♘c4 33
♖c6 ♘e5 34 ♖b6 ♘d7 35 ♖c6 ♘e5 36
♖b6 ♘d7 37 ♖c6 ♖b7 38 ♖c7 ♖xc7

This looks like mutual time trouble with
White's flag falling after his next move.
38...♖b6 is easier.

39 ♘xc7+ 0-1

Game 31
Mihajlovskij-Gershon
World U16 Ch., Menorca 1996

---

1 d4 ♘f6 2 ♘c3 d5 3 ♗g5 c5 4 ♗xf6

White can also vary his move order with 4
e3, when 4...♘c6 5 ♗xf6 gxf6 6 ♕h5 transposes back to the game but having cut out
6...h5!?. Knaak-V.Georgiev, Germany 1999
continued 6...e6 7 0-0-0 f5 8 f4 c4 (8...cxd4!?
9 exd4 ♗b4) 9 g4?! fxg4 10 e4 ♘e7 11 f5
exf5 12 exd5 ♕d6 13 ♖e1 a6 and White had
inadequate compensation.

4...gxf6 5 e3

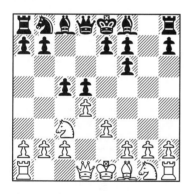

A quiet alternative to the aggressive 5 e4,
the text leads to complex middlegames in
which Black has the bishop pair and central
pawns but his pawn weaknesses make his
structure rather unwieldy and immobile. Another possibility is 5 ♘f3, when an interesting line is 5...♘c6 6 e4!? (quiet moves such as
6 e3 and 6 g3 fail to trouble Black) 6...dxe4 7
d5 exf3 8 dxc6 fxg2 9 ♗xg2 ♕b6 10 ♕f3
♖b8 (10...♕xb2? 11 ♖b1) 11 0-0-0 ♗h6+ 12
♔b1 bxc6 13 ♘a4 with what looks like an

edge.

5...cxd4

After 5...♘c6 White could play 6 ♕h5!,
making life rather awkward for Black. An
alternative is 5...e6 6 ♘ge2 ♘c6 7 g3 ♕b6 8
dxc5 ♗xc5 9 ♗g2 ♕xb2 10 0-0 ♕a3?!
(10...♕b4 is better, intending 11 ♖b1 ♕c4
etc.) 11 e4 dxe4 12 ♘xe4 ♗e7 13 ♘d4 and
White had compensation for his pawn in
Mensch-Gofstein, Paris Ch. 2000. Here after
(5...e6) 6 ♕h5 Black can try 6...♘d7 with the
aim of playing ...f7-f5 and ...♘f6 in order to
displace White's queen and secure Black's
kingside.

6 exd4

Not the only move, and possibly not the
best. White can also play 6 ♕xd4

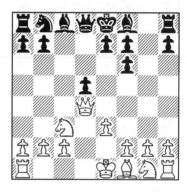

Then 6...e6 7 0-0-0 ♘c6 8 ♗b5 ♗d7 9
♗xc6 (9 ♕h4 is possible here too, as is 9
♕f4!?) 9...bxc6 10 ♘ge2 ♗e7 11 f4 ♕b6 12
♕d3 ♖b8 13 b3 ♖g8 14 e4 ♖xg2 15 f5 gave
White attacking chances for his pawn in Day-
Dlugy, Toronto 1989. 8 ♕h4 is very similar
to an analogous variation of the Chigorin
Defence, for example 8...f5 9 ♕g3 ♗d6 10
♕h3 ♗e5 11 ♘b5 ♕f6 12 c3 a6 13 ♘d4
♗d7 14 ♘gf3 produced a fairly balanced
knights versus bishops and weak pawns contest in Nikolic-Karpatchev, Leutersdorf 2001.

6...♘c6?!

Surprisingly this natural move might actually be a mistake. White's most dangerous
idea in this position is to play 7 ♕h5, which

Black can prevent with 6...h5!?. Maksimovic-Tatai, Vrnjacka Banja 1979 continued 7 ♗e2 h4 8 ♗f3 e6 9 ♘ge2 (9 ♕e2 ♘c6 10 ♗xd5 ♘xd4 11 ♕e4 e5 12 ♗xb7 ♗xb7 13 ♕xb7 ♖b8 14 ♕e4 ♖xb2 was good for Black in Navinsek-B.Avrukh, Ljubljana 1998) 9...♗h6 10 0-0 ♘c6 11 ♖e1 ♗d7 12 ♘c1 ♔f8! 13 ♘3e2 ♕b6 with a good game for Black thanks to the bishop pair and centre pawns. Tatai gave 7 h4 ♗g4! 8 ♗e2 ♖g8 as being favourable to Black, although it doesn't look like very much. Perhaps White should play 7 ♕f3, when 7...e6 8 0-0-0 ♘c6 9 ♘ge2 f5 10 ♔b1 ♗g7 11 h4 ♕b6 12 ♕e3 was about equal in West-Ahn, Elista Olympiad 1998.

7 ♕h5

7...e6

7...♘xd4? is poor in view of 8 0-0-0 e5 9 ♘f3 ♗c5 (or 9...♘xf3 10 ♗b5+ ♗d7 11 ♖xd5 etc.) 10 ♘xe5 with a winning attack. Kravtsov-Lubansky, Vladivostok 1994 continued in interesting fashion: 7...♗e6 8 0-0-0 ♕d7 9 h3 ♗f5 10 g4 ♗g6 11 ♕xd5 ♗h6+ 12 ♔b1 ♗xc2+! 13 ♔xc2 ♘b4+ 14 ♔b3 ♘xd5 15 ♗b5 0-0-0 16 ♗xd7+ ♖xd7 with approximate equality. And in Shrentzel-Hodgson, Tel Aviv 1988 Black chose to sacrifice a pawn for active play with 7...♖g8, when 8 ♕xh7 (8 ♕xd5 is also possible) 8...♖g6 9 0-0-0 ♗f5 10 ♗d3 ♕d7!? (10...♗xd3 11 ♖xd3 ♖xg2 looks playable and recovers White's pawn) 11 ♘ge2 (11 ♗xf5 ♕xf5 12 ♖d2 is better) 11...0-0-0 12 ♕xf7

♘b4 13 ♘g3 ♘xd3+ saw him win the exchange after 14 cxd3 ♖g7 15 ♕h5 ♗g4 etc.

8 0-0-0 ♗b4

Not the only square for the bishop. In B.Maksimovic-A.Rodriguez, Belgrade 1980 Black played 8...♗g7, the game continuing 9 g4 ♗d7 10 ♗g2 ♕b6 11 ♘ge2 0-0-0! (11...0-0 12 ♖d3 gives White a very strong attack) 12 ♕xf7 ♖dg8 13 ♕h5 ♔b8 14 f4! f5! 15 gxf5 ♘xd4 16 ♘xd4 ♗xd4 17 fxe6 ♗xe6 18 ♗f3 ♖c8 19 ♖he1 ♖xc3! 20 ♖xd4 ♕xd4 21 bxc3 ♕xf4+ 22 ♔b2 and the complications had burned out to equality. After the alternative 13 ♘a4!? ♕c7 14 ♘c5 Black can play 14...♘e5! 15 dxe5 ♕xc5 16 ♘d4 ♕f8 17 ♕xf8+ ♖xf8 18 exf6 ♖xf6 with compensation for the sacrificed pawn (Rodriguez). Another idea is 8...♗d7, keeping Black's options open with his king's bishop whilst getting nearer castling long.

9 ♘ge2

Tsesarsky suggested an interesting plan for White in 9 ♘ce2! – after 9...♕a5 10 ♔b1 White threatens to win the h-pawn with 11 ♕h6 and 12 ♕g7, which would cause Black to play 10...h6 (or possibly the retrograde 10...♗f8).

9...♗d7 10 g4!?

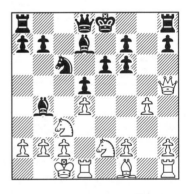

A thematic advance, preventing ...f6-f5 and preparing to tackle the enemy pawn centre with a subsequent f4-f5. After the immediate 10 f4 Black has 10...f5 11 g4 fxg4 12 ♕xg4 ♕f6 with a good game.

10...♞a5 11 a3 ♝d6 12 ♝g2?!

Both here and on the next move White can also consider 12 f4.

12...♝c6 13 ♖he1 ♛d7 14 ♝xd5!?

Sacrificing a piece in order to try to catch Black's king in the centre. White can cause problems for Black with the simple 14 ♛h6.

14...exd5 15 ♞f4+ ♚d8 16 ♞fxd5 ♝xd5 17 ♞xd5 ♞c4 18 ♞xf6 ♛c6 19 ♛g5?

Allowing Black's king to slip away to safety. White should play 19 ♞d5 with good compensation.

19...♚c7 20 ♞d5+ ♚b8 21 ♛g7?

Carried away with thoughts of the attack, White forgets to take care of his own monarch. He should challenge Black's knight with the immediate 21 ♞e3.

21...♖c8! 22 ♞e7?

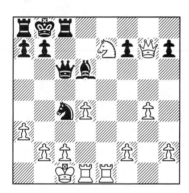

This loses quickly. The best chance is 22 ♛xf7 ♞xa3 23 c3 ♖f8 24 ♛h5 and the game goes on.

22...♛b5

22...♝f4+ 23 ♚b1 ♛b5 is also good.

23 b3 ♝f4+ 24 ♖e3 ♝xe3+ 25 fxe3 ♛a5 0-1

Game 32
Hort-Van der Wiel
Amsterdam 1982

---

1 d4 ♞f6 2 ♞c3 d5 3 ♝g5 c5 4 e3
More flexible than the immediate capture on f6. White maintains this as a possibility, thus keeping Black on his toes, the drawback being that the option of doubling Black's pawns can be lost, depending on the response.

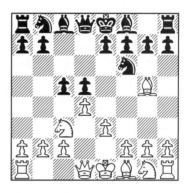

4...♞c6

Both 4...e6 5 ♞f3 ♞c6 and 4...♞c6 5 ♞f3 (5 ♝xf6!?) 5...e6 transpose to Mestrovic-Zivkovic.

5 ♞f3

Either missing or rejecting 5 ♝xf6 gxf6 6 ♛h5, when 6...cxd4 7 exd4 ♞xd4? leads to a strong attack for White after 8 0-0-0 e5 9 ♞f3 ♝c5 10 ♞xe5 etc.

5...♝g4!? 6 dxc5!?

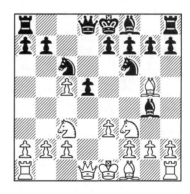

The last two moves have lent the game a sharp and independent flavour. Quieter alternatives give White nothing, for example:

a) 6 ♝xf6 gxf6 7 ♝e2 e6 8 0-0 f5 9 ♖e1 cxd4 (Black could also consider 9...♖g8, or even 9...♛f6 followed by castling queenside)

10 ♘xd4 ♗xe2 11 ♕xe2 ♗g7 12 ♖ad1 0-0 13 ♕h5 with a dynamically equal position in Zilberman-Rotman, Rishon Le Ziyyon 1993. 9 dxc5 ♗xc5 10 ♘d4 h5 11 ♕d3 ♕g5 12 f4 ♕e7 13 ♘xc6 bxc6 14 ♘a4 ♗d6 15 c4 ♕b7 16 ♖ac1 ♖g8 17 ♔h1 h4 18 c5 ♗xe2 19 ♕xe2 ♗e7 20 ♕d2 was about equal in Hoi-Kristiansen, Naestved 1985.

b) 6 ♗e2 e6 7 0-0 ♗e7 8 h3 ♗h5 9 ♘e5 ♗xe2 10 ♘xe2 was Richter-Rohacek, Munich 1941, and now (instead of 10...♘d7) 10...♘xe5 11 dxe5 ♘d7 would have been at least equal.

6...e6 7 h3

This peters out to rather dull equality. In his notes to the game Hort pointed out that 7 ♘a4!? is critical, for example 7...♗xc5 8 ♘xc5 ♕a5+ 9 c3 ♕xc5 10 ♗xf6 gxf6 11 ♗e2 with slightly the better pawn structure for White. Alternatively 7...♕a5+ 8 c3 ♘e4 9 ♕b3! is good for White – 9...♘xc5 10 ♘xc5 ♕xc5 11 ♘e5! ♘xe5 12 ♕xb7, threatening 13 ♕xa8+ and 13 ♗b5+. The quiet 7 ♗e2 leads to stone cold equality after 7...♗xc5 8 0-0 0-0 9 ♘d4 ♗xd4 10 exd4 ♗f5, as in Skembris-Van der Wiel, Groningen 1977.

7...♗xf3! 8 ♕xf3 ♕a5 9 ♗xf6 gxf6 10 ♗b5

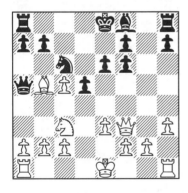

After 10 ♕xf6 ♖g8 Black gets excellent compensation for the pawn.

10...f5 11 0-0 ♗xc5 12 a3 ♗d6 13 b4 ♕b6 14 ♕e2 ♖c8 15 ♘a4 ♕c7 16 c4 a6 17 ♗xc6+ ♕xc6 18 c5 ♕xa4 19 cxd6

♕d7 20 ♕b2 0-0 21 ♕f6 ♕xd6 22 ♕g5+ ♔h8 23 ♕f6+ ♔g8 24 ♕g5+ ½-½

Game 33
Mestrovic-Zivkovic
Croatia Cup, Pula 1997

1 d4 ♘f6 2 ♘c3 d5 3 ♗g5 c5 4 e3 ♘c6

It is probably more accurate to play 4...e6 5 ♘f3 ♘c6 in order to avoid White's capture on f6.

5 ♘f3

As previously noted, 5 ♗xf6 is interesting.

5...e6 6 ♗d3

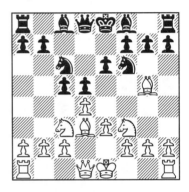

A logical developing move which intends either to open the game up with a later e3-e4 (probably preceded by d4xc5) or establish a knight in the centre with ♘f3-e5 followed by f2-f4. There are a couple of alternatives which make sense, though they are not as strong: 6 ♘e5 seems to be well met by 6...♕b6 7 ♗b5 a6, and 6 ♗b5 ♗e7 7 0-0 0-0 8 dxc5 ♗xc5 9 ♕e2 ♗e7 10 ♖fd1 a6 11 ♗d3 ♘d7 12 ♗xe7 ♕xe7 13 e4 d4 14 ♘b1 e5 15 ♘bd2 ♘c5 gave Black a nice position in Kogan-Savchenko, Cappelle la Grande 1995.

6...♗e7

Black can also prevent dxc5 by playing 6...cxd4 first. Burnazovic-Jelen, Ljubljana 1993 continued 7 exd4 ♗d7 8 0-0 ♗e7 9 ♖e1 0-0 10 a3 ♖c8 11 ♘e2 ♘h5 12 ♗xe7 ♕xe7 13 c3 ♕f6, and now an improvement on 14 ♘e5 is 14 ♘g3 ♘f4 15 ♗f1, which looks slightly better for White.

7 dxc5 ♕a5

After 7...♗xc5 play might continue 8 e4 d4 9 ♘e2 e5 10 0-0 0-0-0 11 ♘g3, when White has some attacking chances on the kingside.

8 0-0 ♕xc5 9 e4 dxe4 10 ♘xe4 ♘xe4 11 ♗xe7 ♕xe7 12 ♗xe4 0-0 13 c3 ♗d7 14 ♕e2 ♖fd8 15 ♖fe1 ♗e8 16 ♕e3 ♖ac8

This position is almost equal, not to mention dull. Nevertheless the players manage to fight on for another 50 moves before peace is agreed.

17 ♗c2 ♖c7 18 ♘g5 h6 19 ♘f3 ♕f6 20 ♖ad1 ♖cd7 21 ♖xd7 ♖xd7 22 h3 ♖d8 23 ♘h2 h5 24 ♘f3 b6 25 ♘g5 ♘e7 26 ♘e4 ♕e5 27 ♕c1 ♘g6 28 ♘g3 ♕f4 29 ♘xh5

This pawn snatch doesn't help White as Black gets a rook to the 7th rank with adequate compensation.

29...♕xc1 30 ♖xc1 ♖d2 31 ♘g3 ♘f4 32

b4 ♗c6 33 ♗e4 ♗xe4 34 ♘xe4 ♘e2+ 35 ♔f1 ♘xc1 36 ♘xd2 ♘xa2 37 ♘b1 ♘c1 38 ♔e1 ♘d3+ 39 ♔e2 ♘e5 40 ♘a3 ♔f8 41 f4 ♘c6 42 g4 f6 43 ♔d3 ♔e7 44 b5 ♘b8 45 ♘c4 ♘d7 46 h4 ♘c5+ 47 ♔e3 ♘b7 48 h5 ♘d8 49 ♘d2 ♘f7 50 c4 e5 51 ♘f3 exf4+ 52 ♔xf4 ♘d6 53 ♘d2 ♔e6 54 ♔e3 ♘f7 55 ♔f4 ♘d6 56 ♔f3 ♘f7 57 ♔e4 ♘d6+ 58 ♔d4 ♘f7 59 ♘f1 f5 60 gxf5+ ♔xf5 61 ♔d5 ♘d8 62 ♔d6 ♘b7+ 63 ♔c7 ♘a5 64 ♘d2 ♔f4 65 ♔b8 ♔e3 66 ♘f1+ ♔d4 67 ♔xa7 ♘xc4 68 ♘g3 ♔e5 69 ♔b7 ½-½

Game 34
Speelman-Saltaev
Hastings Premier 1998/99

---

1 d4 ♘f6 2 ♗g5 d5 3 e3 c5 4 ♘c3 ♘c6 5 a3!?

Speelman often plays such 'half-moves' and here nudging the a-pawn has some subtle effects. In some positions White may threaten to take on c5, in others Black might get his queen trapped with ♘a4, should he be so foolish as to snatch the pawn on b2 at the wrong moment. Of course this does represent a lost tempo...

5...e6

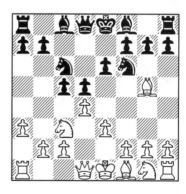

Alternatively Black can play 5...cxd4 6 exd4 ♗f5, when in Lys-Pisk, Prague 1992 Black had a good game after 7 ♗d3 ♘xd4 8 ♗xf5 ♘xf5 9 ♗xf6 gxf6 10 ♕xd5 ♕xd5 11

♘xd5 0-0-0. Perhaps White can do better with 7 ♕d2.

6 ♘f3 ♛b6 7 dxc5 ♗xc5 8 ♗d3 ♗e7 9 h3 0-0

Not 9...♕xb2?? 10 ♘a4.

10 0-0 ♖d8 11 ♕e2 g6 12 ♖fd1 ♗d7 13 ♖ab1 ♗e8 14 e4 dxe4 15 ♘xe4 ♘xe4 16 ♕xe4 ♗xg5 17 ♘xg5 ♕d4 18 c3 ♕xe4 19 ♗xe4 ♖xd1+ 20 ♖xd1 ♖d8

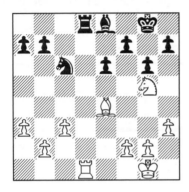

Black seems to be coasting to a draw, yet even the most innocent looking position can contain a dash of poison... In this one White has the more active pieces and a queenside pawn majority.

21 ♖xd8 ♘xd8 22 f4 f6 23 ♘f3 ♗c6 24 ♗xc6 ♘xc6 25 ♔f2 ♔f7 26 ♔e3 ♔e7 27 ♘d4 ♔d6 28 ♘xc6 ♔xc6 29 c4 ♔c5 30 ♔d3 h6 31 b4+ ♔c6 32 ♔d4 ♔d6?

The decisive error. 32...b6! would prevent White from getting his pawns to b5 and c5,

for example 33 b5+ ♔d6 34 h4 e5+ 35 fxe5+ fxe5+ 36 ♔e4 h5 37 a4 ♔e6! (37...♔c5? 38 ♔xe5 ♔xc4 39 ♔f6 sees White come first) 38 ♔d3 ♔d6 39 ♔e4 with a draw.

33 c5+ ♔c6 34 a4 ♔c7 35 b5 ♔d7 36 ♔e4 ♔c7 37 ♔f3 a6 38 ♔e4 axb5 39 axb5 ♔d7 40 ♔f3 ♔e7 41 h4 h5 42 ♔e4 ♔d7 43 ♔d4 ♔c7 44 ♔c4 ♔d7 45 ♔b4 ♔c7 46 ♔a5 ♔c8 47 ♔b6 e5 48 fxe5 fxe5 49 ♔a5 1-0

Game 35
Sagalchik-Ariel
USA Ch., Seattle 2002

1 d4 ♘f6 2 ♘c3 d5 3 ♗g5 c5 4 e4!?

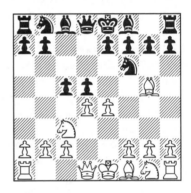

An enterprising idea which resembles an Albin Counter Gambit with colours reversed and a useful extra tempo in 3 ♗g5. Black has a choice about which pawn to take.

4...♘xe4

After 4...cxd4 5 ♕xd4 ♘c6 6 ♗b5 dxe4 7 ♕xd8+ (7 ♗xf6 exf6 8 ♕xe4+ ♕e7 9 ♕xe7+ ♗xe7 10 ♘d5) 7...♔xd8 (thus far Huhn-Oberhofer, Bad Wörishofen 2000) White can play 8 ♗c4 (8 ♖d1+ ♗d7 9 ♘ge2 ♔c8 was just equal in the game). After 4...dxe4 we get the aforementioned reversed Albin Counter Gambit. White has good compensation after 5 d5, for example 5...♗f5 6 ♘ge2 ♕a5 7 ♘g3 ♗g6 8 h4 h6 9 ♗xf6 gxf6 10 ♗b5+ ♘d7 11 ♗xd7+ ♔xd7 12 ♕g4+ ♔e8 13 h5 ♗h7 14 0-0 with a powerful initiative in

Bletz-Hovde, Gausdal 1982. White would meet 5...♘bd7 with 6 ♘ge2 a6 7 ♘g3, which recovers the pawn with a good game. 5...h6 6 ♗f4 e6 7 ♗b5+ ♗d7 8 dxe6 fxe6 9 ♕e2 ♘c6 10 0-0-0 ♘d4 11 ♕e3 ♗e7 12 ♘ge2 was promising for White in Richter-Opocensky, Podebrady 1936.

5 ♘xe4 dxe4 6 d5

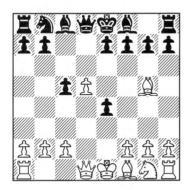

Now we have a gambit. White has an interesting (and probably sensible) alternative in 6 dxc5, for example 6...♕a5+ (6...♗d7 7 ♗e3 e6 8 ♕d2 ♕c7 9 b4 produced a double-edged game in Wade-Palliser, Hampstead 1998, and 6...♕xd1+ 7 ♖xd1 g6 8 ♗c4 ♗g7 9 c3 h6 10 ♗e3 ♘d7 11 ♘e2 e5 12 0-0 0-0 13 ♘g3 gave White an edge in Trescher-Ankerst, Bad Wiessee 1997) 7 ♕d2 ♕xc5 (7...♕xd2+ 8 ♗xd2 e5 was played in Boeven-Bu Xiangzhi, Budapest 1999 and now instead of 9 ♗e3 White's best appears to be 9 b4) 8 0-0-0 ♘c6 9 ♗e3 ♕a5 10 ♕xa5 ♘xa5 11 ♗b5+ (11 ♘e2 ♗g4 12 h3 ♗xe2 13 ♗xe2 gave White adequate compensation for the pawn in Czerniak-Bednarski, Polanica Zdroj 1963) 11...♘c6 12 ♘e2 e6 13 ♖d4 f5 14 ♖hd1 and White had the initiative for his sacrificed pawn in Einarsson-Van der Weide, Reykjavik 1998.

6...♕b6

Preventing White from finding a safe haven for his king on the queenside with 7 ♕d2 and 8 0-0-0. After 6...g6 7 f3 ♕b6 8 fxe4 ♕b4+ 9 ♕d2 ♕xb2 10 ♖d1 h6 11 ♗e3

♗g7 Black stood better in N.Benjamin-Bellin, Brighton 1977, so White should take the opportunity to play 7 ♕d2, intending to castle long. In W.Ernst-Unzicker, Essen 1948 he rightly adopted this plan after 6...♘d7 7 ♕d2 g6 8 0-0-0, and after 8...♗g7 9 ♗h6 0-0 10 ♗xg7 ♔xg7 could have continued more consistently with 11 f3 with dangerous attacking chances; in the game he won back his pawn with 11 ♕c3+ ♘f6 12 ♕xc5 but stood slightly worse after 12...♗g4.

7 ♘e2

Throwing another pawn on the fire, but this could be a case of discretion being the better part of valour... In Rocha-Yakovich, Santo Antonio 1999 White limited his material deficit to a single pawn with 7 b3, after which 7...g6 (7...e5!?) 8 ♕d2 ♗g7 9 ♖c1 ♘d7 10 ♘e2 ♘f6 11 ♘g3 0-0 12 ♗e2 ♖d8 13 c4 e6 was quite double-edged.

7...g6

If there's a reason why Black can't play the consistent 7...♕xb2, then I don't see it. White should probably offer a third pawn with 8 ♖b1, but would he really have enough compensation?

8 ♖b1 ♗g7 9 ♘c3 f5

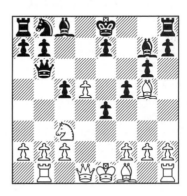

Hanging on to the e-pawn. After 9...♘d7 10 ♘xe4 ♕b4+ 11 ♘d2 ♘f6 12 c3 ♕b6 13 ♘c4 ♕d8 14 ♘e3 White recovered his pawn with a space advantage in Eriksson-Medvegy, Stockholm 2001.

10 ♗e2 h6 11 ♗e3 ♘d7 12 0-0 0-0 13

♕d2 ♔h7 14 f3

The e4-pawn currently inhibits the activity of White's pieces so he quite rightly undermines it.

14...exf3 15 ♗xf3 ♕a5

15...♘f6 is answered by 16 b4.

16 ♕e2 ♗xc3!?

Grabbing a second pawn. Black might have been bothered by the fact that 16...♘f6 17 ♗f4 ♖e8 18 ♘b5 gives White a continuing initiative, consequently deciding to alter the course of the game.

17 bxc3 ♕xc3 18 ♗c1

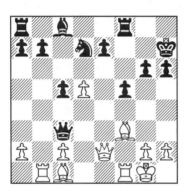

18 ♖be1 is an interesting alternative.

18...♕e5 19 ♕f2 ♕d6 20 ♕h4 f4

After 20...h5?! 21 ♖e1 White has massive pressure. Finkel's suggestion of 21 ♗xh5 gxh5 22 ♕xh5+ isn't clear after 22...♔g7.

21 ♗e4 ♕f6

The idea of 22...♕d4+ virtually forces the exchange of queens. White's initiative starts to diminish.

22 ♕xf4 ♕d4+ 23 ♕e3 ♖xf1+ 24 ♔xf1 ♕xe3 25 ♗xe3 b6 26 ♖e1

Not 26 d6 in view of 26...♗a6+ 27 ♔e1 ♖e8 28 ♗c6 exd6! etc.

26...♘f6 27 ♗f3 ♗a6+ 28 ♔f2 ♖d8 29 ♗c1 ♖d7 30 ♗b2 ♘g8?!

Black should play 30...♗c4!, when 31 d6 ♘g8! leaves White in serious trouble.

31 a4 ♗c4 32 ♖d1 h5?!

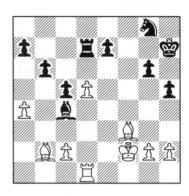

And here Black should play 32...♘f6. Now White gets some play...

33 h3 ♘h6 34 g4 h4 35 ♖e1 ♘f7 36 ♗g2 ♘d8 37 ♖e5 ♘f7 38 ♖e1 ♘d6?! 39 ♖e6 ♗a2 40 ♗c1 ♗b1 41 ♗g5 ♗xc2 42 ♗xe7 ♘c8

Perhaps 42...♘c4 43 ♗xh4 ♔g7 is better. In the game Black manages to get three connected passed pawns but his king is in serious danger.

43 ♗xh4 ♗xa4 44 ♗e4 ♖g7 45 ♗g3 ♗d7 46 ♖f6 a5 47 ♔f3 a4 48 ♗e5 a3 49 ♖f8 a2 50 ♖d8 b5 51 h4!

Suddenly it becomes clear that Black is in a mating net.

51...♘b6 52 h5 ♔h6 53 hxg6 ♖xg6 54 ♖h8+ 1-0

Summary

The sharp 3...c5 is one of Black's best options in the Veresov and leads to double-edged, challenging play. 4 ♗xf6 gxf6 5 e4 is under a cloud but 5 e3 is playable. The play looks rather quiet after 4 e3, although Black has to play carefully to maintain the balance. It can also be used to transpose to the 4 ♗xf6 line whilst avoiding 4...gxf6 5 e3 cxd4 6 exd4 h5.

1 d4 ♘f6 2 ♘c3 d5 3 ♗g5 c5 *(D)* **4 ♗xf6**

4 e3 ♘c6

5 ♘f3 *(D)*

5...♗g4 - *Game 32*

5...e6 6 ♗d3 - *Game 33*

5 a3 e6 5 ♘f3 - *Game 34*

4 e4 ♘xe4 5 ♘xe4 dxe4 6 d5 - *Game 35*

4...gxf6 5 e4

5 e3 - *Game 31*

5...dxe4 6 dxc5 *(D)*

6...♕a5 - *Game 29*; 6...f5 - *Game 30*

3...c5

5 ♘f3

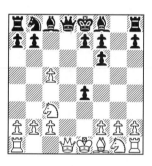

6 dxc5

CHAPTER FIVE

3...c6

1 d4 ♘f6 2 ♘c3 d5 3 ♗g5 c6

This is one of Black's most flexible options, protecting the d5-pawn, allowing his queen to come out to b6 or a5 and leaving open the possibility of playing ...♗f5. Black also avoids placing his queen's knight on the passive d7-square. The most aggressive answer is 4 f3, trying to construct a pawn centre with 5 e4. Black can transpose to the 3...♘bd7 4 f3 c6 lines by playing 4...♘bd7, and possibly this should be his preferred course of action. He has also played 4...♕b6 but this looked quite promising for White in Games 36 & 37 (Richter-Rogmann and Pasman-Georgiev).

One of the objections to 3...c6 (by comparison with 3...♘bd7) is that White can double Black's f-pawns with 4 ♗xf6 and, after 4...exf6, play 5 e3 followed by ♗d3, ♕f3, ♘ge2, 0-0-0 followed by g2-g4 etc. Unfortunately I'm completely unconvinced by this plan as Black can play ...f6-f5 (as in Gurgenidze-Stein) and position his pieces so that White cannot lever open the game with either e3-e4 or g2-g4. I think White should really be playing for c2-c4 with a kingside fianchetto, bringing the knight from c3 to e2, but all this takes time. Besides 4...exf6 Black has also played the extravagant 4...gxf6, but I think that White had a good position in

Kohlhage-Langheinrich before he misplayed the early middlegame.

Morozevich played 4 ♕d3 in his game against Malaniuk, though I'm not sure he'd be that eager to repeat the experience. This move didn't work out too well in Markovic-Cvitan either and, although White's play can be improved in both cases, it doesn't seem as if Black is under any pressure here. I'm similarly unimpressed with 4 ♕d2, though it's not clear that this move should be the unmitigated disaster suggested by Stryjecki-Vokac.

Last but not least there is the modest 4 e3. This was Veresov's own choice again Krogius and, despite looking quiet, it contains a drop of poison. Once again White has the Stonewall f2-f4 plan (especially if Black plays ...♘b8-d7), and after developing his pieces he can sometimes play a later e3-e4.

Game 36
Richter-Rogmann
Berlin 1937

---

1 d4 ♘f6 2 ♘c3 d5 3 ♗g5 c6

Bronstein liked this move, reinforcing d5 and giving Black's queen access to the queen-side. It must always be remembered that 3 ♗g5 leaves b2 unprotected.

4 f3

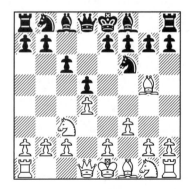

As in most Veresov lines, this is White's most ambitious plan.

4...♛b6

Hitting the b2-pawn, which White is really obliged to sacrifice. Of the alternatives, 4...♝f5 makes sense. White can offer a pawn with 5 e4 dxe4 6 ♝c4, when 6...exf3 7 ♘xf3 creates Blackmar-Diemer style compensation. After 4...♛a5 White can play 5 ♛d2, preparing e2-e4, although this transposes to de Souza-Vescovi from Chapter 2 after 5...♘bd7 (which, by the way, is not mandatory). 4...♘bd7 transposes to 3...♘bd7 4 f3 c6, which is covered in Chapter 1.

5 e4

For 5 ♛d2 see Pasman-Georgiev.

5...♛xb2 6 ♘ge2 e6 7 e5 ♘fd7 8 ♖b1 ♛a3 9 ♖b3 ♛a5 10 ♝d2 ♛c7 11 ♘f4

White can also consider 11 f4, intending to lever open Black's kingside with f4-f5. Richter returns to this idea later, but after first bringing his knight to h5.

11...a6 12 ♝d3 ♝e7

With regard to ...c6-c5 Black probably feared a sacrifice on d5, but he certainly should have tried this, as passive play allows White to engineer an impressive attacking position. After 12...c5 I'm sure that the 'executioner of Berlin' would have played 13 ♘cxd5!?, when White obtains a dangerous attack for the sacrificed piece after, for example, 13...exd5 14 0-0!?. But this would

probably have been better than the mildly suicidal plan of putting his king on the kingside. Over the following moves we see Richter prepare, then execute, a massive kingside onslaught.

13 0-0 0-0 14 ♛e1 ♖e8 15 ♛g3 ♘f8 16 ♘h5 ♘g6 17 f4 ♝d8 18 ♛h3 b5 19 g4 ♛e7 20 g5

Black's last move prepared to meet 20 f5 with 20...♛h4, so Richter changes tack.

20...♝b6 21 ♘e2 c5

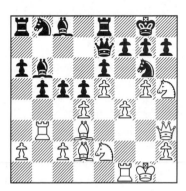

22 ♘f6+! gxf6 23 gxf6 ♛f8 24 ♔h1 cxd4

24...c4 25 ♝b4 and Black loses his queen.

25 ♖g1 ♘d7 26 ♛h5

White finally has a concrete threat to sacrifice on g6. With the storm about to break Black desperately tries to disperse some of the gathering enemy forces.

26...♘xf6 27 exf6 ♖a7 28 ♝b4 ♝c5 29 ♝xc5 ♛xc5 30 ♝xg6 fxg6 31 ♖xg6+ ♔h8

In the event of 31...hxg6 there follows 32 ♛xg6+ ♔f8 33 ♖g3 etc.

32 f7 1-0

White's two threats of fxe8♛ and ♛e5+ cannot be dealt with.

Game 37
Pasman-Kr.Georgiev
EU U20 Ch., Groningen 1977

---

1 d4 ♘f6 2 ♘c3 d5 3 ♝g5 c6 4 f3 ♛b6

5 ♕d2!? ♕xb2 6 ♖b1 ♕a3 7 e4

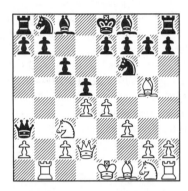

7...e6

In a later game Stean played 7...♘bd7, and 8 ♗d3?! dxe4 9 fxe4 e5! 10 ♘f3 ♗b4 11 ♖b3 ♕a5 12 dxe5 ♘g4 13 e6 ♘de5 14 exf7+ ♘xf7 left White with inadequate compensation for the pawn in Pasman-Stean, Beer Sheeva 1980. Instead White should have driven Black's knight away with 8 e5, when I think that 8...♘g8 9 f4 e6 10 ♗d3 ♕a5 11 ♘ge2 gives White a dangerous looking attacking position. This, as with many Veresov lines, 'requires tests'!

8 ♗d3 ♕a5 9 ♘ge2 h6?!

Weakening Black's kingside. Black should play 9...♘bd7!?, when 10 e5 ♘g8 11 f4 leads to similar play to the line given above.

10 ♗h4 ♘bd7 11 0-0 dxe4?!

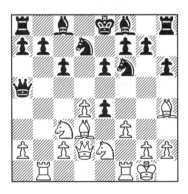

V.Sokolov suggested 11...♗e7!? 12 e5 ♘g8 but then 13 ♗e1!? leaves Black to deal

with the threat of f3-f4-f5, and his bishop on e7 will want to make room for the knight on g8. Sokolov's 13 ♗xe7 is relatively harmless after 13...♘xe7.

12 fxe4 ♗b4 13 a3!?

An ingenious second pawn sacrifice which, if accepted, sets up an awkward pin on Black's bishop. 13 ♖b3 is a reasonable alternative.

13...♗xa3 14 ♖a1 ♕b4 15 e5!?

Already planning the following exchange sacrifice, although this might be getting a bit carried away! 15 ♖fb1 looks very strong to me as after 15...♕f8 there follows 16 e5 ♘d5 17 ♘e4 with tremendous pressure for the two pawns.

15...♘d5 16 ♖xa3! ♕xa3 17 ♘e4 0-0 18 ♘f6+! ♘7xf6

18...gxf6? 19 ♕xh6 f5 20 ♖f3 is decisive, and after 18...♔h8 White has 19 ♘xd5 exd5 20 ♕f4, intending 21 ♘g3 with terrible threats on the kingside.

19 exf6 e5! 20 fxg7 ♔xg7 21 dxe5 ♕c5+ 22 ♔h1 f5

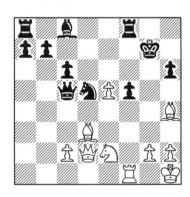

Black can exchange queens with 22...♕e3 but then 23 ♕xe3 ♘xe3 24 ♗f6+ ♔g8 25 ♖f3 ♘g4 26 ♖g3 a5 27 ♘d4! followed by ♘f5 will leave his king in a mating net.

23 exf6+ ♘xf6 24 ♕f4 ♘d5 25 ♕g3+ ♔h8 26 ♕e5+ ♔g8 27 ♕g3+ ♔h8 ½-½

At the board White evidently saw nothing better than this repetition, but he can in fact win with 28 ♖xf8+ (not 28 ♕e5+ ♔g8 29

♖f6 ♖xf6 30 ♗xf6 due to 30...♔f7!) 28...♕xf8 29 c4 ♕g7 30 ♕f2 when Black must give up his knight (just the beginning).

1 d4 ♘f6 2 ♘c3 d5 3 ♗g5 c6 4 ♗xf6 exf6

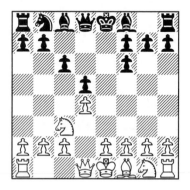

The most natural move, aiming for quick kingside development. For 4...gxf6 see Kohl-hage-Langheinrich.

5 e3

There's definitely an argument for 5 e4, which at least gives White a queenside pawn majority after 5...dxe4 6 ♘xe4. But 6...♕b6!? looks quite awkward. In Klinger-Wetscherek, Oberwart 1991 White continued 7 b3, but then 7...♗b4+ 8 c3 f5 looks quite strong.

5...f5

Immediately addressing the critical e4-square, and preventing pawn levers such as e3-e4 or g2-g4. Black has also tried simple development with 5...♗d6 6 ♗d3 0-0 but this does little to stop White on the kingside. Miles-Tisdall, England 1982 continued 7 ♕f3 ♖e8 8 ♘ge2 ♘d7 9 0-0-0 ♕a5 10 ♔b1 ♘f8 11 g4 b5 12 ♘g3 ♗e6 13 ♘f5 ♗a3 14 ♘e2 ♕b4 15 b3 c5 16 dxc5 ♕xc5 17 h4 with good attacking chances on the kingside. 9 a3 ♕c7 10 e4 dxe4 11 ♘xe4 ♗e7 12 0-0 b6 13 ♖ad1 ♗b7 14 c4 ♖ad8 15 b4 g6 16 c5 f5 17

♘4c3 was slightly better for White in Larsen-Westerinen, Hastings 1972/73.

5...♗f5 leads to similar play to 3...♗f5, with White's best being 6 ♗d3.

6 ♗d3

An alternative plan is 6 g3 ♘d7 7 ♗g2 ♘f6 8 ♘ce2, intending ♘f3, 0-0, b2-b3 and c2-c4. If Black were then to capture on c4 White would retake with the b-pawn. This plan is known in the Trompovsky (1 d4 ♘f6 2 ♗g5) but I cannot find any examples of it in the Veresov.

6...g6 7 ♘ce2 ♘d7 8 ♘f3 ♗d6 9 c4 ♘f6 10 ♘c3 dxc4!?

Black can also hold the centre with 10...♗e6 with what is undoubtedly a good position.

11 ♗xc4 b5 12 ♗b3 0-0 13 0-0 a6 14 ♘e2?

According to Suetin White should play 14 a4 in an attempt to inhibit the thrust with ...c6-c5.

14...♗b7 15 ♖c1 ♕e7 16 ♘f4 c5

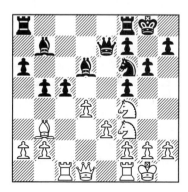

Opening the position for Black's bishop pair. Black is already better.

17 dxc5 ♗xc5 18 ♕e2 ♗d6 19 ♘d4 ♖fe8 20 ♕d3 ♖ad8 21 ♖fd1 ♘g4! 22 ♕d2 ♗b8 23 h3 ♘e5 24 ♕e2 ♕g5

Suddenly Black has some very unpleasant threats against both g2 and the insecurely placed knights on d4 and f4.

25 ♔f1 ♕f6 26 ♔g1 ♘c4 27 ♕f1? ♗xf4 0-1

Game 39
Kohlhage-Langheinrich
Schloss Open, Werther 2000

1 d4 ♘f6 2 ♘c3 d5 3 ♗g5 c6 4 ♗xf6 gxf6 5 e3

5 e4 dxe4 6 ♘xe4 resembles a Bronstein-Larsen Variation of the Caro-Kann Defence (1 e4 c6 2 d4 d5 3 ♘c3 dxe4 4 ♘xe4 ♘f6 5 ♘xf6+ gxf6) except that White has parted with his dark-squared bishop. This has the effect of making 6...♕b6!? look interesting, although after 7 ♘f3 Black curiously decided to decline the b-pawn in Hoi-Hansen, Copenhagen 1982, which went 7...♗f5 8 ♗d3 ♘d7 9 0-0 e6 10 c3 0-0-0 11 b4 ♖g8 12 ♘g3 with mutual attacks in the offing and White's chances looking the more promising. Here 6...f5 7 ♘g5 e6 8 ♕h5 ♕e7 9 ♘1f3 ♘d7 10 0-0-0 ♘f6 11 ♕h4 h6 12 ♘h3 ♘g4 was fine for Black in Shagalovich-Osnos, Leningrad 1967.

White has an interesting alternative in 5 ♕d2, when Miladinovic-Mantovani, Saint Vincent 1998 continued 5...♗f5 6 e3 ♘d7 7 ♘ge2 e6 8 ♘g3 ♗g6 9 ♗d3 ♗d6 10 ♘ce2 ♕c7 11 c4 dxc4 12 ♗xc4 with a nice game for White.

5...e5

A very ambitious move which deserves to be taken seriously. After the relatively meek 5...♗f5 White gets a good game with 6 ♘ge2

♘d7 7 ♘g3 ♗g6 8 h4 h6 9 ♗d3, which was very promising in R.Watson-Klappert, Oberjoch 2001. Wade-Kieninger, Reykjavik 1966 was less dangerous for Black after 6 ♗d3 ♗g6 7 h4 ♘d7 8 h5 ♗xd3 9 ♕xd3 e5 10 ♕f5 ♕e7 11 ♘ge2 ♕e6 12 ♕xe6+ fxe6.

6 ♕h5

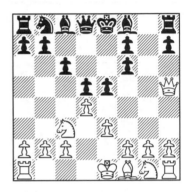

6...♗d6

In Wade-Kinzel, Varna 1962 Black made a quick exit after 6...e4? 7 f3 f5? 8 fxe4 fxe4? 9 ♕e5+ 1-0. In the main game Black also pushes ...e5-e4, which looks strategically dubious to me. But at least he doesn't lose a rook!

7 0-0-0 e4 8 f3

My first thought in this position was to play 8 g3 (intending 9 ♗h3) but then Black could answer with 8...f5 9 ♗h3 ♕f6 and 10...♕g6. I therefore suggest 8 g4!? in order to prevent ...f6-f5, after which White will continue undermining operations with 9 f3.

8...f5 9 g4 ♗b4 10 gxf5?!

A very risky move due to the weakening of White's queenside. 10 ♘ce2 would have been a good idea as after 10...exf3 (10...♕f6 looks better) 11 ♘xf3 fxg4 White has 12 ♘e5 with good play.

10...♗xc3 11 bxc3 ♘d7 12 ♗h3

Removing the defence of the c4-square is not a clever idea. 12 fxe4 ♘f6 13 ♕h6 ♘xe4 is also quite good for Black, but 12 ♕h6 offers reasonable counterplay.

12...♕e7 13 f4?

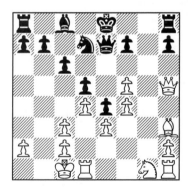

White seems oblivious to the danger facing his king. He had to try for some counterplay with 13 ♕h6.

13...♘b6 14 ♕g5?!

This loses in short order. White could have tried defending the c4-square with 14 ♗f1 but after 14...♕a3+ 15 ♔d2 ♘a4 16 ♘e2 ♘b2 Black's knight will get there anyway.

14...♕a3+ 15 ♔d2 ♘c4+ 16 ♔e2 ♕xc3 17 ♗g4 ♕xe3+ 18 ♔f1 h6 19 ♕g7 ♕xf4+ 20 ♔e2 ♖f8 21 ♘h3 ♕e3+ 22 ♔f1 h5 0-1

Game 40
Markovic-Cvitan
Bosnian Team Ch., Neum 2002

---

1 d4 ♘f6 2 ♘c3 d5 3 ♗g5 c6 4 ♕d3 ♕a5

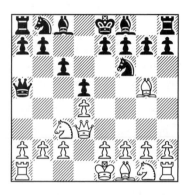

For 4...g6 see Morozevich-Malaniuk, while 4...♘bd7 leads to lines covered in Chapter 2.

5 ♗xf6

Retreating the bishop with 5 ♗d2 is well met by 5...♘a6 6 ♘d1 ♕b6 7 f3 (7 ♘f3 ♘e4 8 e3 ♘b4 is less than nothing for White) 7...c5 8 c3 e6 9 e3 ♗d7 10 ♘h3 ♗d6, and Black had the better game in Pimenov-Moisieev, Yerevan 1955. In the event of 5...♕a6!? White should consider 6 ♕g3 because 6 e4 ♕xd3 7 ♗xd3 dxe4 8 ♘xe4 ♘xe4 9 ♗xe4 ♘d7 was equal in Vokac-Vesselovsky, Czech Republic 1999. If Black plays 5...g6 6 f3 and only then 6...♕a6 White doesn't have this option, and Hector-Gdanski, Gothenborg 1997 was about equal after 7 e4 ♕xd3 8 ♗xd3 b6 9 ♗g5 ♗g7 10 ♘ge2 e6 11 b4 ♘bd7 12 0-0 ♗b7.

On the other hand the immediate 5 f3 is worth considering, and after 5...b5 6 ♗d2 b4 7 ♘d1 ♕b6 8 e4 ♗a6 9 ♕e3 ♗xf1 10 ♔xf1 e6 11 ♘e2 c5 12 c3 ♘c6 a double-edged game arose in Sobolevsky-Kosikov, Kiev 1998.

5...exf6 6 e4 ♗b4 7 exd5 0-0!

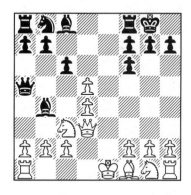

An interesting pawn sacrifice. After the immediate 7...cxd5 White plays 8 ♕b5+ as the isolated pawn on d5 might be more of a factor after the exchange of queens. Recapturing with the queen is good enough for equality, Leonidov-Sanakoev, Voronezh 1997 going 7...♕xd5 8 0-0-0 ♗xc3 9 ♕xc3 0-0 10 ♘f3 ♗e6 11 b3 ♕d6 12 ♗c4 ♗xc4

13 ♕xc4 ♘d7 14 ♖he1 ♖fe8 15 g3 a5 when the slight weakness of White's king position is sufficient compensation for the inferior quality of his pawn majority.

8 ♘ge2 cxd5

This seems like the sensible move but the weakness of the d5-pawn is now a permanent factor. In Mestrovic-Bronstein, Sarajevo 1971 the famous Russian Grandmaster continued to offer a pawn sacrifice with 8...♗a6!? 9 0-0-0 ♖d8 10 ♖g1 ♗f8 and had dynamic compensation after 11 g4 ♖b8 (11...♘b4!? is also worth considering) 12 ♘f4 ♘b4 13 ♕c4 b5 14 ♕b3 ♕c7. This seems like the best way for Black to treat the position.

9 0-0-0 ♘c6 10 ♕b5

Even better might be 10 a3 ♗d6 11 ♕b5 as Black can't tuck his bishop away on f8.

10...♕xb5 11 ♘xb5 ♖d8 12 ♘f4 ♗a5 13 c3 a6 14 ♘a3 ♗c7 15 ♘d3 ♖e8 16 ♘c2 ♗g4 17 ♖d2 ♗f5 18 ♘e3 ♗xd3 19 ♗xd3

White has a nice advantage here because of the weakness of the d5-pawn. The problem, of course, is how to actually win!

19...♗f4 20 ♖e2 g6 21 g4?!

A rash looking move which throws away White's advantage. After the natural 21 ♖he1 Black is under some pressure.

21...♖e6 22 ♔d1 ♖d8 23 h3 b5 24 ♖he1 ♗c7 25 ♘c2 ♖dd6 26 ♖e3 ♔f8 27 ♗f1 ♘a5!? 28 b3 ♘c6 29 b4 ♘e7 30 ♘a1

♖xe3 31 ♖xe3 f5

With the disappearance of the doubled pawn Black is no longer worse.

32 ♘b3 fxg4 33 hxg4 ♖f6 34 ♔e1 ♗f4 35 ♖e2

35 ♖h3 ♔g7 36 ♘c5.

35...♖d6 36 ♖e3 ♗f4 37 ♖h3 ♔g7 38 ♘c5 h6 39 ♗d3 ♘c8 40 ♔f1 ♗d2 41 ♗e2 ♘e7?!

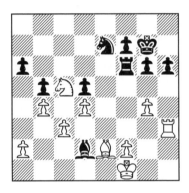

A rather passive move which renews Black's difficulties. He should play 41...♘d6!?, when 42 ♖d3 ♘c4 43 ♖f3 ♖xf3 44 ♗xf3 ♗xc3 45 ♗xd5 ♘a3 leads to a draw.

42 ♖d3 ♗f4 43 ♗d1 g5 44 a4 bxa4 45 ♗xa4 ♖d6 46 ♖d1 ♘g6 47 ♗c2 ♘h4 48 ♗d3 ♖f6 49 ♔e2

Possibly showing undue concern over Black's idea of 49...♗e3. White should play the cold-blooded 49 ♗xa6, after which 49...♗e3 50 ♔e2 ♗xf2 51 ♗b7 ♘g6 52 ♘d3 offers excellent winning chances.

49...♗d6 50 ♘xa6 ♘g2 51 ♘c5 ♘f4+ 52 ♔f1 h5 53 gxh5 g4 54 ♗c2?!

After this Black gets enough counterplay to draw. White can retain some winning chances with 54 ♗e2, when 54...♘h3 55 ♘d3 ♘xf2 56 ♘xf2 g3 57 ♖d3 ♖xf2+ 58 ♔e1 ♘h2 59 ♗f3, threatening the d5-pawn, leaves Black with some problems left to solve.

54...♖h6 55 ♘d3 ♖xh5 56 ♘xf4 ♗xf4 57 b5 ♗c7 58 ♔g1 ♖h3 59 ♗f5 ♖xc3

Finally a draw is on the cards.

60 ♗xg4 ♗b6 61 ♗e2 ♖b3 62 ♔g2 ♔f6 63 ♖h1 ♗xd4 64 ♖h4 ♔e5 65 ♖h1 ½-½

Game 41
Morozevich-Malaniuk
Alushta 1994

---

1 ♘c3 ♘f6 2 d4 d5 3 ♗g5 c6 4 ♕d3 g6 5 f3

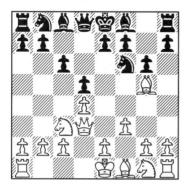

It is well worth considering 5 ♗xf6, securing a higher quality pawn majority at the cost of the bishop pair after 5...exf6 6 e4 dxe4 7 ♕xe4+. In theory, at least, it makes more sense for Black to keep the queens on with 7...♗e7 as 7...♕e7 8 0-0-0 ♕xe4 9 ♘xe4 f5 10 ♘d2 ♗e6 11 ♗c4 ♗xc4 12 ♘xc4 ♘d7 13 ♘f3 left White with an edge in Schmidt-Rasmussen, Aarhus 1984. However, in Alburt-Polugaevsky, Moscow 1966 White was anyway better after (7...♗e7) 8 0-0-0 f5 9 ♕e3 0-0 10 ♗c4 ♘d7 11 h4 ♘f6 12 ♘f3 ♘g4 13 ♕e2 ♗b4 14 ♖de1.

5...♕a5

Designed to inhibit White's e2-e4 plan. Favouring White is 5...♗g7 6 e4, for example 6...0-0 (or 6...♘a6 7 e5 ♘d7 8 ♕d2 h6 9 ♗e3 with a space advantage) 7 0-0-0 b5 8 e5 b4 9 ♘ce2 ♘e8 10 ♗d2 (the immediate 10 h4 also looks interesting, so as to meet 10...f6 with 11 exf6 exf6 12 ♗d2) 10...a5 11 h4 c5 12 dxc5 ♘d7 13 ♕xd5 ♘c7 14 ♕e4 ♘xc5 15 ♕c6 left Black with only nebulous com-

pensation for the pawn in Muratov-Airapetian, Yerevan 1981. White can also keep open the option of castling short with 7 e5, for example 7...♘e8 8 ♗e3 f6 9 f4 ♗f5 10 ♕d2 ♕b6 11 ♖b1 and the central pawn wedge remains intact.

Black can try 5...♗f5 in this position because 6 e4? meets with 6...dxe4 7 fxe4 ♘xe4! 8 ♘xe4 ♕d5 9 ♘c3 ♗xd3 10 ♘xd5 ♗xf1 11 ♘c7+ ♔d8 12 ♘xa8 ♗xg2 etc. The problem is that after 6 ♕d2 it isn't clear whether 5...♗f5 has achieved much. White might gain time on the bishop with a later g2-g4.

Finally there is 5...h6, when 6 ♗xf6 (6 ♗h4 is possible) 6...exf6 7 e4 brings about a position akin to those arising after 5 ♗xf6 but with ...h7-h6 and f2-f3 included. It's not clear who this will favour, practical tests being required.

6 h4?!

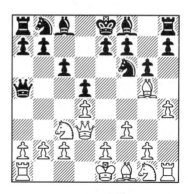

Morozevich is an interesting and creative player but occasionally his ideas walk on the wild side. The reasoning behind this move is that an immediate 6 e4 dxe4 sees Black threatening the bishop on g5 with his queen. Another way to try to solve this problem is with 6 ♗xf6, although after 6...exf6 7 e4 ♗b4 8 exd5 Black can sacrifice a pawn with 8...0-0! 9 0-0-0 ♘a6! along the lines of the Mestrovic-Bronstein game, given as a note within Markovic-Cvitan. There is also 6 ♗d2, but this seems okay for Black after 6...♗g7 7 e4 dxe4 8 fxe4 e5! (rather than 8...0-0 9 e5 with a space advantage for White).

**6...b5 7 e4 b4 8 ♘ce2 ♗a6 9 ♕e3 dxe4!
10 fxe4 ♘bd7 11 ♘f3 ♗g7**

Intending to break open the centre with 12...e5. White's reply prevents this but runs into other problems.

12 ♗xf6 exf6!

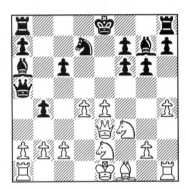

An excellent and unstereotyped idea with which Black aims to exert pressure on the e-file.

**13 h5 0-0 14 hxg6 hxg6 15 ♘c1 ♗xf1
16 ♔xf1 ♖fe8**

Threatening to demolish White's centre with 17...f5 18 e5 c5 etc.

17 ♕d3 c5 18 c3

Trying to keep hold of the central dark squares. After 18 d5 ♘e5 19 ♘xe5 ♖xe5 the threat is 20...f5, putting White in all sorts of trouble.

18...bxc3 19 bxc3 ♖ac8

Black has an interesting alternative in 19...♖ab8, when Malaniuk suggested White should play 20 ♔f2 (20 ♘d2 cxd4 21 cxd4 f5! is very dangerous) 20...♖b2+ 21 ♔g3 – not that this looks very comfortable for White!

**20 ♘b3 ♕a4 21 ♘bd2 ♕a3! 22 ♘c4
♕a6 23 d5 ♘b6 24 ♘fd2 ♖cd8**

Threatening ...f6-f5.

**25 ♖e1 f5 26 exf5 ♖xe1+ 27 ♔xe1
♘xd5 28 ♖h3 ♕f6 29 ♘e4 ♕xf5 30 ♖f3
♕d7 31 ♘cd6 ♘xc3! 32 ♕c4 ♕e6**

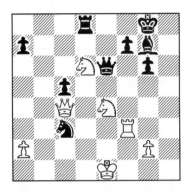

A good alternative is 32...♘xe4, when 33 ♖xf7 ♘xd6 34 ♖xd7+ ♘xc4 35 ♖xd8+ ♗f8 also gives Black excellent winning chances.

**33 ♕xe6 fxe6 34 ♖g3 ♘xe4 35 ♘xe4 c4
36 ♖xg6 ♔f7 37 ♖g3 ♗d4?!**

37...♗b2 stops the rook coming to a3 and leaves White in serious trouble, although even now he's not out of the woods.

38 ♖a3 ♔e7 39 ♖a4! ♖c8?!

Black should try 39...c3 since after 40 ♖c4 (40 ♔d1 e5, planning 41...♖g8, is also good for Black) 40...♖b8 41 ♘xc3 (41 ♖xd4 ♖b1+ 42 ♔e2 c2) he has the stunning 41...♖b4!.

40 ♘d2 ♗c3 41 ♔e2 ½-½

Game 42
Stryjecki-Vokac
Czech Extra League 2001

1 d4 ♘f6 2 ♘c3 d5 3 ♗g5 c6 4 ♕d2

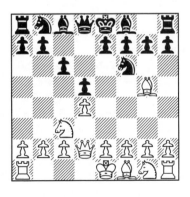

As with 4 ♕d3 White prepares queenside castling and keeps the option of playing f2-f3 and e3-e4. The queen is slightly less exposed on d2 but does not support the e4-square.

4...♗f5

A natural developing move, but possibly not the best. 4...b5 is an attempt to launch an attack on the queenside even before White's king has gone there. White can consider changing plans with 5 ♗xf6 (5 f3 is also possible and leads to positions from Chapter 2 after 5...♘bd7) 5...gxf6 6 e4!? b4 7 ♘ce2 dxe4 8 ♕xb4 ♕b6, and now 9 ♕c3 looks interesting, rather than 9 ♕xb6? axb6 which gave Black the bishop pair and a clear advantage in Johnsen-Akesson, Gausdal 1996.

Summerscale-Lalic, Coulsden 1999 saw 4...h6, and after 5 ♗xf6 exf6 6 e4 ♗b4 7 exd5 ♗xc3 8 ♕xc3 ♕xd5 9 ♕e3+ ♗e6 10 ♘e2 ♘d7 11 ♘f4 ♕a5+ 12 ♕d2 ♕xd2+ 13 ♔xd2 the resulting ending was only slightly worse for Black. 4...♘bd7 transposes to Chapter 2.

5 f3 ♘bd7

Black can prevent White from playing e2-e4 on his next move with 5...♗g6, which also means not having to worry about White attacking the bishop with a later ♕f4. White should probably play 6 ♘h3 with the idea of ♘f4xg6. Instead 6 h4 h6 7 ♗xf6 exf6 8 h5 ♗h7 9 e4 dxe4 10 ♘xe4 ♗e7 11 ♘h3 ♘d7 was very solid for Black in Sliwa-Doda, Polanica Zdroj 1966.

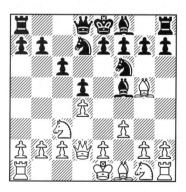

6 0-0-0

The immediate 6 e4 is rather dubious after 6...dxe4 7 ♕f4 ♕a5 8 0-0-0 e6 9 ♗xf6 ♘xf6 10 fxe4 ♗g6 11 ♗d3 ♗b4 12 ♘ge2, and now according to Bogolyubov Black's best is 12...e5! with a clear advantage. 12...0-0-0 13 e5 ♘d5 14 ♘xd5 ♕xd5 15 ♗xg6 fxg6 16 a3 ♕xg2 was also better for Black in Spielmann-Bogoljubov, Moscow 1925.

A better way of enforcing e2-e4 is with 6 ♕f4 ♗g6 7 e4 ♕b6 8 0-0-0 e6 as in Kulaots-Veingold, Parnu 1996. Then the immediate 9 e5 is best, with an interesting struggle in prospect, rather than the game's 9 ♕e3.

The quiet 6 e3 is inconsistent – in Rubinetti-Sunye Neto, Moron 1982 Black emerged with a good game after 6...h6 7 ♗h4 e6 8 g4 ♗g6 9 ♗g3 h5 10 g5 h4 11 ♗f2 ♘g8 12 e4 ♗b4 as his king's knight was re-emerging neatly to e7.

6...h6

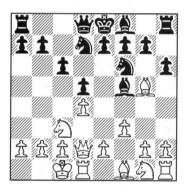

Black must be careful not to play 6...♕a5, when 7 e4 dxe4 8 fxe4 ♗g4 (8...♘xe4? 9 ♘xe4) 9 ♗e2 ♗xe2 10 ♘gxe2 0-0-0 11 ♖hf1 gave White the better chances in Demeny-Bach, Odorheiu Secuiesc 1993. The natural 6...e6 also appears to allow 7 e4, although after 7...dxe4 8 fxe4 Black can play 8...♗xe4. Filchev-Pelitov, Bulgaria 1956 continued 9 ♖e1 (9 ♘xe4? ♘xe4 exchanges queens) 9...♗b4 10 a3 ♗xc3 11 ♕xc3 ♕b6 12 ♘f3 h6 13 ♗h4 ♗h7 14 ♘e5 with healthy compensation for the sacrificed pawn.

7 ♗h4

Perhaps White should avoid any loss of time and opt for the immediate 7 ♗xf6 ♘xf6 8 e4. Then 8...dxe4 allows White to recover his pawn with 9 ♕f4 with a broad pawn centre, so Sandipan-Yurtaev, Guntur 2000 went 8...♗d7 9 e5 ♘g8 10 f4 e6, and now 11 ♔b1 would have been relatively best, with a complex game in prospect. In the game Black was doing very well after 11 ♘f3?! ♕a5 12 ♔b1 ♗b4.

7...♗h7

A useful waiting move. Black is in no hurry to push the e-pawn since doing so would only encourage White to make his central break. On 7...e6 White could play 8 e4 thanks to the pin on the knight. Hence the text. In Smirnov-Zavgorodniy, Lvov 2002 Black's attempt to start an attack on the queenside with 7...b5 was met with the razor sharp 8 e4!?, when there followed 8...dxe4 9 d5 cxd5 10 ♗xf6 ♘xf6 11 fxe4 ♗d7 12 e5 ♘h7? (12...b4 seems best, with Black reaching a solid position after 13 ♘xd5 ♘xd5 14 ♕xd5 e6). Smirnov chose the interesting 13 e6, but White's simplest is 13 ♕xd5, when 13...e6 14 ♕xd7+ ♕xd7 15 ♗xb5 earns a good pawn and a huge lead in development.

8 e4

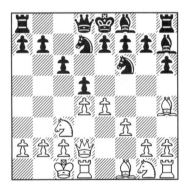

Anyway!

8...dxe4 9 ♖e1 e3

Black is evidently worried about the compensation White would have after 9...exf3 10

♘xf3 e6 11 ♗c4, with pressure on the e- and f-files akin to the Blackmar-Diemer Gambit. Declining the gambit is not bad, and is certainly less dangerous.

10 ♕xe3 e6 11 ♗c4?!

Perhaps White should have played 11 ♗d3, but then 11...♗xd3 12 ♕xd3 ♕a5 is no worse for Black.

11...♗e7 12 ♗b3 0-0 13 ♘h3 c5

Initiating counterplay on the queenside, Black being helped by the fact that the rook is no longer on d1.

14 ♗xf6?

A somewhat careless pawn grab which gives Black an uninhibited dark-squared bishop. 14 ♔b1 is safer.

14...♗xf6 15 dxc5 ♕c7 16 ♘a4 ♖ac8 17 ♖d1 b5! 18 ♘c3

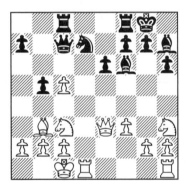

White has no good move. After 18 cxb6 there follows the spectacular 18...♕xc2+! 19 ♗xc2 ♖xc2+ 20 ♔b1 ♖xb2+ 21 ♔c1 (21 ♔a1 ♖b1 mate — Black's bishops call all the shots!) 21...♖c8+ etc.

18...♘xc5 19 ♖d2 ♘xb3+ 20 axb3 ♕a5 0-1

White has no satisfactory defence to the threats of 21...♕a1+ and 21...♖xc3.

Game 43
Veresov-Krogius
USSR Team Ch. 1953

1 d4 ♘f6 2 ♘c3 d5 3 ♗g5 c6 4 e3

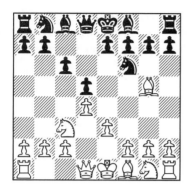

Once again we see that Veresov himself prefers this quiet and unassuming move. 4 ♘f3 seems less precise in view of 4...♕b6!, e.g. 5 ♖b1 ♘bd7 6 e3 g6 7 ♗d3 ♗g7 8 0-0 0-0 9 h3 (9 e4 dxe4 10 ♘xe4 ♘xe4 11 ♗xe4 ♘f6 12 ♗d3 ♗g4 13 c3 ♕a5! was quite promising for Black in Potterat-Cvitan, Bad Ragaz 1992) 9...♖e8 10 ♘e2 e5 11 dxe5 ♘xe5 12 ♘xe5 ♖xe5 13 ♗f4 ♖e8 with equality. Here 9...c5 invites 10 ♗xf6! ♘xf6 11 ♘a4, when trying to avoid losing a pawn with 11...♕a5 12 ♘xc5 ♕xa2 runs into 13 ♕d2! etc.

4...♕b6 5 ♖b1

White has also tried the gambit of the b-pawn with the variation 5 ♗d3 ♕xb2 6 ♘ge2, an idea which would not be possible if the knight were already committed to f3. White had some compensation for the pawn in the game Gardner-Levit, Chicago 1989 after 6...♘bd7 (the alternative try 6...♕b6 7 0-0 ♘bd7 8 e4 leads to similar play) 7 0-0 g6 8 e4 dxe4 9 ♘xe4 ♘xe4 10 ♗xe4 ♗g7 11 ♕d3.

5...♗f5 6 ♗d3 ♗xd3

This leaves White with a nice positional edge. His doubled pawns cover key squares and he has the makings of a 'minority attack' on the queenside with an advance of the b-pawn. Preferable is 6...♗g6 but this still looks nice for White after 7 ♘f3 e6 8 0-0 ♗e7 9

b4!? etc.

7 cxd3 ♘bd7 8 ♘f3 e6 9 0-0 h6 10 ♗h4 ♗e7 11 b4 0-0 12 ♘a4 ♕d8 13 ♕b3 b5 14 ♘c5 ♘xc5 15 bxc5 a5 16 ♖fe1 ♘d7 17 ♗g3 ♖c8 18 e4 ♗f6 19 ♗d6 ♖e8 20 ♖e2

Black's main problem is that he is very passive, enabling White to improve at leisure.

20...♘f8 21 ♖be1 ♕d7 22 ♘e5 ♗xe5 23 dxe5 ♘g6 24 g3 ♕d8 25 f4 dxe4

With the position being so unpleasant for Black this exchange is understandable. But now the problem is that White can penetrate on the d-file.

26 dxe4 f6 27 exf6

27 a4 looks very strong as after 27...b4 White can play 28 f5 ♘xe5 29 ♖d1, threatening 30 ♗xe5, and in response to 29...♘f7 there comes 30 fxe6 ♘xd6 31 e7+ etc.

27...♕xf6 28 ♕d3 e5!

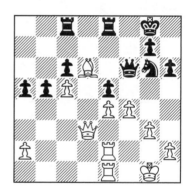

Suddenly the Black pieces start to cooperate.

29 f5 ♘h8 30 ♕c3 ♘f7 31 ♖d1 a4 32 ♔g2 ♖cd8 33 ♖ed2 ♖d7 34 h4 ♖ed8 35 ♕b4 ♔h7 36 ♖d3 g6 37 fxg6+ ♕xg6 38 ♖f1 ♕e6 39 ♕d2 ♘xd6 40 ♖d1 ♕g4 41 ♖xd6 ♕xe4+ 42 ♔h2 ♖xd6 43 cxd6 ♖d7 ½-½

Black must have been relieved to get away with a draw, but in the final position he could and should continue.

Summary

3...c6 is a solid move against which I think there are two good choices for White. The first is to play 4 f3, making a gambit of the b-pawn after 4...♕b6 and transposing to Chapter 2 after 4...♘bd7 5 ♕d2!?. The second is to play 4 e3, when Black's position is not as comfortable as it might appear.

1 d4 ♘f6 2 ♘c3 d5 3 ♗g5 c6 *(D)* **4 f3**

   4 ♗xf6 *(D)*
      4...exf6 - *Game 38*; 4...gxf6 - *Game 39*
   4 ♕d3
      4...♕a5 - *Game 40*; 4...g6 - *Game 41*
   4 ♕d2 - *Game 42*
   4 e3 - *Game 43*

4...♕b6 *(D)*
   4...♘bd7 5 ♕d2 - *Game 12*
5 e4 - *Game 36*
   5 ♕d2 - *Game 37*

3...c6

4 ♗xf6

4...♕b6

CHAPTER SIX

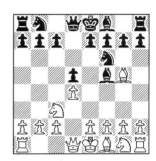

3...♗f5

1 d4 ♘f6 2 ♘c3 d5 3 ♗g5 ♗f5

This simple developing move is seen quite often, Black developing the bishop to its most natural square and hoping to inhibit e2-e4. The drawback is that the bishop can be exposed on f5, either to ♘xd5 combinations, a g2-g4 thrust or by having to retreat or exchange after a challenge with ♗d3.

Despite the sound appearance of 3...♗f5 Black certainly needs to know what he's doing against 4 f3. The complications arising from 4...♘bd7 5 ♘xd5!? (Bairamov-Smagin) appear to burn out to approximate equality but only after considerable excitement. The best answer may well be 4...c5, though the accuracy with which this must be played is shown by the fact that Black lasted only 15 moves in Jagielsky-Pytlakowski! And even after the sound 4...♗g6 International Master Strikovic also managed just 15 moves against Khachian. Generally speaking I don't like 4 f3 lines, but here it is genuinely interesting and there are many pitfalls for Black.

Another reasonable treatment for White is 4 ♗xf6. I don't usually like this move either but in this position it's not too bad; Black's light-squared bishop is not on the best square and may later lose time retreating. After 4...gxf6 5 e3 e6 6 ♗d3 ♗g6 White tried to take advantage of the bishop's location with

7 f4 in Maryasin-Tyomkin, and Black seemed to be okay in this game, although it wasn't as good as Tyomkin thought. In Kupreichik-Westerinen White adopted a different approach, with 6 ♘ge2 followed by ♘g3 and h2-h4, but I thought that his e3-e4 was a bit rash. If Black plays 4...exf6 he has to follow up very carefully; he can improve on Gufeld-Ujtumen by dropping the bishop back to e6 on move five, as by move six it is already a bit too late.

4 ♘f3 isn't very good because of 4...♘e4 (Bochkarev-Vinokurov) but 4 e3 seems interesting. I would not be too enthusiastic about following the game Ciocaltea-Tabor as the game was distinctly dubious for White. The simple 5 ♗d3 is quite promising.

Game 44
Bairamov-Smagin
USSR 1982

---

1 d4 ♘f6 2 ♘c3 d5 3 ♗g5 ♗f5 4 f3

As usual in the Veresov, this is White's sharpest response.

4...♘bd7

This seems like a very solid move, developing a piece and supporting the knight on f6. But White has a tactical trick which throws the game into wild complications.

The alternatives are as follows:

a) 4...e6? is very bad in view of 5 e4!.

b) 4...h6 5 ♗xf6 (after 5 ♗h4 Black might play 5...e6, when 6 e4 ♗h7 7 ♗xf6 ♕xf6 8 exd5 ♗b4 is an interesting pawn sac) 5...gxf6 (5...exf6 is more solid) 6 e4 dxe4 7 fxe4 ♗h7 8 ♘f3 ♗g7 9 ♗d3 0-0 10 0-0 ♘d7 11 ♕d2 left Black's bishops looking rather miserable in Schumacher-Tack, Antwerp 2000.

c) 4...c6 5 ♕d2 ♘bd7 transposes to Stryjecki-Vokac from Chapter 5. White has alternatives here. 5 g4!? ♗g6 6 h4 h6 7 ♗f4 e6 8 e3 ♗d6 9 ♘h3 gave White a space advantage on the kingside in Long-Sholl, Moline 1992, while Ciocaltea gave 5 e4 dxe4 6 ♗xf6 exf6 7 fxe4 ♗g6 8 ♘f3 ♘d7 with an 'unclear' assessment.

For 4...c5 see Jagielsky-Pytlakowski, and for 4...♗g6 see Khachian-Strikovic.

5 ♘xd5

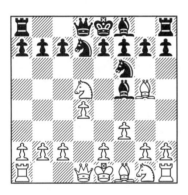

After Summerscale's suggestion of 5 g4 ♗g6 6 h4 I think that Black can play 6...h5 7 ♗xf6 exf6! (7...♘xf6 looks quite good for White after 8 g5 ♘g8 9 ♘h3, intending 10 ♘f4) 8 ♘xd5 hxg4 with a strong position because 9 fxg4? loses a piece after 9...♗e4!.

5...♘xd5 6 e4 h6

6...f6 is a little played continuation which has the benefit of allowing the bishop a retreat square on f7. 7 ♗h4 ♗e6 8 exd5 ♗xd5 9 c4 ♗f7 10 f4 (trying to dissuade Black from carrying out thematic pawn break but...) 10...e5 (Black plays it anyway!) 11 fxe5 ♗b4+

12 ♔f2 g5 (and continues to play very energetically) 13 e6 (13 ♗g3 fxe5 makes White's king feel very uncomfortable) 13...♗xe6 14 a3 ♗e7 15 ♗g3 0-0 16 ♗d3 f5

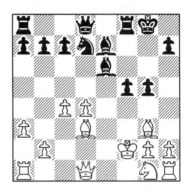

Matters are delicately balanced. White has better control of the centre but Black has the superior development and good kingside attacking prospects. Tallova-Babula, Czech Extra League 2000 continued 17 ♕e2 ♗f7 18 ♔f1 (18 ♗xc7!? ♕xc7 19 ♕xe7 – pawn grabbing is not always advisable, but this may have been preferable to the game) 18...♗g6 19 ♘f3 (19 ♗xc7!?) 19...♗f6 20 ♕e6+ ♖f7 21 h4 (a double-edged decision; it is extremely dangerous for White to open the kingside with his own king still stuck there) 21...♘f8 (21...♘c5!?) 22 ♕e2 f4 23 hxg5 fxg3 24 ♗xg6 ♘xg6 25 ♖d1?? (what a shame – a stupid blunder in an otherwise well contested game, where the sensible 25 gxf6 ♕xf6 would have left all to play for) 25...♗xg5 0-1 (based on notes by Aaron Summerscale).

Black should avoid 6...♗xe4 7 fxe4 ♘5b6 as after 8 ♘f3 White has the bishop pair and control of the centre. D.MacDonald-Rix, Hastings 1991/92 continued 8...g6 9 a4 a6 10 a5 ♘c8 11 ♗c4 ♗g7 12 e5 c5 13 c3 ♕c7 14 ♕b3 and Black was in serious trouble.

7 ♗h4

After 7 ♗c1 Black can develop at top speed with 7...e5! 8 ♘e2 (both 8 exd5 and 8 exf5 can be answered by 8...♕h4+, when Black recovers his pawn with an excellent game) 8...♗xe4 9 fxe4 ♕h4+ 10 ♘g3 ♘5f6 11 ♕d3 0-0-0 and White was under serious pressure in Herz-Bree, Wuerttemberg 2000.

7...♘e3

7...♘7b6 is also interesting for after 8 exf5 ♘e3 9 ♕d3 Black has 9...♕xd4.

8 ♕d3

White has also tried 8 ♕e2 at this point, but the current theoretical verdict is that this is favourable for Black after 8...♘xf1 9 exf5 ♘b6 10 0-0-0 ♕d5! (10...♕d6 11 g4! was played in Khachian-Elkin, USSR 1986, and now Khachian gave 11...♘c4! 12 ♕xc4 ♕f4+ 13 ♔b1 ♘d2+ 14 ♖xd2 ♕xd2 15 ♘e2 with compensation for the exchange) 11 ♔b1 (or 11 b3 ♕xf5 12 ♗f2 ♘xh2 etc.) 11...♘c4! 12 ♖xf1 (12 ♕xf1? ♕b5) 12...♕xd4! 13 c3 ♕xh4 14 g3 ♕g5 15 ♕xc4 ♕xf5+ and Black was a good pawn up in Khachian-Obukhov, USSR 1986.

8...♘xf1 9 exf5 ♘c5!

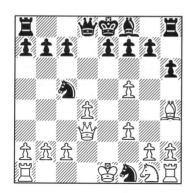

The start of some pyrotechnics with the knights which should lead to an equal game with best play. After 9...♘xh2 10 ♖xh2 the cramping effect of the pawn on f5 will make life difficult for Black.

10 ♕b5+?!

In this complex and difficult position White goes astray. Capturing the knight gives Black the better endgame after 10 dxc5 ♕xd3 11 cxd3 ♘e3 12 ♔e2 ♘xf5 in the form of the weak squares in front of White's d-pawn. He had to play 10 ♕c3!, when

10...♘a4 11 ♕d3 ♘xb2 12 ♕b5+ ♕d7 13 ♕xb7 ♖d8 14 ♔xf1 ♘c4 gives Black excellent counterplay, but 11 ♕b3 is better, e.g. 11...♘b6 12 ♘e2 (Black meets 12 0-0-0 with 12...♕d5, and 12 ♗f2 with 12...♕d7) 12...♕d5 13 ♖xf1 ♕xf5 14 0-0-0 with White having a shade the better of it thanks to his extra space, or 11...♕xd4 12 ♕b5+ ♕d7 13 ♕xd7+ ♔xd7 14 0-0-0+ ♔c6 15 ♖xf1, which is slightly better for White because the cramping pawn on f5 will leave Black with some weak pawns whether he liberates his kingside with ...e7-e6 or ...g7-g6.

10...c6 11 ♕xc5 ♘e3 12 ♔e2

Not 12 ♗g3 ♕xd4!, or 12 ♔f2 ♘xf5 13 ♕xf5 ♕xd4+ 14 ♔g3 g5.

12...♘xg2 13 ♗g3 e6 14 ♕e5 ♗e7! 15 fxe6

After 15 ♕xg7 Black gets the better endgame with 15...♗f6 16 ♕g4 ♕xd4 17 ♕xd4 ♗xd4, and 15 ♔f1 can be met with 15...♘h4 16 fxe6 0-0.

15...0-0 16 c3 ♗f6 17 ♕h5

A better defence might have been 17 ♕c7, e.g. 17...♕xc7 18 ♗xc7 fxe6, which is equal, or 17...♕d5 18 ♔f2 ♘h4 19 ♕xb7, which is far from clear.

17...fxe6 18 ♔f2 ♘h4 19 ♕g4 ♘f5 20 ♘e2 ♕b6 21 b4 ♖ae8 22 ♖hd1 ♗g5 23 ♕e4 e5! 24 ♗xe5 ♗f6!

The most important defender is the bishop on e5, so Black sets about removing it from office. Doing this 'combinatively' with

24...♘d6 25 ♕g6 ♖xe5 is not clear after 26 ♕xd6 because Black has had to part with his superb knight.

25 ♔e1 ♘d6 26 ♕g4 ♘c4 27 f4 ♗xe5 28 dxe5

After 28 fxe5 ♖f1+! the queen goes.

28...♖xe5! 29 ♖d7

And here 29 fxe5?? allows mate in one.

29...♖xe2+ 30 ♔xe2 ♕e3+ 31 ♔d1 ♕xc3 32 ♖c1 ♘b2+ 33 ♔e2 ♖e8+ 34 ♔f2 ♘d3+ 35 ♖xd3 ♕xd3 36 ♖g1 ♕d2+ 37 ♔g3 ♖e3+ 0-1

Game 45
Jagielsky-Pytlakowski
Poland 2000

---

1 d4 ♘f6 2 ♘c3 d5 3 ♗g5 ♗f5 4 f3 c5

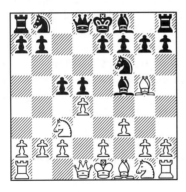

As in many lines this is the most incisive response to 4 f3. Black immediately counter-attacks by challenging the d4-pawn and makes room for his queen to come out to b6 or a5. White now responds with an equally sharp reply.

5 e4 dxe4

The alternative is 5...cxd4, when 6 ♗xf6 dxc3 7 ♗xc3 dxe4 8 ♕xd8+ ♔xd8 9 0-0-0+ gives White more than enough initiative for the pawn in the endgame, for example Krogius-Aronin, USSR Ch Semi Final 1952 went 9...♔c7 10 ♗c4 e6 11 fxe4 ♗xe4 12 ♘e2 ♘c6 13 ♖hf1 ♗g6 14 ♘f4 ♗f5 15 h3 h5, and now 16 ♗e2 h4 17 ♘d5+ ♔c8 18

♘e3 ♗g6 19 ♘c4 would have maintained the pressure. 6 ♕xd4 ♘c6 7 ♗b5 seems natural but favoured Black after 7...dxe4 8 ♗xc6+ bxc6 9 ♕c5 ♕c8 10 ♗xf6 exf6 in Klemp-Lindemann, Spree 1997.

6 ♗b5+

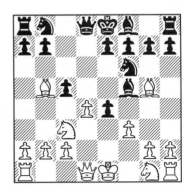

White can also play a kind of reversed Albin Counter Gambit with 6 d5, for example 6...♕a5 7 ♗xf6 exf6 8 fxe4 ♗d7 9 ♘f3 ♗d6 10 ♗e2 0-0 11 0-0 b5 12 a4 b4 13 ♘b5 ♗f4 14 ♘d2 and White had an edge in D.Farrand-Harari, Eastman Plate Final 1999. 7 ♕d2 makes sense as White's threat to recapture the e4-pawn with 8 fxe4 ♘xe4? 9 ♘xe4 almost forces Black to accept the gambit pawn with 7...exf3, when 8 ♘xf3 leaves White with compensation.

6...♗d7 7 ♗xd7+

White has an interesting alternative in 7 dxc5, for example 7...♕a5 8 ♗xf6 ♗xb5 9 b4 ♕xb4? (9...♕a3 is forced) 10 ♖b1 won a piece and the game in Peperle-Ertelt, correspondence 1974.

7...♘bxd7 8 d5 exf3 9 ♕xf3 g6 10 0-0-0 ♕b6 11 ♘h3 ♘e5?!

A flimsy looking manoeuvre which leads to Black's pieces becoming uncoordinated. After 11...♗g7 12 ♖he1 White has sufficient pressure to force Black to return the e-pawn if he wants to castle. Black's best might be 11...h6, after which 12 ♗xf6 ♘xf6 13 d6 0-0-0 leaves me wondering if White has sufficient compensation for the pawn.

12 ♕e2 ♘fd7 13 d6! exd6 14 ♘d5 ♕a5??

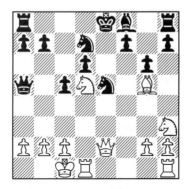

Black has to play 14...♕c6 when the position still looks unclear.

15 ♕b5! 1-0

15 ♕e1 would have been equally effective. In either case Black must lose his queen as capturing White's allows mate with 16 ♘c7.

Game 46
Khachian-Strikovic
Candas Open 1996

1 d4 ♘f6 2 ♘c3 d5 3 ♗g5 ♗f5 4 f3 ♗g6

A prophylactic move, anticipating White's central pawn expansion with e2-e4.

5 ♕d2

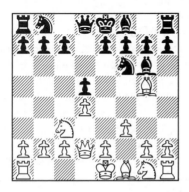

White can also offer a gambit with 5 e4, for example 5...dxe4 (if Black declines the pawn with 5...c6 White can offer another one

with 6 e5 ♘fd7 7 ♘ge2 f6 8 ♗e3!?, for example 8...fxe5 9 dxe5 ♘xe5 10 ♘d4 with compensation) 6 ♕d2 e6 7 fxe4 ♗b4 8 ♕e3 ♘g4 9 ♕d2 ♘f6 10 ♕e3 ♘g4 11 ♕f4?! (White should have allowed the repetition with 11 ♕d2) 11...♕xd4 12 ♘ge2 ♗xc3+ 13 ♘xc3 h6 14 ♕xg4 hxg5 15 ♕xg5 and White stood worse in Spassky-Filip, Amsterdam (Candidates) 1956, although he did eventually manage to draw.

The immediate 5 ♘h3 is also worth considering, for example 5...e6 6 ♘f4 ♗d6 (6...♗e7 7 ♕d2 ♘bd7 8 0-0-0 would lead back to the game) 7 ♕d2 c6 8 h4 (a preliminary 8 0-0-0 is more circumspect) 8...h6 9 ♘xg6 ♗g3+ 10 ♔d1 fxg6 11 ♗f4 ♘h5 12 ♗xg3 ♘xg3 13 ♖h3 ♘xf1 14 ♕d3 0-0 15 ♔e1 ♘g3 16 ♖xg3 ♕xh4 17 ♕xg6 ♖f7 18 ♖d1 ♘d7 19 e3 e5 and Black had freed himself and taken over the initiative in Lipski-Kholmov, Warsaw 1989.

5...♘bd7

Khachian has played this position several times and showed that it is deceptively dangerous for Black. Khachian-Goletiani, Erevan Open 1996 went 5...e6 6 0-0-0 ♗b4 7 ♘h3 ♘bd7 8 a3 ♗e7 9 ♘f4 c5 10 dxc5 ♘xc5 11 e4 dxe4 and now 12 ♕e3!? looks interesting. 12 ♗b5+ ♔f8 13 ♕e2 ♕a5 14 ♘xg6+ hxg6 15 fxe4 a6 was the game continuation, when 16 e5 axb5 left Black somewhat better.

6 0-0-0 e6 7 ♘h3 ♗e7 8 ♘f4 ♘g8!?

Black had no doubt been relying on this to free his game, but he comes under considerable pressure anyway. The problem with the natural 8...0-0 is that White can play 9 h4, when 9...h6 10 ♘xg6 causes serious damage to Black's pawn structure.

9 ♗xe7 ♘xe7 10 e4 c6 11 h4 h6 12 ♗d3 dxe4

This turns out to be a surprisingly serious mistake. Black should keep his outpost on d5 intact and play 12...♗h7.

13 ♘xg6 ♘xg6 14 ♘xe4 ♕c7?

Missing White's reply? Actually this position is far from easy for Black as after 14...♘b6 White has 15 ♘c5, and 14...0-0 walks into an attack after 15 h5 ♘e7 16 g4, threatening 17 g5.

15 ♕b4 1-0

Game 47
Maryasin-Tyomkin
Israeli Open Ch., Tel Aviv 1999

---

1 d4 d5 2 ♘c3 ♘f6 3 ♗g5 ♗f5 4 ♗xf6 gxf6

Recapturing towards the centre like this is Black's most ambitious line. For 4...exf6 see Gufeld-Ujtumen.

5 e3 e6

5...♕d7 also seems quite reasonable, intending ...♘c6 and ...0-0-0. White's best is probably 6 ♘ge2 ♘c6 7 ♘g3 ♗g6 8 h4 h6 9 h5 ♗h7 10 ♗d3 ♗xd3 11 ♕xd3 when the main problem with Black's setup is that it is not very active.

6 ♗d3

The standard continuation, but not a very threatening one. For the more dangerous 6 ♘ge2 see Kupreichik-Westerinen.

6...♗g6

Black can also play 6...♗xd3 when the game Schweber-Szmetan, Buenos Aires 2001 continued 7 cxd3 ♘c6 8 ♘ge2 f5, and now 9 0-0 followed by a minority attack on the queenside (a2-a3, b2-b4, ♖c1, ♘c3-a4-c5) would have been best. In the game White played 9 ♘g3?! but 9...f4 10 ♘h5 fxe3 11 fxe3 ♕g5 12 ♕f3 ♗h6 handed Black the initiative.

7 f4!?

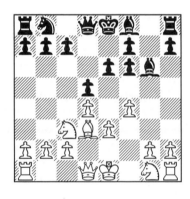

An interesting approach which threatens to ruin Black's pawn structure with 8 f5. The standard 7 ♘ge2 is innocuous after 7...c5 (or 7...♘d7 8 h4 c6 9 h5 ♗xd3 10 cxd3 f5 11 ♘f4 ♗d6 12 g3 ♕b6 with equality in Speelman-Ledger, England 1997) 8 0-0 ♘c6 9 dxc5 (9 f4 f5 10 dxc5 ♗xc5 was good for Black due to the weakness of e3 in Ippolitti-Panno, Buenos Aires 1998) 9...♗xc5 10 e4 d4 11 ♘b1 ♕d7 12 ♘d2 0-0-0 13 f4 f5 and Black stood well in Ostapenko-Bocharov, Novosibirsk 1998.

7...f5!?

A simple yet radical way to prevent f4-f5. The other way to take the sting out of this plan is by exchanging bishops on d3, but after 7...♗xd3 8 cxd3 c5 9 dxc5 ♗xc5 10 d4 ♗b4 11 ♘f3 ♘c6 there was equality in Maryasin-Cherepkov, Minsk 1981. Perhaps 8 ♕xd3 ♘d7 9 f5 is worth investigating.

Allowing White to play f4-f5 turns out rather badly for Black, for example 7...♘c6?! 8 f5 ♗xf5 (8...exf5 9 ♕f3) 9 ♗xf5 exf5 10 ♕f3; or 7...c5?! 8 f5! exf5 9 ♕f3 ♘c6 10 ♘ge2 ♕d7 11 0-0 and White stood better in Chernyshov-Ovetchkin, Smolensk 2000.

8 ♘f3 ♗h5

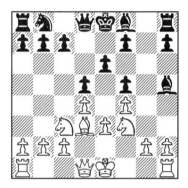

Bringing the bishop back into play. Another possibility is 8...c5, when 9 0-0 (or 9 ♗b5+ ♘c6 10 ♘e5 ♕c7 intending 11...f6) 9...♘c6 10 ♘e5 cxd4 11 ♘xc6 bxc6 12 exd4 ♕b6 was good for Black in Buhmann-Komljenovic, St.Ingbert 1987.

9 ♗e2 ♘d7 10 ♘e5 ♗xe2 11 ♕xe2 ♘xe5 12 dxe5

Perhaps 12 fxe5 (threatening 13 ♕b5+) would have been better, although this still looks at least equal for Black after 12...a6 (12...c6 and 12...♗h6 look like good alternatives) 13 0-0-0 ♕g5, preventing White's positional threat of 14 g4 and securing a good game.

12...a6?!

I would prefer the solid 12...c6. Black evidently wanted to retain the option of playing ...c7-c5 but he's playing with fire while his king is in the centre.

13 0-0-0 ♗b4 14 e4!?

With his position starting to creak from a strategic point of view, White launches an interesting attack involving the sacrifice of his knight. Quiet moves leave Black better thanks to his superior pawn structure.

14...♗xc3 15 exd5 ♗b4 16 dxe6

This seems to leave White with slightly inadequate compensation. After 16 ♕c4 Black would be forced to return the piece with 16...♕e7 (16...♗f8 17 dxe6 ♕e7 18 exf7+ ♕xf7 19 e6 is very dangerous for Black) 17 d6 ♗xd6 18 exd6 cxd6 but, although this leaves him a pawn up, the situation is far from clear after 19 ♖he1.

16...♕e7 17 exf7+ ♕xf7 18 e6 ♕f6 19 ♖d7 ♗d6 20 g3 0-0 21 ♖e1 ♖ae8 22 ♖f7 ♕g6 23 ♕c4 b5 24 ♕d5 ♖e7 25 ♖xe7 ♗xe7 26 ♕c6 ♖d8 27 ♕xc7?!

27 ♕xa6 is preferable. Tyomkin then gave 27...♕f6 28 ♕xb5 ♕d4 but White can defend with 29 ♕d3 ♕b4 30 c3 ♕a5 31 ♕c4 with everything left to play for.

27...♕f6 28 c3 b4 29 ♔c2

After 29 ♖e5 Black has 29...bxc3 (not 29...♗d6? 30 ♖xf5!) 30 bxc3 ♕f8 when White's king has serious problems, not to mention the immediate threat of 31...♗d6.

29...bxc3 30 bxc3 ♖d6 31 ♕c8+ ♔g7 32 ♖e5 ♕h6 33 h4 ♕h5-+ 34 ♖e1 ♕f3 35 ♕c4 ♕f2+

There was nothing wrong with the cold-blooded 35...♕xg3, though Black was understandably nervous about opening the g-file when short of time. The text is good enough.

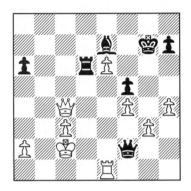

36 ♕e2 ♕xe2+ 37 ♖xe2 ♔f6 38 h5 ♖xe6 39 ♖g2 ♔f7 40 ♔d3 ♖h6 41 ♖h2 ♖d6+ 42 ♔e3 ♖e6+ 43 ♔d3 ♖e1 44 ♖b2

There are too many weak white pawns, and with the following move White brings out the rook, hoping to generate counterplay.
44...♖g1 45 ♖b6 ♖xg3+ 46 ♔c4 ♖g4 47 ♖xa6 ♖xf4+ 48 ♔d5 ♖f1!

White can no longer stop the f-pawn.
49 c4 f4 50 ♔e4 f3 51 ♖a5 f2 52 ♔f3 ♗h4 0-1

Game 48
Kupreichik-Westerinen
Dortmund 1975

---

1 d4 ♘f6 2 ♘c3 d5 3 ♗g5 ♗f5 4 ♗xf6 gxf6 5 e3 e6 6 ♘ge2 c5

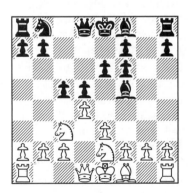

In Miles-Hort, Amsterdam 1982 Black played 6...♗d6 in order to meet 7 ♘g3 ♗g6 8 h4 with 8...♗xg3. Miles, in turn, used the position of Black's bishop on d6 to play 7 ♘b5 ♗e7 8 ♘g3 ♗g6 9 c4, and after 9...c6 10 ♘c3 h5 could have secured a slight edge with 11 ♗d3 according to Hort. Another playable move is 6...♕d7 though this seems slightly better for White after 7 ♘g3 ♗g6 8 h4 h6 (8...h5? 9 ♗e2) 9 h5 ♗h7 10 ♗d3 ♗xd3 11 ♕xd3 ♗d6 12 ♘ce2, intending a later c2-c4.

7 ♘g3

7 g3 is not as innocuous as it looks. Kacheishvili-Buehl, Kona 1998 continued 7...♘c6 8 dxc5 ♗xc5 9 ♗g2 ♕d7 10 e4 dxe4 11 ♘xe4 ♗xe4 12 ♗xe4 0-0-0 13 ♕xd7+ ♖xd7 14 ♗xc6 bxc6 15 ♘c1 and Black's weak pawns made life difficult for him.

7...♗g6 8 h4

After the immediate 8 ♗d3 Black is not forced to exchange bishops, which made life awkward for White in Braga-Rodriguez Cespedes, Bayamo 1984. After 8...♘c6 9 0-0 cxd4 10 exd4 ♕b6 11 ♘ce2 0-0-0 White was already in trouble as both b2 and d4 were attacked.

8...h6 9 e4?!

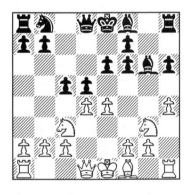

True to form, Kupreichik begins to play very sharply, opening up the centre. Objectively stronger is 9 h5 ♗h7 10 ♗d3, when 10...cxd4 11 exd4 ♗xd3 12 ♕xd3 ♘c6 13 0-0-0 is somewhat better for White due to his superior pawn structure and more active pieces.

9...cxd4

Krnic claimed that 9...dxe4 was bad in view of 10 d5, but 10...f5! is far from clear. Krnic only gave 10...exd5 11 ♕xd5 ♕xd5 12 ♘xd5 which, admittedly, is unpleasant for Black.

10 ♗b5+ ♘c6 11 exd5

White can also try 11 ♕xd4!? although this looks very comfortable for Black after 11...a6 12 ♗xc6+ bxc6 13 0-0 ♗d6, intending ...♗e5.

11...a6!

After 11...exd5 12 ♕xd4 Black's badly weakened pawn structure will leave him with problems, for example 12...♕e7+ 13 ♘ge2 0-0-0 14 ♗xc6 bxc6 15 0-0-0 and Black's king looks vulnerable.

12 dxc6 axb5 13 cxb7 ♖b8 14 ♘ce2 ♗b4+ 15 ♔f1 e5 16 f4 ♕d7!

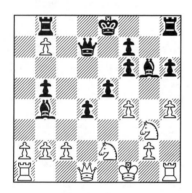

Black prevents f4-f5, which would shut his bishop out of play and give White a great square for his knight on e4. 16...d3? doesn't work because of 17 f5! dxe2+ 18 ♕xe2 ♖xb7 (18...♗h7 19 ♕xb5+ picks up the bishop on b4) 19 fxg6 fxg6 20 ♕e4, hitting b4, b7 and g6!

17 c3 ♗c5 18 cxd4 exd4 19 ♖c1 ♗b6 20 f5!

The best move. 20 ♘xd4? doesn't work due to 20...♕xd4 21 ♖c8+ ♔d7, and 20 ♖c8+ ♖xc8 21 bxc8♕+ ♕xc8 22 ♘xd4 0-0 gives

Black a strong pair of bishops in an open position.

20...♗xf5 21 ♘xd4 ♗xd4 22 ♖c8+ ♔e7

In the event of 22...♖xc8? 23 bxc8♕+ ♕xc8 24 ♕xd4 0-0 25 ♔g1 White's king scuttles away to safety and he's left with the better pawn structure.

23 ♕e1+!

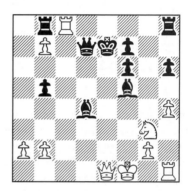

Heading for a draw by repetition. 23 ♕xd4?? ♗d3+! is one to avoid! .

23...♔d6 24 ♕d1! ♔e7

Attempting to avoid the repetition with 24...♔e6? runs into 25 ♘xf5 ♔xf5 26 ♖c5+! ♔e6 (26...♔g6 27 ♕h5+ ♔h7 28 ♖d5 recovers the piece with the better game) 27 ♕b3+ ♔e7 28 ♖d5 and White regains the piece with a large advantage in the form of Black's weak pawns and poor king position.

25 ♕e1+ ½-½

Game 49
Gufeld-Ujtumen
Tbilisi 1971

---

1 d4 ♘f6 2 ♘c3 d5 3 ♗g5 ♗f5 4 ♗xf6 exf6

A solid reply, keeping a nice row of pawns on the kingside and preparing to develop his king's bishop. Black's problems stem from his pawn structure; his lack of central pawns means that he has to control the centre with pieces and may find himself with a qualitatively inferior pawn majority should White play a later e2-e4.

5 e3 c6

Black's best plan is to retreat his bishop from f5 to e6, play ...f6-f5 and then bring his knight from b8 to e4 via d7 and f6. With this in mind, 5...c6 makes perfect sense, though there are a number of alternatives:

a) 5...♗e6 also looks logical. The standard 6 ♗d3 doesn't get anywhere after 6...f5 7 ♕f3 g6 8 ♘ge2 c6 9 ♘f4 ♘d7 10 h4 ♘f6, which gave Black an excellent game in Tiberkov-Spassov, Sofia 1988. Consequently I suggest 6 ♘f3 f5 7 ♘e2!? (7 ♗d3 ♘d7 8 ♘e2 ♗d6 9 0-0 0-0 10 ♘d2 ♘f6 11 ♖c1 c6 12 c4 dxc4 13 ♗xc4 was a bit better for White in Maljutin-Tiviakov, Forli 1992, but in my view White is even better off putting his bishop on g2) with a possible sequel being 7...♗d6 8 g3 c6 9 ♗g2 ♘d7 10 0-0 ♘f6 11 c3 0-0 12 ♕c2, intending b2-b3 and c3-c4 with some pressure. This slow plan is known from the Trompovsky.

b) 5...♘c6 looks considerably less logical because it moves the knight to a square which is four moves from e4. Tartakower-Spielmann, Copenhagen 1923 continued 6 ♗d3 ♕d7 7 ♘ge2 ♘b4 (7...♗b4 8 0-0 0-0 9 a3 ♗xc3 10 ♘xc3 ♘e7 11 ♘e2 c6 12 c4 favoured White in Christiansen-Biyiasas, Hastings 1979/80) 8 ♗xf5 ♕xf5 9 0-0 ♗d6 10 a3 ♘a6 (10...♘c6 11 ♘b5 ♕e6 12 c4 was also better for White in Tartakower-Pokorny, Maehrisch Ostrau 1923) and now instead of

11 ♘g3 ♗xg3 12 fxg3, as in the game, 11 ♘b5 ♗e7 12 ♘g3 ♕d7 13 ♕d3 c6 14 ♘c3 looks better for White.

c) 5...♗b4 doesn't seem quite right either after 6 ♗d3 (6 ♘ge2 c6 7 ♘g3 ♗g6 8 ♗d3 ♗xd3 9 ♕xd3 g6 10 e4 was also an edge for White in Tartakower-Colle, Budapest 1929) 6...♗xd3 7 ♕xd3 ♘c6 (7...♗xc3+ 8 bxc3 c6 9 ♘e2 0-0 10 0-0 ♘d7 11 ♘g3 b5 12 f3 ♘b6 13 e4 gave White the more promising game in Tal-Vladimirov, USSR Ch., Baku 1961) 8 ♘ge2 ♕d7 9 0-0-0 0-0-0 10 g3 ♗xc3 11 ♕xc3 ♘e7 12 ♘f4 and White stood slightly better in Veresov-Bronstein, Moscow 1959. Stein-Lazarev, Kiev 1960 went 6...♗g6 7 ♘ge2 c6 8 a3 ♗a5 9 h4 ♘d7 10 h5 ♗xd3 11 ♕xd3 ♕e7 12 0-0-0 ♗xc3 13 ♘xc3 0-0 14 ♘e2, planning ♘g3, with an edge for White, while 6...♕d7 7 ♕f3 ♗xd3 8 cxd3 c6 9 ♘ge2 0-0 10 0-0 ♖e8 11 e4 dxe4 12 dxe4 ♗xc3 13 bxc3 was seen in Veresov-Lapienis, Novgorod 1961. Black's most logical move is 6...♗e6, when White should probably try 7 ♘ge2 0-0 8 a3, for example 8...♗d6 9 ♘b5 ♗e7 10 ♘f4 c6 11 ♘c3 ♗d6 12 ♕h5 g6 13 ♕f3 f5 14 h4 with the more promising position.

6 ♗d3

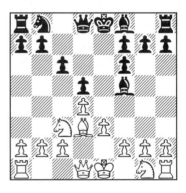

White has also tried 6 ♘ge2, after which 6...g6 7 ♘f4 ♗d6 8 ♗d3 ♗xd3 9 ♘xd3 f5 10 ♕f3 ♘d7 was equal in Speelman-Popovic, Groningen 1976.

6...♗xd3

I chose this game as the main line because it is a good illustration of White's strategy rather than a model of defence by Black. The exchange on d3 is very helpful for White as it becomes difficult for Black to control the e4-square. The most 'logical' move is 6...♗e6 but then 7 ♕f3 (7 ♘ge2 f5 8 ♕d2 ♘d7 was fine for Black in Tartakower-Grünfeld, Vienna 1921) 7...♗b4 8 ♘ge2 0-0 9 a3 seems to prevent Black from setting up his ...f6-f5 blockade.

Gufeld and Stetsko give 6...♗g6 but don't mention White's most promising looking move which is 7 ♕f3!?, intending ♘1e2 and perhaps a later g2-g4. They also give 6...♕d7, when an interesting plan for White is 7 ♗xf5 ♕xf5 8 ♕d3 ♕g4 (8...♕xd3 9 cxd3 leaves White with the better endgame) 9 ♔f1 followed by ♘ge2. White would then have a variety of interesting middlegame plans, including h2-h3 and g2-g4 or just e3-e4. Black doesn't have any compensation for his weakened pawn structure.

7 ♕xd3

7...♗b4

Black's position is sound enough but he is on the negative side of the board, defending against White's aggression rather than instituting his own ideas. The alternatives also see White pressing, for example 7...♘a6 8 ♘ge2 ♗d6 9 e4 0-0 10 0-0 dxe4 11 ♘xe4 ♖e8 12 ♕f3 ♕d7 13 ♖ad1 and White an edge because of his healthier pawn majority in Tal-

Soderborg, Varna 1962. Another possibility is 7...♗d6 8 e4 0-0 9 exd5 cxd5 10 ♘ge2 ♕a5 11 0-0 ♘c6 12 a3, leaving Black with some concerns regarding his isolated d-pawn in Wade-Garcia, Cienfuegos 1975.

8 ♘ge2 0-0

Bronstein-Vasiukov, Moscow 1959 went 8...♘d7 9 e4 (after 9 0-0-0 Black can contemplate 9...♘b6 10 g4 ♕e7 followed by 11...0-0-0 as his king is relatively safe on the queenside) 9...♘b6 10 exd5 ♘xd5 11 0-0 ♘xc3 12 ♘xc3 0-0, and now 13 a3 (rather than 13 ♘d1 as played in the game) 13...♗d6 14 ♘e4 would have given White a slight but persistent advantage.

9 0-0-0

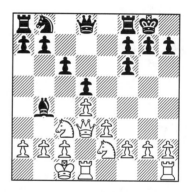

The dynamic treatment, and quite promising now that Black has committed his king to the kingside. An alternative plan is to play for e3-e4, for example Tartakower-Norman, Hastings 1926/27 went 9 0-0 ♖e8 10 e4 ♗xc3 11 ♘xc3 dxe4 12 ♘xe4 ♘d7 13 ♖fe1 with a typical edge thanks to White's queenside pawn majority – not that it is easy to win this kind of position...

9...♘d7 10 g4! ♖e8 11 h4 b5 12 ♔b1 ♘b6 13 ♘g3 ♖b8

An optimistic move. Perhaps Black should play 13...♗xc3 while he still has the chance, reducing the attacking chances of both sides. After 14 ♕xc3 ♘c4 15 h5 followed by 16 ♘f5 White has the more comfortable game.

14 ♘ce2 ♘c4 15 ♘f5 ♖b6?

The attack against a2 will not get anywhere as White can simply defend with ♘e2-c1. 15...a5 is a better try, followed by ...a5-a4.

16 g5 ♖a6 17 ♘c1 ♕a5?

This attempt to attack falls woefully short. Black should defend the kingside with either 17...g6 or 17...♗f8.

18 gxf6 g6

After 18...♗d2 White sets in motion a mating attack with 19 ♘h6+ gxh6 20 ♖hg1+ etc.

19 h5! gxf5

Had Black played 19...♘xb2 he would have allowed White to crown the game with a queen sacrifice: 20 hxg6 ♘xd3 (20...hxg6 21 ♘h6+ ♔f8 22 ♘g4, or 20...fxg6 21 ♖xh7 ♘xd3 22 ♖g7+ ♔f8 23 ♘h6 followed by mate) 21 ♘h6+ ♔f8 22 g7 mate.

20 ♕xf5 ♖e6 21 ♕f4!

White must preserve the f4-pawn, for after 21 ♖hg1+ ♔f8 22 ♕xh7? Black can escape with 22...♖xf6.

21...♔f8

After 21...♕d8 White's most effective line is 22 ♘d3, when 22...♗d6 23 ♕g5+ ♔f8 24 ♕g7+ ♔e8 25 ♕g8+ ♗f8 26 ♘c5 gets very ugly for Black.

22 ♖hg1 ♗d6

On 22...♘d6 White decides the game most easily with 23 a3 (23 c3 should also be good), for example 23...♕xa3 24 ♘b3 ♕a4 (24...♕b6 25 bxa3 is hopeless for Black because White's knight will reinforce the attack

by coming to c5) 25 bxa3 ♕xa3 26 ♕h6+ ♔e8 27 ♖g8+ ♔d7 28 ♘c5+ ♔c7 29 ♘xe6+ fxe6 (or 29...♔b6 30 ♖b8+ ♔a5 31 ♖d3 etc.) 30 ♕xh7+ ♔b6 31 ♖b8+ ♔a5 32 ♖d3 ♕b4+ 33 ♖b3 ♕e1+ 34 ♔b2 ♘c4+ 35 ♔a2 ♕xf2 36 f7 followed by the crowning of another queen.

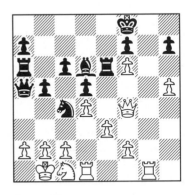

23 ♕h6+ ♔e8 24 ♖g8+ ♔d7 25 ♕g7 ♗e7

25...♕b4 26 ♘b3 ♕a4 27 a3 is decisive.

26 fxe7 ♖xe7 27 ♕xh7 ♘d6 28 h6 b4 29 ♕d3 f5 30 ♖g7 c5 31 dxc5 1-0

Game 50
Bochkarev-Vinokurov
Voronezh Open 2001

1 d4 ♘f6 2 ♘c3 d5 3 ♗g5 ♗f5 4 ♘f3

Black's reply is the most direct argument against this move, the other disadvantage is that it obstructs the f-pawn. If White wants to play quietly then the immediate 4 e3, as in Ciocaltea-Tabor, is the best course.

4...♘e4

Clearly Black has a number of choices here, of which 4...e6 is probably the most solid. Rodchenkov-Gorbunova, Togliatty 2001 continued 5 e3 ♗b4 (5...♗e7 is very sound) 6 ♗d3 ♗g4!? (ambitiously playing for ...e7-e5; 6...♗xd3 7 cxd3 strengthens White's centre, but 6...♗g6 looks very solid) 7 0-0 ♘c6!? 8 h3 ♗h5 9 a3 ♗d6 (9...♗xc3 10 bxc3 e5 favours White after 11 dxe5 ♘xe5 12 g4)

10 ♘b5 h6 11 ♘xd6+ ♕xd6 12 ♗f4 ♕e7 13 c4 with White holding the advantage due to his bishop pair and potential pressure on the c-file.

5 ♗h4

Perhaps 5 ♘xe4 dxe4 6 ♘g1 is better, although this hardly inspires much confidence in White's position.

5...c5 6 dxc5

Not very desirable but the threat of 6...♕a5 left White little choice in the matter.

6...♘xc3 7 bxc3 ♕a5 8 ♖b1 ♘c6 9 ♖xb7

A rather desperate looking attempt to hit back which results in disaster. White should either set about developing his kingside with 9 e3 or play 9 ♕xd5 ♕xc3+ 10 ♕d2.

9...♕xc3+ 10 ♘d2?

Probably missing Black's reply. White had to play 10 ♕d2, when 10...♕a1+ 11 ♕d1 ♕xa2 leaves him much worse but still fighting.

10...♘d4! 11 ♕c1

After 11 e3 there follows 11...♘xc2+ 12 ♔e2 ♗g4+ 13 ♘f3 d4 with a truly horrific position for White.

11...g5!?

Throwing in another pawn to accelerate development. A more prosaic continuation was 11...♘xc2+ 12 ♔d1 ♕xc5 with an extra pawn and a strong position.

12 ♗xg5 f6 13 ♗f4 e5 14 e4

This game is not a great advert for the Veresov. White finally plays this thematic

advance when the game is totally lost.

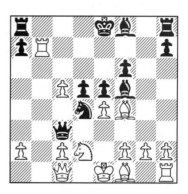

14...dxe4 15 ♗a6 exf4 16 0-0 ♖g8 17 ♔h1 ♗h6 18 ♖e1 f3 19 ♕a1 fxg2+ 20 ♔g1 ♗xd2 21 ♗e2 ♘xe2+ 0-1

One could hardly say that White's resignation was premature!

Game 51
Ciocaltea-Tabor
Baja 1971

---

1 d4 ♘f6 2 ♘c3 d5 3 ♗g5 ♗f5 4 e3

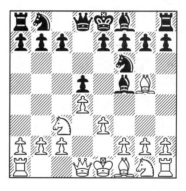

Once again this simple move is one of White's best options.

4...e6

This looks sensible but White has an interesting and dangerous reply. Black should probably prefer 4...♘bd7, though there too White has some interesting ideas. Weenink-Euwe, Amsterdam 1930 continued 5 ♗d3

♗xd3 6 ♕xd3 c6 7 ♘f3 e6 8 e4 dxe4 9 ♘xe4 ♕b6?! (an attempt to mix it up which rebounds badly; 9...♗e7 is the solid option, when White has only a minimal space advantage) 10 ♗xf6 gxf6 11 0-0 0-0-0 and now just 12 ♕e2 (rather than 12 a4?!) would leave White with a promising game, 12...♕xb2 giving White a dangerous initiative after 13 a4. Also worth considering is 6 cxd3 c6 7 f4!?, when Mestrovic-Kecic, Ljubljana 1995 continued 7...e6 8 ♘f3 ♗e7 9 0-0 h6 10 ♗h4 0-0 11 ♕e2 with White's central pawns giving him the slightly easier game. Instead of the trade on d3 Black has dropped the bishop back to g6: 5...♗g6 6 f4!? e6 7 f5 ♗xf5 8 ♗xf5 exf5 9 ♘xd5 h6 10 ♗xf6 ♘xf6 11 ♘xf6+ ♕xf6 12 ♕f3 ♗d6 13 ♘e2 0-0 14 0-0 ♕e7 15 ♘c3 c6 16 ♖ae1 ♗b4 17 ♕xf5 ♗xc3 18 bxc3 ♕a3 19 ♕d3 ♕xa2 20 c4 ♕a5 21 c5 was better for White in Mestrovic-Kurajica, Cateske Toplice 1968.

Another solid try is 4...c6, although after 5 ♗d3 ♗g6 I think that White's most interesting move is 6 f4!? (6 ♘f3 ♘bd7 7 0-0 e6 8 ♘e5 ♕b6 was fine for Black in Rellstab-Keres, Kemeri 1937), with the sunnier prospects for White after 6...e6 7 ♘f3.

5 g4!?

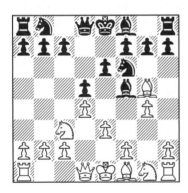

Unstereotyped and audacious play. White gains time on the bishop and space on the kingside. Having said that, the quiet 5 ♗d3 might be better, offering White good chances for an edge after 5...♗xd3 6 cxd3. Karaklajic-

Minic, Belgrade 1962 continued 6...♗e7 7 ♘f3 (7 f4!? is worth considering) 7...0-0 8 0-0 ♘e8 9 ♗xe7 ♕xe7 10 ♖c1 (10 ♕c2 with the idea of 11 b4 seems more logical to me) 10...♘d7 11 e4 ♘b6 12 ♖e1 ♘f6 13 e5 ♘e8 14 ♕b3 a5 15 a4 ♕b4 and Black had equalised. Alternatively 6 ♕xd3 c5 7 ♗xf6 gxf6 8 dxc5 ♘d7 9 e4 dxe4 10 ♕xe4 ♘xc5 11 ♕f3 ♗g7 was fine for Black in Bronstein-Fischer, Mar del Plata 1960. This leaves 5...♗g6 6 ♘f3 ♗e7 7 ♘e5 ♘bd7 8 f4 a6 9 ♕f3 ♗xd3 10 cxd3 c5 11 0-0!? cxd4 12 exd4 which brought about an interesting structure in Sakharov-Shiyanovsky, USSR 1958. White's doubled d-pawns cover important squares and his pieces are very actively placed.

5...♗g6 6 ♘ge2 c5

In Navinsek-Gjuran, Ljubljana 2001 Black tried to equalise by exchanging pieces with 6...♗e7 7 ♘f4 ♘e4, but after 8 ♗xe7 ♕xe7 9 ♘xg6 hxg6 10 ♘xe4 dxe4 White was better thanks to his superior pawn structure. The game continued 11 ♕e2 ♕d6 12 h4 g5 13 h5 ♘d7 14 0-0-0 0-0-0 15 ♕b5 with quite unpleasant pressure on Black's position. Black should certainly consider 6...h6, making room for his bishop to retreat.

7 ♘f4 ♕b6 8 ♗b5+ ♘c6 9 a4!? cxd4 10 a5 ♕c7 11 ♗xf6 gxf6 12 ♕xd4 0-0-0

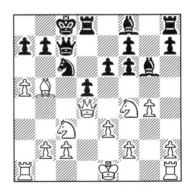

Giving up a pawn in order to make his king safe. 12...e5 runs into 13 ♘cxd5!, but simply 12...♗e7 looks fine. Ciocaltea's suggestion of 13 a6 0-0 14 ♕a4 looks unimpressive after 14...♘e5.

13 ♗xc6 ♛xc6 14 ♘xg6 hxg6 15 ♛xf6

Not 15 ♛xa7?? ♗c5 and the queen goes.

15...d4 16 0-0-0 ♗h6

White meets the spectacular 16...♗a3 with 17 ♘b1! which favours White after 17...♗c5 18 exd4 ♗xd4 19 ♛xf7. The other move is 16...♗e7, although after 17 ♛xe7 dxc3 18 ♛xf7 cxb2+ 19 ♔xb2 Black is still struggling to demonstrate equality.

17 ♘e2 dxe3 18 g5! ♛b5 19 gxh6 ♛xe2 20 h7?!

With the benefit of hindsight it appears that the alternative 20 fxe3 might have been better.

20...exf2??

In this complex and tricky position Black loses the plot, sacrificing a rook for totally inadequate compensation. Ciocaltea gave 20...♛h5 as Black's best and claimed a clear advantage for White after 21 ♛c3+ ♔b8 22 ♖d7. But Black can defend with 22...♖c8 23 ♛b3 ♛f3, covering b7. Two other moves seem playable: 20...♖de8 and 20...♖df8.

21 ♖xd8+ ♖xd8 22 ♛xd8+ ♔xd8 23 h8♛+ ♔e7

Both 23...♔c7 24 ♛c3+ and 23...♔d7 24 ♛d4+ lose on the spot.

24 ♛h4+ f6 25 ♛b4+ ♔e8 26 ♛a4+ ♔f8 27 ♛a3+ ♔g7 28 ♛d3 ♛e1+ 29 ♛d1 ♛xa5 30 ♔b1 ♛e5 31 ♛d2! ♛xh2 32 ♛d7+ 1-0

Black is losing his entire queenside after 32...♔f8 33 ♛c8+ ♔g7 34 ♛xb7+ ♔g8 35 ♛a8+ ♔g7 36 ♛xa7+, when White can win easily by capturing on h2.

Summary

The natural 3...♗f5 leaves White with several attractive options and requires accuracy from Black if he wants a playable game. Once again I like the simple 4 e3 followed by 5 ♗d3, but I'd also be tempted to play 4 f3 or 4 ♗xf6.

1 d4 ♘f6 2 ♘c3 d5 3 ♗g5 ♗f5 *(D)* **4 f3**
>   4 ♗xf6 exf6 - *Game 49*
>>   4...gxf6 5 e3 e6 *(D)*
>>>   6 ♗d3 - *Game 47*; 6 ♘ge2 - *Game 48*
>   4 ♘f3 - *Game 50*; 4 e3 - *Game 51*

4...♘bd7
>   4...c5 - *Game 45*; 4...♗g6 - *Game 46*

5 ♘xd5 ♘xd5 6 e4 *(D) - Game 44*

3...♗f5   *5...e6*   *6 e4*

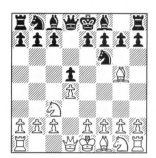

CHAPTER SEVEN

3...h6, 3...♘c6, 3...g6 and Others

1 d4 ♘f6 2 ♘c3 d5 3 ♗g5

In this chapter we'll consider four of Black's less usual options, namely 3...g6, 3...h6, 3...♘e4 and 3...♘c6. The first two seem perfectly sound but I have my doubts about options three and four.

I've played 3...g6 myself in one game as I guessed that my opponent would play for a Stonewall set-up with 4 e3 and 5 f4, and I wanted my queen's knight on the more active c6-square rather than d7 (compare Chapter 3). One of the reasons it has not been popular is the old myth that White should be prevented from doubling Black's pawns with 4 ♗xf6 (Miles-Spassov). Yet Black has a good plan starting with 6...f5 and followed by bringing the queen's knight to f6 via d7. The pawn on g6 supports this advance and produces a position which looks quite good for Black.

If there is an objection to 3...g6 then it lies in 4 ♕d2 (Reprintsev-Kachar). Here White prepares to exchange Black's dark-squared bishop with ♗h6, castling long. He can also think about building a broad pawn centre with f2-f3 and e2-e4 and levering open the h-file with h2-h4-h5. Comparing with the 4 ♕d2 lines from Chapter 2 it is clear that playing this move after ...g7-g6 is a clear improvement.

3...h6 has been similarly dismissed because of 4 ♗xf6, yet once again the assessment of this plan as being good for White is premature to say the least. In Bellin-Penrose Black could have played 6...f5 with quite a good game, which casts doubt over the whole plan with ♗d3, ♘ge2 etc. I think that White is much better off adopting a kingside fianchetto, repositioning the knight on c3 (probably to e2) and playing b2-b3 followed by c2-c4. This is quite a heavy positional treatment but I think it is White's best way to play. White's main alternative to 5 e3 is (4 ♗xf6 exf6) 5 e4, the aim being to get a pawn majority on the queenside which is healthier than Black's on the kingside. The problem is that the two bishops become considerably more active after 5 e4 than had the position remained closed. Spassky-Korchnoi was fine for Black, but perhaps White can improve with 7 ♕d2.

I can't say that I like 4 ♗h4 after 3...h6 as Black gets an improved version of just about every Veresov line if these two moves are inserted. Bellon-Spassky was just one example of what Black can do, and he also has moves such as 4...♘bd7 and 4...e6.

3...♘e4 was well met by 4 ♘xe4 dxe4 5 e3 in Maryasin-Manor, and 3...♘c6 4 f3 also looked promising for White in Sammalvuo-

Ronman. These offbeat attempts to take White 'out of the book' appear to be a little misplaced against Veresov practitioners as the opening tends to appeal to individuals who like to improvise.

Game 52
Miles-Spassov
Surakarta-Denpasar 1982

1 d4 ♘f6 2 ♘c3 d5 3 ♗g5 g6 4 ♗xf6

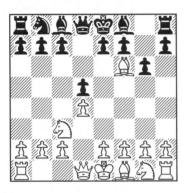

I can't say that I particularly like this capture here. After ...exf6 Black can easily adopt the plan with ...f6-f5, ...c7-c6 and a transfer of his knight to f6 via d7. In fact 3...g6 is quite useful for this.

4...exf6 5 e3

Because it tends to steer the game away from the main lines the Veresov attracts more than its fair share of oddball practitioners. In Chernyshov-Beliavsky, Ohrid 2001 the interesting course was 5 ♕d3!? f5 6 ♕g3 ♗g7 (6...♗d6?! 7 ♕e3+ ♗e7 8 ♕e5 wins a pawn for what is probably inadequate compensation) 7 ♘b5!? ♘a6 8 ♕a3 c5?! (Black could equalise with 8...♕e7 but he wants more) 9 dxc5 0-0 10 e3 ♕e7 11 ♘d6 ♘xc5 12 ♕xc5 ♖d8 13 0-0-0 and White had the better game thanks to the isolated d-pawn. After 5...♗g7 White can play 6 e4 dxe4 7 ♕xe4+ ♕e7 8 ♕xe7+ ♔xe7 9 0-0-0 as in Zoeller-Baeumer, Germany 1992, when he might claim a slight advantage.

There's a strong argument for establishing a qualitatively superior pawn majority with 5 e4 dxe4 6 ♘xe4, even though this hasn't done terribly well in practice. After 6...♗g7 7 ♘f3 0-0 8 ♗e2 f5 9 ♘c5 b6 10 ♘b3 ♗b7 11 0-0 ♘d7 12 c3 ♘f6 13 ♖e1 a6 14 a4 ♖e8 15 a5 ♘d5 16 ♗f1 White had a slight edge in Alburt-Marjanovic, Bucharest 1978.

5...♗g7 6 ♗d3 0-0?

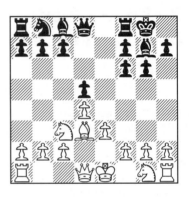

Black should take this opportunity to play 6...f5 before he's prevented from doing so. White's next two moves secure the advantage by ruling out this possibility.

7 ♕f3! c6 8 g4! ♖e8 9 0-0-0 a5

White could meet 9...b5 10 ♘ge2 b4 with 11 ♘a4, for example 11...♕a5 12 b3 ♘d7 13 ♔b1 ♘b6 14 ♘c5, keeping the queenside closed while continuing to prepare the assault on the opposite side of the board. Consequently Black first advances his a-pawn in order to rule out the possibility of White putting his knight on a4.

10 ♘ge2 a4 11 a3!

White can construct a queenside blockade and his next two moves make it difficult for Black to make progress there. After 11 h4 b5 12 h5 b4 13 ♘b1 b3 Black forces open some lines and gets counterplay.

11...b5 12 ♘a2 ♘a6 13 c3 ♘c7 14 h4 ♘e6 15 e4!

Switching play to the centre. Black's queenside pawn advances have noticeably weakened his structure (especially c6) and this central action by White brings these weaknesses to light.

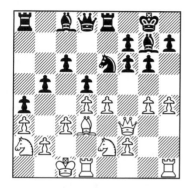

15...♘c7 16 ♘b4 ♕d6 17 exd5 ♘xd5 18 ♘xd5 cxd5 19 h5 ♕c6 20 ♚b1 ♖e4

Offering the exchange like this looks like the only chance. If Black waits any longer he will be crushed on the kingside. 20...♗f8 is answered by 21 hxg6 fxg6 22 g5 fxg5 23 ♖xh7! ♚xh7 24 ♕f7+ followed by mate, whilst 20...♗e6 21 ♘f4 leaves Black wondering what to do next.

21 hxg6

White could also capture the rook immediately with 21 ♗xe4, for example 21...dxe4 22 d5!? ♕c4 (22...exf3 23 dxc6 fxe2 24 ♖d8+ ♗f8 25 c7 and Black is completely tied up) 23 ♕e3 ♗xg4 24 ♖d2 with Black having inadequate compensation.

21...hxg6 22 ♘f4 f5 23 g5 ♗d7?

Black had to play 23...b4, for example 24

axb4 a3 25 ♗xe4 fxe4 26 ♕e2 ♗a6 etc.

24 ♗xe4 fxe4 25 ♕g3 ♗f5 26 ♚a1 ♖c8 27 ♘g2 ♗e6 28 ♘e3

Now there's no more doubt as White's king is securely protected and his knight is well placed to come to g4 and f6.

28...♕d7

After 28...b4 29 cxb4 ♕b6 White wins with 30 ♘g4! ♗xd4 (30...♗xg4 31 ♕xg4) 31 ♖xd4! ♕xd4 32 ♘f6+ followed by mate.

29 ♖h4! ♕e7 30 ♖dh1 ♕c7 31 ♕xc7 ♖xc7 32 ♘g4 ♗f8 33 ♘f6 ♚e7 34 ♖f4 ♖c8 35 ♖h7 ♗xf6 36 ♖xf6 ♖b8 37 ♚b1 ♖c8 38 ♚c1 ♖b8 39 ♚d2 ♖c8 40 ♖xg6 ♗f5 41 ♖xf7+ 1-0

Game 53
Reprintsev-Kachar
Geller Memorial, Moscow 1999

---

1 d4 ♘f6 2 ♘c3 d5 3 ♗g5 g6 4 ♕d2

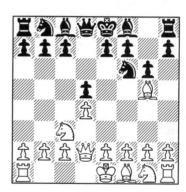

I take the view that this is White's most logical move. I don't like the plan with 4 e3 ♗g7 5 f4?! in this position as Black's queen's knight can come to c6 rather than d7. Walton-Davies, Lancaster Rapidplay 2002 went 5...0-0 6 ♘f3 c5 7 ♗d3 ♘c6 8 0-0? ♘g4! 9 ♕e1 ♘xe3! etc. 4 ♘f3 is also rather questionable in view of 4...♘e4!.

4...♗g7

After 4...h6 the arguments are stronger than ever that White should capture on f6, for example 5 ♗xf6 exf6 6 0-0-0!? (6 e4 dxe4

7 ♘xe4 ♗g7 8 0-0-0 0-0 9 ♗c4 is the 'normal' way to play) 6...f5 (6...♗g7 7 ♕e3+ ♗e6 8 ♘h3 intending 9 ♘f4 looks better for White) 7 ♕e3+ ♗e6 8 ♕e5 ♖g8 9 ♘h3 ♘d7 10 ♕e3 (followed by 11 ♘f4) with chances for an edge. A more aggressive idea for White is 5 ♗f4 ♗g7 6 ♘f3 c6 7 e3 ♘bd7 8 ♗e2 0-0 9 ♘e5 followed by attacking on the kingside with the g- and h-pawns, although Black could also react more actively with 5...c5!?, for instance. As usual there are very few practical examples.

5 ♗h6

Not just an attacking move – Black's king's bishop is the 'good' one, without which he has a certain vulnerability on the dark squares...

5...0-0

With the disappearance of his fianchettoed bishop Black is well advised to put his king on the queenside. For example he might play 5...♗xh6 6 ♕xh6 c5 (6...♕d6 7 ♘f3 ♘c6 8 e3 ♗f5 9 0-0-0 0-0-0 was fine for Black in Muratov-Reprintsev, Moscow 1991) 7 e3 cxd4 (7...♘c6 8 0-0-0 ♕a5 9 dxc5 ♕xc5 10 ♘ge2 ♗e6 11 ♘d4 0-0-0 was defensible for Black in Prins-Petrosian, Leipzig Olympiad 1960) 8 exd4 ♘c6 9 ♗b5 ♗d7 10 ♘f3 ♕b6 11 0-0 0-0-0 12 ♕e3 e6 13 a4! and White had promising attacking chances on the queenside in Sulava-Duda, Metz 2000.

6 0-0-0

The immediate 6 ♗xg7 gives White extra

options: 6...♔xg7 7 e3 (7 0-0-0 c6 8 f3 leads to the Begun-Smirnov example, quoted below) 7...♘bd7 8 f4 b6 9 ♘f3 ♗b7 10 ♗e2 produced an unusual kind of Stonewall set up in Spal-Prandstetter, Ceske Budejovice 1992, as White was the one with the better bishop. Mestrovic-Grosar, Portoroz 1996 featured the wild 6 h4!?, when 6...♘c6 7 h5 (7 ♗xg7 ♔xg7 8 h5 looks quite good) 7...♗xh6 8 ♕xh6 ♘xd4 9 0-0-0 ♘g4 10 ♕d2 ♘xf2 11 ♕xd4 ♘xh1 12 ♕h4 e5! was double-edged.

6...c6 7 f3 b5 8 h4!

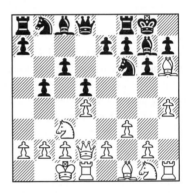

This natural attacking move seems very unpleasant for Black, although it's not the only way to treat the position. 8 ♗xg7 ♔xg7 9 e4 b4 10 e5 bxc3 11 exf6+ exf6 12 ♕xc3 was slightly better for White in Begun-Smirnov, Belorus Ch., Minsk 1966.

8...♘h5!

Ducking rather than punching seems appropriate in this position. The attempt to create something on the queenside appears to fall short, for after 8...b4 9 ♘b1 ♕a5 10 h5 ♗xh6 11 ♕xh6 ♕xa2 White's attack proves to be the stronger: 12 e4 b3 13 c3 dxe4 (13...c5 14 hxg6 fxg6 15 e5 ♗f5 16 ♗d3) 14 hxg6 fxg6 15 ♗c4+ e6 16 fxe4, threatening 17 e5.

9 g4 ♘g3 10 ♖h3 ♘xf1 11 ♖xf1 f5?

Not what you would call 'cold-blooded defence'. Black should aim to keep the kingside closed with 11...f6!, when 12 ♗xg7

♔xg7 13 h5 g5 14 e3 e5 15 ♘ge2 ♗e6 16 ♘g3 ♘d7 is far from clear.

12 ♗xg7 ♔xg7 13 h5!

Going for the throat.

13...fxg4

It is too late for Black to blockade the kingside as after 13...f4 there follows 14 hxg6 hxg6 15 e3 ♕d6 16 ♘ge2, threatening 17 ♖dh1 with a winning attack.

14 ♖h1 ♕d6

If Black keeps the h-file closed with 14...g5 there is 15 ♕xg5+ ♔h8 16 h6 ♖f7 17 ♕e5+ ♔g8 (or 17...♖f6 18 fxg4) 18 ♖h5! followed by 19 ♖g5+.

15 hxg6 ♕xg6 16 ♘h3!

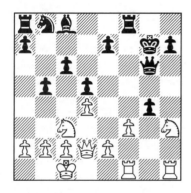

16...gxh3

This doesn't give Black enough for the queen but he might be losing in any case. After 16...b4 17 ♘a4 g3 18 ♖fg1 there's little to stop White charging down the g- and h-files.

17 ♖fg1 ♗e6 18 ♘d1 ♘d7 19 ♘f2

There's no need to take the queen just yet – White can watch his opponent stew.

19...♖f6 20 ♕c3

White could win by capturing his opponent's queen, but he should be careful to avoid 20 ♘xh3? ♗xh3 21 ♖xg6+ ♖xg6 22 ♖xh3? ♖g1+ etc.

20...♕g2 21 ♖xg2+ hxg2 22 ♖g1 ♖g6 23 ♕xc6

The harvest of pawns commences. Meanwhile the guy on g2 is going nowhere.

23...♖g8 24 e4 ♔f7 25 ♕xb5 ♖g5 26 f4 1-0

When the rook moves away, 27 f5 will win a piece.

> ## Game 54
> ## Bellin-Penrose
> *British Ch., Clacton 1974*

1 d4 d5 2 ♘c3 ♘f6 3 ♗g5 h6

Immediately asking White's bishop this question makes a lot of sense, although it has been frowned upon by successive generations of writers for encouraging White to play a move he'd like to make anyway.

4 ♗xf6 exf6

The most solid and popular option. White should meet 4...gxf6 with 5 e3 when Spassky-Uusi, USSR Team Ch 1960 gave White some pressure after 5...e6 6 ♕h5 c5 7 0-0-0 cxd4 8 exd4 ♘c6 9 f4 ♗b4 10 ♘ge2 f5 11 h3 ♗d7 12 g4 ♘e7 13 ♗g2 ♕c7 14 ♖hf1, with Black unable to castle long due to the pressure against f7. Instead 5 ♕d3 e6 6 0-0-0 ♘d7 7 e4 c6 8 exd5 cxd5 9 f4 f5 10 g4 fxg4 11 f5 ♘b6 was unconvincing in Malich-R.Byrne, Leipzig 1960, as was 5 e4 dxe4 6 ♘xe4 f5 7 ♘g3 c5 8 d5 ♕b6 9 ♖b1 e6 in Zakharov-Simagin, Moscow 1961.

5 e3

With this move White intends a simple plan of attack with ♗d3, ♕f3, ♘ge2 and 0-0-0 and then launching a kingside pawn storm with g2-g4 and h2-h4. The problem is that Black can try to prevent the pawn storm element of this strategy with ...f7-f5. For 5 e4 see Spassky-Korchnoi.

5...c6 6 ♗d3

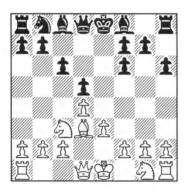

An alternative plan of development might be possible here, namely 6 g3 intending ♗g2, ♘f3, 0-0, ♘ce2, b2-b3 and c2-c4. There's a lot to be said for this slow preparation of c2-c4 – White will be in a position to recapture with a pawn should Black take it and his bishop on g2 will have considerable influence on the centre.

6...♗d6?

Allowing White to execute his plan. Black's best is ...f6-f5, for example 6...g6 7 ♘ge2 f5 8 ♕d2 ♘d7 followed by 9...♘f6, which favoured Black in Balashov-T.Giorgadze, USSR Ch. 1979, or 6...f5 7 h4 h5 8 ♘ce2 ♕b6 9 b3 g6 10 ♘f3 ♘d7 11 0-0

♗h6 as in Bellin-Kharitonov, Lodz 1980. White's problem is that if g2-g4 is his only pawn lever, what does he do if Black manages to stop it?

7 ♕f3 0-0 8 ♘ge2 ♖e8 9 0-0-0

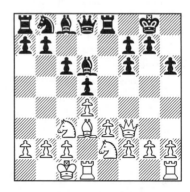

There is a strong argument for the immediate 9 g4 as after 9...b5 he is able to neatly reposition his knights with 10 ♘g3 b4 11 ♘ce2. Rabinovich-Sorkin, Herzliya 1993 continued 11...g6 12 h4 a5 13 0-0-0 a4 14 ♖dg1 ♗f8 15 g5 fxg5 16 hxg5 hxg5 and now White should have played 17 ♖h8+! (in the game 17 ♘h5 allowed Black to defend with 17...♗e7) 17...♔xh8 18 ♕xf7 ♗h3 19 ♖h1 g4 (or 19...♕d7 20 ♕xg6) 20 ♘f4 and Black is helpless.

9...b5 10 g4 ♘d7 11 h4 b4 12 ♘a4 g6?!

Black should set about removing the knight on a4 with 12...♘b6, when Clark-Barbagello, Correspondence 1986 went 13 ♘xb6 (13 ♘c5 looks better to me) 13...axb6 14 ♔b1 ♕e7 (Black should prevent White's next with 14...♗e7) 15 g5! b3 16 cxb3 ♕a7 17 ♘c1, leaving his king completely secure before delivering mate on the other side of the board.

13 ♖dg1 ♗e7 14 g5! fxg5 15 h5! g4

The attempt to secure Black's kingside with 15...♔g7? loses to 16 hxg6 fxg6 17 ♗xg6! ♔xg6 18 ♕h5+ etc.

16 ♖xg4 g5 17 ♖gg1 ♕a5?

Superficially this looks strong, but Black is leaving his kingside up for grabs. Black should probably try 17...♗f8.

18 b3 ♘f6

Black may have been intending to play 18...♘b6 here, only now realising that 19 ♘c5 ♕xa2 20 ♔d2 is very good for White in view of the threat to win Black's queen with 21 ♖a1. The fantastic 19 ♗g6!? fxg6 20 hxg6 is worth considering.

19 ♘g3 ♗g4 20 ♕g2 ♔h8 21 ♗f5 ♗xf5 22 ♘xf5 ♗f8 23 f4 ♘e4 24 fxg5 ♘xg5

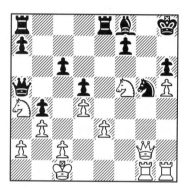

Black's best defence is 24...hxg5. Now White finds a way through.

25 ♖h4 ♖e4 26 ♖f4! ♖ae8 27 ♘xh6! ♗xh6 28 ♖f6 ♕d8

After 28...♖4e6 there follows 29 ♖xh6+ ♖xh6 30 ♕xg5 etc.

29 ♖xh6+ ♔g7 30 ♖xc6 f6 31 ♕f1 ♖xe3

In the event of 31...♖4e6 White has 32 ♖xe6 ♖xe6 33 ♕f5 ♕e8 34 ♘c5.

32 ♖xg5+! fxg5 33 ♖g6+ 1-0

Black finds himself in a mating net after 33...♔h8 34 ♕f7.

Game 55
Spassky-Korchnoi
Candidates Match, Belgrade 1977

---

1 d4 ♘f6 2 ♘c3 d5 3 ♗g5 h6 4 ♗xf6 exf6 5 e4 ♗b4

After the simple 5...dxe4 6 ♘xe4 ♗e7 White should play 7 ♘f3 0-0 8 ♗e2 ♘d7 9 0-0 f5 10 ♘ed2 (10 ♘g3 ♘f6 11 ♗d3 g6 left the knight on g3 looking strange in Kleopas-

Yanofsky, Havana 1966) with what looks like a slight edge due to the queenside pawn majority (Black's kingside majority cannot produce a passed pawn). These positions closely resemble those arising from the Exchange Ruy Lopez.

6 exd5 ♕xd5

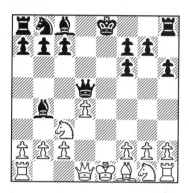

It is sensible to regain the pawn immediately. In Wade-Perez, Havana 1965 Black tried to play in gambit style with 6...0-0 7 ♘f3 ♖e8+ 8 ♗e2 ♕e7 but after 9 ♕d2 ♘d7 10 0-0 ♘b6 11 ♖fe1 ♗d7 12 a3 ♗xc3 13 bxc3 ♘xd5 14 c4 White had a clear edge.

7 ♘f3

Perhaps White should play 7 ♕d2, which led to the better game after 7...♕a5 8 ♗c4 ♗xc3 9 bxc3 0-0 10 ♘e2 in Vogler-Wegener, Wiesbaden 1994.

7...0-0 8 ♗e2 ♕a5 9 ♕d2 ♘d7! 10 a3 ♘b6 11 ♖b1!?

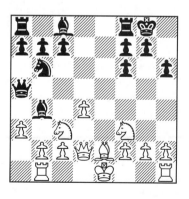

After 11 0-0 &xc3 12 ♕xc3 ♕xc3 13 bxc3 ♘d5 14 c4 ♘c3 Black gets slightly the better endgame, so Spassky tries to improve his chances by leaving his king in the middle.

11...&xc3 12 ♕xc3 ♕xc3+ 13 bxc3 ♘d5 14 ♔d2 ♘f4 15 &f1 b6 16 g3 ♘h3

Korchnoi prefers to get bishop for knight rather than damage White's pawn structure. Stean claimed that Black was also slightly better after 16...&b7 17 gxf4 &xf3 18 ♖g1 g5 but this seems to be patently untrue after 19 ♖g3 g4 (or 19...&h5 20 h4) 20 h3 etc.

17 &xh3 &xh3 18 ♘e1 ♖fd8 19 ♘d3 ♖ac8 20 ♖he1 ♔f8 21 ♖b5 c6 22 ♖b4 c5?!

In view of White's reply Black should prepare this with 22...♖c7!.

23 ♖a4! cxd4

Black's pawns become targets after either 23...♖c7 24 dxc5 bxc5 25 c4, intending ♖a5, or alternatively 23...a5 24 dxc5 bxc5 25 ♔c1. Therefore Korchnoi is forced to seek simplification.

24 ♖xd4!

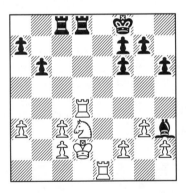

White has to be careful about the safety of his rook, for example 24 cxd4 is answered by 24...a5! (threatening 25...&d7), and after 25 ♘b2 there follows 25...♖a8 (threatening 26...b5) 26 ♖c4 &e6 winning the pawn on d4.

24...♖d7 25 ♖xd7 &xd7 26 ♖e4 g5 27 c4 &e6 28 ♔c3² ♔e7 29 ♖d4 b5?!

Around here Black is losing the plot. He should play 29...a5! either now or on the next move.

30 ♘b2 bxc4 31 ♘xc4 ♖c5 32 ♔b4 ♖f5 33 f4 gxf4 34 ♖xf4

The game has seen quite a turnaround, with White now standing clearly better. Black's kingside majority is useless whereas White has a passed c-pawn.

34...♖h5 35 ♖f2 ♖d5 36 ♘a5 ♖d6 37 a4?!

The wrong pawn move as it is vulnerable on this square. White should push his c-pawn.

37...♖b6+ 38 ♔c5 &d7 39 ♖f4 ♖e6 40 c3 f5! 41 ♘b3 ♖e5+?

Missing an immediate draw with 41...♖e2!, after which 42 ♖h4 can be met by 42...♖e4! etc.

42 ♔b4 ♖e2 43 ♘c5! &e6!?

After 43...♖b2+ 44 ♔c4 ♖xh2 White can play 45 ♘xd7 ♔xd7 46 ♖xf5 with some practical chances in the rook endgame.

44 ♖h4 ♖b2+ 45 ♔a5 ♖c2 46 ♔b4?!

White can keep his winning chances alive with 46 ♔a6! ♖xc3 47 ♘b7, winning the a7-pawn. Now it's a dead draw.

46...♖b2+ 47 ♔a5 ♖c2 48 ♔b4

After the sequence 48 ♔a6 ♖xc3 49 ♘b7 ♖c4! 50 ♖xc4 &xc4+ 51 ♔xa7 ♔e6 52 a5 ♔e5 53 a6 f4 54 gxf4+ ♔xf4 55 ♘d6 &xa6 56 ♔xa6 ♔g4 Black will eliminate White's last pawn.

48...♖b2+ ½-½

Game 56
Bellon Lopez-Spassky
Linares 1981

1 ♘c3 d5 2 d4 ♘f6 3 ♗g5 h6 4 ♗h4 ♗f5

Black must decide how to benefit from the insertion of the moves 3...h6 and 4 ♗h4, and I don't believe that this is the best way. After 4...♘bd7 5 f3 there is at least one advantage for White in having the bishop on h4 in that the variation 5...c6 (5...c5 might be Black's best here) 6 e4 dxe4 7 fxe4 e5 8 dxe5 ♕a5?? would now just drop a piece. One of Black's best moves in this position might be 4...g6 because White no longer has the opportunity to exchange Black's dark-squared bishop with ♕d2 and ♗h6. Another good idea is 4...e6 followed by 5...c5 because 5 e4 is well met by 5...♗b4, transposing into a line of the MacCutcheon French which is supposed to be quite good for Black.

5 f3?!

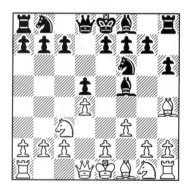

Spassky had probably guessed that the aggressive Bellon would play this way, and designed his choice of 4...♗f5 accordingly. The right way to play the position is with 5 e3 as after 5...e6 6 ♗d3 the fact that Black has moved his h-pawn means that he can no longer retreat his bishop to g6. Myagmarsuren-Koskinen, Lugano Olympiad 1968 continued 6...♗xd3 7 ♕xd3 c6 8 ♘f3 ♘bd7

and now 9 0-0, intending either e3-e4 or ♘f3-e5, is best. In the game White attempted to exploit Black's ...h7-h6 with 9 h3?! ♗d6 10 g4 but the problem is that he hasn't castled so it represents nothing more than a loss of time. The game continued 10...♕c7 11 ♗xf6 ♘xf6 12 e4 dxe4 13 ♘xe4 ♘xe4 14 ♕xe4 ♕a5+ 15 c3 ♕d5 and Black stood well. Here 7 cxd3 might be stronger, especially in conjunction with 8 f4. Take a look at the analogous positions from Chapter 6.

5...c6 6 ♕d2

If White wants to play e2-e4 he has to surrender the bishop pair. Kharitonov gives the line 6 ♗xf6 exf6 7 e4 dxe4 8 fxe4 ♗h7 9 a3 ♗d6 10 ♘f3 0-0 11 ♗d3 ♘d7 with an 'unclear' assessment. Chances seem fairly balanced to me.

6...♘bd7 7 ♘h3?

This move is probably a mistake, but Black's position is unappealing in any case. Kharitonov gave 7 e3 and 7 g4 ♗h7 8 e3 e5 9 0-0-0, although neither of these looks very attractive to me after 7...e5 and 9...♗b4 respectively.

7...♗xh3 8 gxh3 e5 9 dxe5?

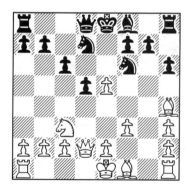

In playing this and his next move White probably missed Black's 10th. White should play 9 e3 but then 9...♕c7 followed by ...0-0-0 looks good for Black.

9...♘xe5 10 ♕e3?

10 0-0-0 is certainly a better try. Now comes the thunderbolt...

10...♘fg4! 11 hxg4

White loses on the spot after 11 ♗xd8 ♘xe3, and 11 ♕xe5+ ♘xe5 12 ♗xd8 ♖xd8 is also very bad.

11...♕xh4+ 12 ♕f2 ♕f6! 13 a3

An even worse continuation is 13 0-0-0? ♘xg4!. White could have tried to stay on the board with 13 ♘d1 ♘c4 14 ♖b1 d4, as un-appealing as this is.

13...♘c4 14 ♘d1

Or 14 0-0-0 ♗xa3 etc.

14...♘xb2 15 ♕e3+ ♗e7 16 ♘xb2 ♕xb2 17 ♖d1 ♕xa3 18 ♕xa3 ♗xa3 19 e4 dxe4 20 fxe4 b5 21 ♗g2 ♖d8 22 ♔e2

After 22 e5 there follows 22...♖xd1+ 23 ♔xd1 ♔d7 24 ♖f1 ♖f8 when White's fun is at an end.

22...♔e7 23 e5 ♖xd1 24 ♖xd1 ♖c8 25 h4

25 ♖a1 ♗c5 26 ♖a6 ♗b6 and Black protects everything.

25...a5 26 ♖d3 b4 27 ♖d4 a4 28 ♔d3 c5 29 ♖f4 ♗b2 30 ♗d5 ♖d8 31 c4

White also has to resign after either 31 ♔e4 ♖xd5 32 ♔xd5 a3 or 31 ♖xf7+ ♔e8 32 ♔e4 ♖xd5 etc.

31...bxc3 0-1

Game 57

Maryasin-Manor

Israeli Team Ch. 2002

---

1 d4 ♘f6 2 ♘c3 d5 3 ♗g5 ♘e4

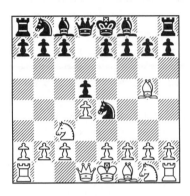

A kind of Bird's Defence to the Veresov, the analogous Spanish Opening line going 1 e4 e5 2 ♘f3 ♘c6 3 ♗b5 ♘d4. Actually it looks rather worse than the Bird because White can play e2-e3 and a later c2-c4 without weakening his king position.

4 ♘xe4 dxe4

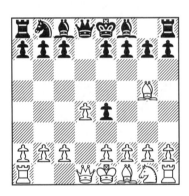

5 e3

White's most aggressive move is 5 f3, which needs to be handled with the utmost precision. The game Roesch-Henkel, Nuremberg 1990 continued 5...♗f5 (Black could also play 5...♕d5 6 ♗f4 ♘c6 7 e3 e5 8 dxe5 ♕c5 with a good game) 6 fxe4 ♗xe4 7 ♘f3 ♘d7?! (7...♘c6! 8 c3 ♕d5 followed by 9...0-0-0 is better) 8 e3 c6 9 ♗f4 (not 9 ♗d3?? ♗xf3 10 ♕xf3 ♕a5+ winning the bishop on g5) 9...e6 10 ♗d3 ♘f6 11 0-0 ♗d6 12 ♗g5 ♗xd3 13 ♕xd3 ♗e7 14 ♘e5 0-0 15 ♖f3 ♕d5 16 ♖af1 with massive pressure.

Another possibility is 5 ♕d2, for example 5...c5!? 6 dxc5 ♕xd2+ 7 ♗xd2 e5 8 b4 ♘c6 9 e3 ♗e6 10 a3 g6 11 ♘e2 and Black was struggling to find adequate compensation in Schneider-Langeweg, Porz Open 1991. 5...♘c6 might be better, e.g. 6 d5 h6 7 ♗f4 e5 with a good game for Black, or 7 ♗h4 ♘e5.

5...c5

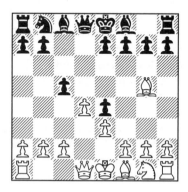

Black has also played 5...c6 but this seems rather too quiet to offset Black's structural problems. C.Bauer-L.Adams, Mainz 1997 continued 6 ♕d2 ♘d7 7 ♘e2 h6 8 ♗h4 ♕b6 9 0-0-0 (9 c4 also looks quite good) 9...e6 10 a3 a5, and now (instead of 11 g4) 11 ♘c3 f5 12 f3 looks very good for White.

6 ♕d2

The more I look at this position the less appealing it seems for Black. In ECO D Bagirov gave 6 dxc5 ♕a5+ 7 ♕d2 as being an edge for White, although this doesn't seem at all true after 7...♕xc5 8 ♗h4 ♘c6, with healthy development and the danger for White that his dark-squared bishop will be shut out of the game (by ...f7-f6 and ...e7-e5).

6...♘c6

Black has also played 6...♕d5, when Fomina-Limberg, Tallinn 2000 continued 7 ♗f4 cxd4 8 c4! ♕d7 9 exd4 e6 10 a3 ♗d6 11 ♖d1 0-0 12 ♘e2 ♕c7 13 ♗xd6 ♕xd6 14 ♘c3 f5 15 ♗e2 ♘c6 16 ♘b5 ♕e7 17 c5 with a clear advantage to White due to the pawn structure and the fact that a knight can land

on d6 at any time. 17 d5 is also promising here.

6...g6 is not sufficiently energetic. In Bukal-Jelen, Zagreb 1997 White gained a decisive advantage after 7 f3 (7 dxc5 also looks good) 7...♗g7 8 c3 exf3 9 ♘xf3 0-0 10 ♗c4 ♘c6 11 0-0 b6 12 ♕e1 h6 13 ♕h4! etc.

7 d5

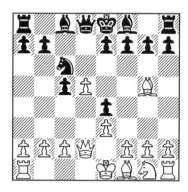

7 c3, intending 8 f3, is playable but lacks the energy of the text.

7...♘e5 8 0-0-0 g6 9 f4! exf3

More or less forced, but this leads to the acceleration of White's development.

10 ♘xf3 ♘xf3 11 gxf3 ♗g7 12 d6!

A hammer blow, cutting right across Black's plans to peacefully castle.

12...f6

After 12...♕xd6 there follows 13 ♗b5+! ♔f8 (13...♗d7 14 ♗xd7+ ♔xd7 15 ♕a5 wins the queen) 14 ♕a5 etc.

13 ♗b5+ ♔f7 14 ♗f4

14 d7 is even more deadly because 14...fxg5 15 ♕d5+ e6 16 dxc8♕ ♕xc8 17 ♕e4 leaves Black facing the unpleasant threat of 18 ♗d7.

14...♗e6 15 ♕c3 f5

In the event of 15...♕b6 there follows 16 ♗c4 ♗xc4 17 ♕xc4+ e6 18 d7, threatening 19 ♖d6.

16 ♗e5

It might have been better to play 16 ♕xc5, picking up another pawn.

16...♗xe5 17 ♕xe5 ♕b6?

Cracking under the pressure. Black had to play 17...a6, when 18 ♗e2 exd6 19 ♖xd6 ♕e7 20 ♖hd1 is very unpleasant but far from over.

18 ♗d7 1-0

Game 58
Sammalvuo-Ronnman
Vantaa 1991

---

1 d4 ♘f6 2 ♘c3 d5 3 ♗g5 ♘c6

Black hopes to discourage the advance of White's e-pawn by putting pressure on the d4-pawn but, in this game at least, it has the opposite effect. However, Black's play can be improved...

4 f3

The most ambitious move, preparing e2-e4. The quiet 4 e3 seems quite good to me, for example after 4...e6 I like 5 a3!? followed by 6 f4, 7 ♗d3 and 8 ♘f3 because Black cannot advance his c-pawn in order to counter-attack the d4-pawn. 5 ♘f3 ♗e7 6 ♗d3 h6 7 ♗h4 b6 8 0-0 ♗b7 9 ♗b5 0-0 was rather innocuous in Tartakower-Nimzowitsch, Copenhagen 1923.

4...♗f5 5 ♗xf6 gxf6?

It is much better to recapture with the e-pawn as after 5...exf6 6 e4 dxe4 7 fxe4 Black can play 7...♕e7, hitting the e4-pawn and preparing ...0-0-0. After 8 ♗b5, 8...♗xe4 9 ♘xe4 ♕xe4+ 10 ♕e2 ♕xe2+ 11 ♘xe2 0-0-0 can follow with an advantage for Black.

6 e4 dxe4 7 fxe4 ♗g6 8 ♘f3

There's a strong argument for the immediate 8 ♗b5.

8...♗h5

Probably overlooking White's brilliant 10th move. Black should probably play 8...a6 followed by ...♕d6 and ...0-0-0, or perhaps ...♗h5. With the b5-square protected Black's chances are far superior.

9 d5 ♘e5??

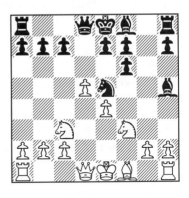

9...♘b8 is mandatory, when Black has a playable (if somewhat inferior) game.

10 ♘xe5!

This spectacular queen sacrifice wins by force. It is surprising that Black missed it as the theme is well known.

10...♗xd1 11 ♗b5+ c6 12 dxc6

Threatening both 13 cxb7+ and 13 c7+.

12...bxc6 13 ♗xc6+ ♕d7 14 ♗xd7+ ♔d8 15 ♘xf7+ 1-0

Summary

White's most dangerous response to 3...g6 is 4 ♕d2, aiming for a vigorous attack against Black's king. 4 ♗xf6 is playable against both this and 3...h6, but here White should adopt a slow plan based on a kingside fianchetto and playing for c2-c4.

Both 3...♘e4 and 3...♘c6 look dubious and White can apply pressure in rather simple fashion. I wouldn't recommend either of them.

1 d4 ♘f6 2 ♘c3 d5 3 ♗g5 h6 *(D)*

   3...g6 *(D)*

      4 ♗xf6 - *Game 52*; 4 ♕d2 - *Game 53*

   3...♘e4 - *Game 57*

   3...♘c6 - *Game 58*

4 ♗xf6

   4 ♗h4 - *Game 56*

4...exf6 *(D)*

   5 e3 - *Game 54*; 5 e4 - *Game 55*

3...h6

3...g6

4...exf6

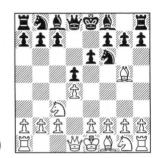

CHAPTER EIGHT

3...e6 (Including Transpositions to the French)

1 d4 ♘f6 2 ♘c3 d5 3 ♗g5 e6

3...e6 is one of Black's most natural moves, the drawback being that Black should know something about the French Defence before playing it. The point is that 4 e4 lands Black straight into a Classical French (usually reached via 1 e4 e6 2 d4 d5 3 ♘c3 ♘f6 4 ♗g5) and is White's usual option.

Aware of the fact that Veresov players are likely to want to stay off the beaten track I suggest that White therefore avoids transposing to the French for just one more move in order to cut out options such as the Mac-Cutcheon Variation (4 e4 ♗b4!?) and some variations of the Burn (4 e4 dxe4 5 ♘xe4 ♘bd7). He can do this by playing 4 ♘f3.

After 4 ♘f3 ♗e7 White can enforce the e2-e4 advance by first capturing on f6, 5 ♗xf6 ♗xf6 6 e4 transposing to the French but possibly not the version that Black is hoping for. We have in fact reached the old Anderssen Attack (normally it comes via 1 e4 e6 2 d4 d5 3 ♘c3 ♘f6 4 ♗g5 ♗e7 5 ♗xf6!? ♗xf6 6 ♘f3), which has been virtually ignored by modern masters but seems to me to be very dangerous (see Tartakower-Lilienthal and Norman-Hanlon). Black can transpose to one form of the Burn Variation by playing 6...dxe4 and here I suggest the trendy 8 ♗c4 (see Shirov-Akopian). Black can also meet 5

♗xf6 with 5...gxf6!? in order to reach another form of Burn but my antidotes are contained within Almasi-Andersson and Shirov-Topalov.

There are a couple of other possibilities after 4 ♘f3, namely 4...c5 and 4...♗b4. These are covered within Lobron-Murei and Hector-Berg respectively.

Game 59
Tartakower-Lilienthal
Paris (match) 1933

---

1 d4 d5 2 ♘c3 ♘f6 3 ♗g5 e6 4 ♘f3 ♗e7 5 ♗xf6 ♗xf6 6 e4

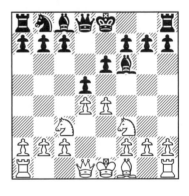

The game has transposed to a supposedly harmless variation of the French Defence, the so-called Anderssen Attack. Yet a closer look at this position has convinced me that Black's task is by no means easy. He can also fall victim to a sharp and devastating attack on his king... Lev Psakhis states in *The Complete French* (Batsford, 1992): 'Black shouldn't be in a hurry to castle' and Alexander Alekhine played this line extensively in simultaneous displays, no doubt attracted by White's attacking chances...

6...b6

A cautious move, delaying castling while continuing development. Here are some examples of the alternatives:

a) 6...c5 is the theoretically approved move but White might gain an edge with 7 exd5 exd5 8 dxc5 (Black must also be careful after 8 ♗b5+ ♘c6 9 0-0 0-0 10 dxc5 ♗xc3 11 bxc3 ♗g4 12 ♖e1 etc.) 8...0-0 9 ♕d2 ♖e8+ (9...♕e7+ 10 ♕e3 ♗xc3+ 11 bxc3 ♕xe3+ 12 fxe3 ♗e6 13 ♘d4 gave White a slight pull in Ljubojevic-Messing, Zagreb 1977) 10 ♗e2 ♗xc3 11 ♕xc3 ♕e7 12 ♕e3 ♕xe3 13 fxe3 ♘d7 14 0-0-0 and White had an edge in Negulescu-Schneider, Washington 1998.

b) 6...♘c6 puts pressure on d4 and effectively forces White to close the centre with 7 e5 but, meanwhile, Black has obstructed the c-pawn. The game might continue 7...♗e7 8 a3 (after the immediate 8 ♗d3 Black can free his position with 8...♘b4 followed by ...c7-c5) 8...♗d7 (8...f5 9 h4 0-0 10 ♘e2 ♕e8 11 ♘f4 ♘d8 12 c4 c6 13 ♖c1 favoured White, with pressure and more space, in Speelman-Knox, Morecambe 1975) 9 ♗d3 a5 10 h4 h6 (after 10...0-0 Black falls victim to 11 ♗xh7+ ♔xh7 12 ♘g5+ etc.) 11 ♕e2 ♘a7 12 ♖h3 c5 13 dxc5 ♗xc5 14 ♖g3 ♕b6 15 ♘d1 g6 16 c3 0-0-0 17 b4 and White had a promising position in Alekhine-Williams, Bridgeport 1932.

c) 6...a6 7 ♗d3 0-0 8 e5 ♗e7 9 h4 h6 10 ♘e2 c5 11 c3 ♘c6 12 a3 was pleasant for White in Alekhine-Macias, Alicante 1935.

d) 6...g6 7 h4 h5 8 ♗d3 c6 was played in Alekhine-Fuentes, Madrid 1935, and now 9 e5 ♗g7 10 ♘e2 looks very comfortable.

e) 6...c6 7 ♗d3 ♘d7 8 ♕e2 0-0 9 0-0-0 ♗e7 10 e5 ♖e8 11 h4 ♘f8 12 ♘g5 f6 13 f4 f5 14 g4 ♘g6 15 ♖df1 with a powerful attack for White in Alekhine-Linares, Panama 1939.

7 ♗d3

If White first closes the centre with 7 e5 ♗e7 8 ♗d3 Black can counter-attack with 8...c5! etc.

7...♗b7 8 ♕e2 dxe4

Tartakower suggested that 8...0-0 might be an improvement in order to meet 9 e5 ♗e7 10 h4 with 10...h6. Nevertheless this looks quite promising for White after 11 ♘d1 followed by c2-c3 and ♘e3.

9 ♗xe4 c6 10 0-0-0 ♕c7

Preparing to complete development with 11...♘d7 and 12...0-0-0. White decides to strike first...

11 ♘e5 ♗xe5

After 11...♘d7 White reinforces the knight with 12 f4.

12 dxe5 ♕xe5 13 ♕d3! 0-0

In reply to 13...♕c7 White has 14 ♘b5, e.g. 14...♕f4+ 15 ♔b1 0-0 16 g3 ♕e5 17 f4 ♕f6 18 ♘c7 or 14...cxb5 15 ♗xb7 ♕xb7 16 ♕d8 mate.

14 ♗xh7+

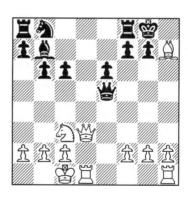

14...♔h8 15 ♗e4 f5

After 15...g6 White continues the attack with 16 h4.

16 ♗f3 ♘a6 17 ♕c4 ♕f6 18 ♖d6 ♖fe8 19 ♖e1 b5 20 ♕f4 e5

After 20...b4 White plays 21 ♘b5! with

lots of horrible threats.

21 ℟xf6 exf4 22 ℟xe8+ ℟xe8 23 ℟xf5 1-0

After 23...b4 24 ♘e2 Black will lose more of his pawns.

1 d4 d5 2 ♘c3 ♘f6 3 ♗g5 e6 4 ♘f3 ♗e7 5 ♗xf6 ♗xf6 6 e4 0-0 7 ♗d3

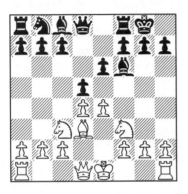

Now that Black has castled White can push with 7 e5, when 7...♗e7 8 ♗d3 c5 will transpose back to the game. If he wants to maintain the tension a better way of doing so might be 7 ♕d2, when B.Ivanovic-Franke, Berlin 1988 continued 7...b6 8 0-0-0 a5?! 9 h4 ♗a6 10 ♗xa6 ♘xa6 11 ♔b1 c6 12 ♘g5 b5 (White meets 12...h6 with 13 f4 as the opening of the h-file would be fatal) 13 e5 ♗e7 14 f4 b4 15 ♘a4 c5 16 dxc5 ♘xc5 17 ♘xc5 ♗xc5 18 ♕d3 g6 19 h5 1-0. An instructive demolition job. Instead 7...dxe4 8 ♘xe4 transposes to a line of the Burn Variation in which White has committed his queen to d2 – see Shirov-Akopian for details.

7...c5

After 7...℟e8 8 e5 ♗e7 9 h4 c5 10 ♗xh7+ ♔xh7 11 ♘g5+ ♔g8 12 ♕h5 White obtained a strong attack in the game Alekhine-Asgeirsson, Reykjavik 1931.

8 e5 ♗e7 9 h4 f6

9...cxd4 10 ♗xh7+ is dangerous for Black, for example 10...♔xh7 11 ♘g5+ ♔h6 12 ♕d3 g6 13 h5 ♗xg5 14 hxg6+ ♔h4 15 ♕g3 fxg6 16 ℟xh4+ ♔g7 17 0-0-0! (after Euwe's old recommendation of 17 ℟g4 Black can defend with 17...♔f7) 17...dxc3 18 ℟dh1 cxb2+ 19 ♔b1 ♕xh4 20 ♕xh4 ♔f7 21 ♕f6+ ♔e8 22 ♕xg6+ etc.

A much tougher defence is offered by 9...h6, but again Black comes under fire: 10 dxc5 (10 g4 looks inadequate after 10...cxd4 11 ♘e2 f6) 10...♗xc5 (10...♘d7 11 ♕e2 ♘xc5 12 0-0-0 ♗d7 13 g4 led to sporting play in Napierala-Liedtke, Kassel 1998) 11 g4!? ♕b6 12 ♕d2 ♗xf2+?? (12...♘c6 is somewhat better for White after 13 ♘a4 ♕b4 14 ♘xc5, so the critical line appears to be 12...♗d7 13 0-0-0 ♗xf2 14 ♔b1 with attacking chances for the pawn) 13 ♕xf2 ♕xb2 14 ♔d2 with an extra piece for White in Charousek-Maroczy, Budapest 1895.

10 ♘g5!

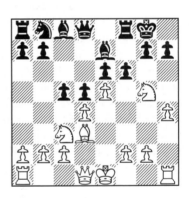

In Pillsbury-Maroczy, London 1899 White played relatively quietly with 10 dxc5, after which 10...♘c6 11 exf6 gxf6 12 ♕d2 ℟f7 13 0-0-0 ♗xc5 14 g4 produced a double-edged game. However, the text is much stronger if followed up correctly.

10...fxg5 11 ♕h5 h6 12 ♕g6 ℟f5 13 g4 ♗d7 14 hxg5?

A far more effective continuation is 14 ♘xd5!, which seems to be winning for White after 14...♗e8 (14...exd5 15 ♗xf5) 15 ♕xe6+

♜f7 16 ♛g6 etc.

14...♗xg5?

Returning the favour, after which White is on top again. Black can weather the storm with 14...♜xg5, for example 15 ♛h7+ ♚f7 16 ♜xh6 ♛g8 and Black's king manages to slip away.

15 gxf5 ♗e8 16 ♛xe6+ ♗f7 17 ♛d6 ♛xd6 18 exd6 cxd4 19 ♘e2 ♘c6 20 f4 ♗f6 21 a3 ♜d8 22 ♚f2 ♜xd6 23 ♜ag1 ♚f8 24 ♘g3 ♘a5 25 b3 ♘c6 26 ♜e1 a6 27 ♘h5 ♗xh5 28 ♜xh5 ♚f7 29 ♜h2 ♘d8 30 ♗e2 ♚f8 31 ♗h5 ♘f7 32 ♚f3 ♜d8 33 ♗xf7 ♚xf7 34 ♜e6 ♜c8 35 ♜d6 ♜c3+ 36 ♚g4 d3 37 cxd3 ♜xb3 38 ♜xd5 ♜xa3 39 ♜c2 ♜b3 40 ♜c8 ♜b2 41 ♜c7+ ♗e7 42 ♜dd7 ♜e2 43 ♚f3 1-0

Game 61
Shirov-Akopian
European Club Ch., Halkidiki 2002

---

1 d4 d5 2 ♘c3 ♘f6 3 ♗g5 e6 4 ♘f3 ♗e7 5 ♗xf6 ♗xf6 6 e4 dxe4 7 ♘xe4 0-0 8 ♗c4

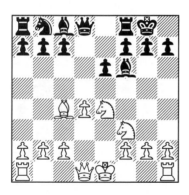

Envisaging a piece set-up in which White's queen comes to e2. An alternative approach is 8 ♛d2 (White's queen would have to be on this square had he answered 6...0-0 with 7 ♛d2) 8...b6 9 0-0-0 ♗b7 10 ♗d3 ♘d7 11 h4 ♗e7 and now an aggressive try for White is 12 ♘fg5!? h6 13 ♜h3!?, as played in a few games by England's aggressive Grandmaster

Mark Hebden.

8...♘c6!?

Black varies from the usual piece formation of ...♘d7, ...b7-b6 and ...♗b7. This is in fact quite difficult for Black after 8...♘d7 9 ♛e2 ♗e7 10 0-0-0!?, when Topalov-Kramnik, Monte Carlo 1997 went 10...c6 11 h4 b5 12 ♗d3 ♛c7 13 ♚b1 ♘f6 (13...c5!? 14 dxc5 ♘xc5 is interesting, giving up a pawn in an attempt to gain counterplay) 14 ♘xf6+ ♗xf6 15 ♛e4 g6 16 h5 ♗b7 17 hxg6 hxg6 18 ♘e5 ♜fd8 19 ♛g4 (the immediate 19 ♘xg6 is met by 19...♜xd4, but now this is a genuine threat) 19...♗xe5 20 dxe5 ♛xe5 21 ♗xg6! with a very dangerous attack.

9 c3 e5 10 d5

Gaining space in the centre. 10 dxe5 is at best harmless.

10...♘e7

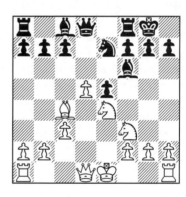

This is looking like Black's main line, despite the doubling of his kingside pawns. Two alternatives have been tried:

a) 10...♘b8 should be met with 11 ♛e2 because 11 0-0 ♗g4 12 h3 ♗xf3 13 ♛xf3 ♗e7 14 ♗b5 a6 15 ♗a4 ♘d7 16 ♜ad1 ♗d6 17 b4 ♘f6 18 ♘xf6+ ♛xf6 19 ♛xf6 gxf6 20 ♗c2 favoured White but was nevertheless rather drawish in Ivanchuk-Ehlvest, Reggio Emilia 1989. Therefore the only way White can really trouble his opponent is by castling long. Leko-Khalifman, Budapest (match) 2000 continued (11 ♛e2) 11...♗f5 12 0-0-0 ♘d7 13 ♘g3 ♗g6 14 ♗d3! (preventing

14...e4, this is a big improvement on Bolo-gan-M.Gurevich, Belfort 1999 which saw Black obtain excellent counterplay after 14 h4 e4! 15 ♘xe4 ♖e8 16 ♘xf6+ ♕xf6 17 ♕d2 ♘b6 etc.) 14...♗xd3 15 ♕xd3 ♘c5 16 ♕e3 b6 17 h4!? (17 ♘e4 was also better for White but Leko decides to play it much more sharply) 17...♖e8 (this was Black's last chance to play 17...e4!?, when 18 ♘xe4 ♖e8 would have given Black some compensation for his pawn; now he winds up very passively placed) 18 ♘e4 ♘xe4 19 ♕xe4 g6 20 g4 ♗g7 21 h5 and Black had serious problems, stemming from the fact that his bishop has been made 'bad' by the inhibiting effect of the e4-pawn.

White has a promising alternative in 12 ♗d3 here, when 12...♗xe4 13 ♗xe4 ♘d7 14 0-0-0 ♗e7 15 g4 ♗d6 16 ♔b1 ♖b8 17 h4 set in motion a powerful kingside attack in Short-M.Gurevich, Shenyang 2000.

b) 10...♘a5!? is dangerous for Black, Baklan-Goloshchapov, Ordzhonikidze Zonal 2000 continuing 11 ♗d3 b6 12 h4!? (12 ♕c2 g6 13 ♘xf6+ ♕xf6 14 0-0 ♗g4 15 ♘d2 ♘b7 was fairly even in Levenfish-Bondarevsky, Leningrad 1939) 12...g6 (12...♘b7 is better) 13 h5 ♗g4 14 ♕d2 ♗g7 15 hxg6 hxg6 16 ♘fg5 with dangerous attacking chances.

11 ♘xf6+ gxf6 12 ♘h4

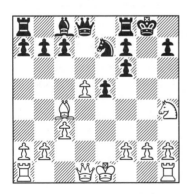

White has a major alternative in 12 ♕d2, which worked out well after 12...♕d6 13 0-0-0 ♗g4?! 14 ♕e3 ♔h8 15 h3 ♗d7 16 g4

in Tischbierek-Izoria, Ohrid 2001. However, after 12...♔h8 13 0-0-0 ♗g4 14 ♗e2 ♕d6 15 ♘h4 ♖g8 16 g3 ♖ad8 Black stood well in Anand-Shirov, Sydney (Olympic Exhibition) 2000.

12...♘g6 13 ♕h5

In Bezgodov-Akopian, Ohrid 2001, White tried to improve with 13 g3!? b5 (13...♘xh4 14 gxh4 ♔h8 15 ♖g1 ♖g8 16 ♖g3 is slightly better for White according to Bologan) 14 ♗b3 a5 15 ♕d2 f5 16 0-0-0 ♖a6 17 ♘g2 a4 18 ♗c2 a3 19 b4 ♖d6 and now 20 f4 would have been slightly better for White according to Bologan. In the game White played 20 ♘e3, when Bologan suggests 20...f4 21 ♘f5 ♗xf5 22 ♗xf5 c6 with a good game for Black.

13...♕d7

An interesting alternative is 13...♔h8!?, when 14 0-0-0 (Finkel has suggested 14 ♗d3!?) 14...f5 15 ♘f3 ♘f4 16 ♕h6 ♕d6 17 ♕xd6 cxd6 18 g3 led to an edge for White in the endgame in Bologan-Kacheishvili, Ohrid 2001. Here 15 ♘xf5?! is better for Black after 15...♘f4 16 ♕f3 ♗xf5 17 g3 ♕d7 18 gxf4 ♗g4 19 ♕e4 ♗xd1 20 ♖xd1 exf4, and 15 g3 is ineffective after 15...♘xh4 16 gxh4 ♕f6 17 ♖hg1 ♗d7.

14 h3 ♕a4

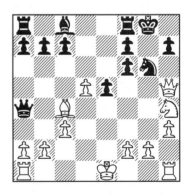

The game Short-M.Gurevich, England (British League) 2000 went 14...♘xh4 15 ♕xh4 ♕f5 16 0-0-0 ♗d7 17 f4 ♕xf4+ 18 ♕xf4 exf4 19 ♖hf1 with an edge for White, although in his notes to the game Gurevich indicated that his 14th move was dubious. What does he have in mind as an improvement? Perhaps 14...b5, when 15 ♗d3 can be met by 15...e4! 16 ♗xe4? ♖e8, winning.

15 b3 ♕a5 16 0-0

Perhaps White should play simply 16 ♖c1 to protect the c3-pawn.

16...♕xc3 17 d6 ♔g7?

Preferable is 17...♘f4, when 18 ♕h6 ♕d2 19 ♕xf6 ♕xd6 is excellent for Black.

18 dxc7 ♕d4 19 g3 ♕d7 20 ♖ac1 ♕xh3

After 20...♕xc7 there follows 21 ♗e6 ♕d8 22 ♘f5+ ♔h8 23 ♖fd1 and Black must part with the queen.

21 ♗d3 ♕e6 22 ♗e4 ♕b6 23 ♖fd1 1-0

Game 62
Almasi-Andersson
Ubeda 1997

1 d4 d5 2 ♘c3 ♘f6 3 ♗g5 e6 4 ♘f3 ♗e7 5 ♗xf6 gxf6 6 e4

White has to play this before Black plays 6...f5.

6...dxe4 7 ♘xe4 b6

The game has transposed into the Burn Variation of the French with 5...gxf6. The fianchetto of Black's queen's bishop is the solid line, which aims first of all to tuck Black's king away on the queenside. Of Black's alternatives, 7...f5!? is the most energetic and direct treatment, leading to ultra-

sharp positions. White should probably respond with 8 ♘c3, supporting the d4-d5 pawn push, when Pavlovic-Sakaev, Vrnjacka Banja 1998 continued 8...♗f6 (8...a6 9 ♕e2 b5 is an interesting plan, 10 0-0-0 b4 11 ♘a4 ♕d5 12 c4 leading to sharp play in Grischuk-Sakaev, Moscow 2002) 9 ♕d2 c5 (9...♘c6 10 ♗b5 is good for White but 9...0-0!? is an interesting alternative, Gipslis-Chernin, St. John 1988 becoming rather complicated after 10 g4 fxg4 11 ♖g1 e5! 12 ♗d3 ♗g7 13 dxe5 ♔h8 14 0-0-0 f5!) 10 d5 0-0 (10...exd5 11 ♕e3+ wins back the pawn with an edge, for example 11...♗e6 12 ♕xc5 ♘d7 13 ♗b5 ♖c8 14 ♕e3 0-0 15 0-0 a6 16 ♗xd7 ♕xd7 17 ♘d4 ♕d6 18 ♘ce2 ♔h8 19 ♖ad1 ♖g8 20 f4, Arnason-Bjarnason, Reykjavik 1989) 11 0-0-0 e5

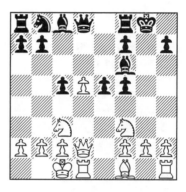

12 h4 (preparing to put the knight on g5, while 12 ♔b1 ♘d7 13 g4!? e4 14 ♘g1 fxg4 15 ♘xe4 ♗g7 16 h3 ♕b6 17 c3 ♘e5 18 hxg4 ♗xg4 19 ♖e1 ♖fe8 also led to a razor-sharp struggle in Saulin-Kiriakov, Moscow 1999) 12...♘d7 13 ♖g1 (13 d6 ♘b6 14 ♕e3 e4 15 ♘g5 ♗d7 16 g4! ♗d4 17 ♖xd4 cxd4 18 ♕xd4 f6 was very messy in Lau-Sakaev, Dortmund 1991) 13...e4 14 ♘g5 ♘e5 15 ♗e2 (Sakaev gave 15 f3 h6 16 ♘h3 ♗g7 17 fxe4 ♕xh4 as an alternative – which is also very complicated) 15...h6 16 ♘h3 ♗g7 17 ♘f4 b5!? (certainly consistent but possibly not the best; Black can also play 17...♕xh4, when the attempt to smash through the king-

side with 18 g4 is insufficient after 18...fxg4 19 ♘xe4 ♗f5 20 ♖h1 ♕d8 21 ♘g3 ♗g6 according to Sakaev) 18 g4 b4 19 ♘a4 fxg4 20 ♘h5 with a complex and double-edged game.

Returning to the position after 12 h4, Black has also played 12...♗g7, but after 13 d6 ♗e6 14 ♘g5 ♘c6 the position of the knight on c6 did not prove that helpful in Klovans-Dizdar, Groningen 1991. That game continued 15 g4 ♘d4 16 gxf5 ♗xf5 17 ♗d3 ♕d7 18 ♗xf5 ♕xf5 19 ♘d5 ♔h8 20 c3 ♘c6 21 ♘e3 ♕d7 22 ♕d5, when White was taking control. 12...a6?! is another try, but in such a sharp position this kind of relaxed build-up looks too slow.

For the trendy 7...a6!? see Shirov-Topalov.

8 ♗c4

8 ♗b5+ c6 9 ♗c4 is a common inaccuracy, giving Black the useful ...c7-c6 for nothing.

8...♗b7 9 ♕e2 c6 10 0-0-0 ♕c7 11 ♖he1 ♘d7 12 ♔b1 0-0-0

Castling immediately is not mandatory, Black can also keep his options open with 12...h5 13 ♘c3 ♘f8, as in Goloshchapov-Volkov, Novgorod 1999.

13 ♗a6 ♗xa6

Black has tinkered with a number of different moves in this position but the respective strategies are basically the same. White exchanges light-squared bishops and then tries to engineer a central breakthrough with

c2-c4 and d4-d5. Black, on the other hand, will try to restrain d4-d5 and perhaps even attack the d4-pawn with a subsequent ...f6-f5 and ....♗f6.

Another plan for Black is to generate play on the half-open g-file. One thing he should be quite wary of, however, is playing ...f6-f5 prematurely. This lessens control of the centre and invites a white knight to step in to e5. Here are some examples of the alternatives in action:

a) 13...♖he8 14 ♗xb7+ ♔xb7 15 c4 (the passive 15 c3 has also been played but should hardly trouble Black after 15...♘f8 followed by ...♘g6) 15...♘f8 16 ♕c2 f5 17 ♘c3 ♗f6 18 ♖e3 (18 d5!?) 18...♖e7 19 ♖ed3 ♘g6 20 d5 (20 g3 is interesting, keeping the tension a little longer) 20...♖ed7 21 ♕a4 ♘e7 22 dxc6+ ♘xc6 23 ♘b5 ♖xd3 24 ♖xd3 ♕b8 25 ♕d1 ½-½, Korchnoi-Andersson, Reykjavik 1988.

b) 13...♖hg8 14 g3 f5 15 ♘ed2 h5 16 ♗xb7+ ♔xb7 17 ♘c4 is similar to the game.

c) 13...♘f8 14 g3 ♘g6 15 h4 h5 16 ♗xb7+ ♔xb7 17 ♖d3 f5 18 ♘eg5 ♗d6 (18...♗f6 19 c4 ♖d7 20 ♖ed1 ♖hd8 21 a3 was also better for White in Izeta-Alvarez, Lleida 1991) 19 ♘d2 ♗f8 20 f4 ♗g7 21 ♘b3 ♗f6 22 ♘f3 ♘e7 23 c4 ♖hg8 24 ♘g5 and White had an advantage in Guliev-Radjabov, Baku 1998.

d) 13...f5? is poor due to 14 ♗xb7+ ♔xb7 15 ♘eg5 ♖df8 16 d5!, when White had achieved his breakthrough very easily in Timman-Andersson, Yerevan Olympiad 1996.

d) Last but not least Black played 13...b5!? in Neelakantan-Speelman, Calcutta 1998. Black's idea is that White will not be able to achieve his thematic c2-c4 and d4-d5 breakthrough. The game went 14 ♗xb7+ ♔xb7 15 c4 bxc4 16 ♕xc4 ♘b6 17 ♕b3 ♗a8 18 ♖c1 ♖b8 19 ♕c2 ♖hc8, defending everything.

14 ♕xa6+ ♔b8

This is probably slightly stronger than 14...♕b7, which forces White's queen back to its best square after 15 ♕e2.

15 g3

The queen is optically impressive on a6 but nothing more. 15 ♕e2 may be White's best after which 15...♖he8 16 c3 ♘f8 17 g3 f5 18 ♘ed2 ♘g6 19 ♘c4 was marginally better for White in Leko-Andersson, Ubeda 1997. 15...♘f8!? and 15...♖hg8 are also possible and lead to similar play.

15...f5 16 ♘ed2 h5

The thematic means of gaining counter-play after White's g2-g3. 16...♗f6 17 ♕e2 was slightly better for White in A.Sokolov-Andersson, Bar 1997, when White's knights homed in on e5.

17 ♕e2 h4 18 ♘c4 hxg3 19 hxg3 ♗f6 20 ♖d3 b5?!

This is often a good idea, although here White rapidly generates pressure against c6. Black should settle for 20...♖he8 with a solid enough position.

21 ♘cd2 ♘b6 22 ♖c1 ♖d5 23 c4 bxc4 24 ♘xc4 ♔a8

A further mistake since Black receives in-adequate compensation for the pawn. He should eliminate White's knight before it comes to e5.

25 ♘ce5 ♕b7 26 ♘xc6 ♖c8 27 ♖dc3 ♘a4 28 ♖c4 ♘b6 29 ♖4c2 ♖d7 30 ♘a5 ♖xc2 31 ♖xc2 ♕e4 32 ♘b3 ♕xe2 33 ♖xe2 ♖d8 34 ♖c2 ♘d5 35 ♘a5 ♖h8 36 a3 a6 37 ♔a2 ♔a7 38 ♘c4 ♖h7 39 ♖c1 f4 40 gxf4 ♘xf4 41 ♘d6 ♘d3?!

41...♘d5 improves, when Black should still be able to hold the draw.

42 ♖c7+ ♔b6 43 ♘e8 ♖h8 44 ♖xf7 ♗xd4 45 ♘xd4 ♖xe8 46 ♖f6 ♘c5 47 f4 ♔b7 48 b4 ♖d8 49 ♘xe6 ♖d2+ 50 ♔b1 ♘e4 51 ♖h6 ♖f2 52 ♔c1 ♔a7 53 ♖h3 ♔b6 54 ♔d1 a5 55 bxa5+ ♔xa5 56 ♔e1 ♖a2 57 ♖e3 ♘f6 58 ♘d4! ♘g4 59 ♖g3 ♘f2 60 f5 ♘e4 61 ♖e3 ♘g5 62 f6 ♔b6 63 ♖c3 ♖g2 64 ♖c6+ ♔b7 65 ♖c5 ♘f7 66 ♘e6 ♔b6 67 a4 ♖g4 68 a5+ ♔a6 69 ♘c7+ ♔a7 70 ♘d5 ♔a6 71 ♔d2 ♖a4 72 ♘c7+ ♔b7 73 ♔e3 ♔a7 74 ♘e6 ♘h6 75 ♔d3 ♔a6 76 ♖h5 ♖a3+ 77 ♔c4 ♘f7 78 ♘c7+ ♔b7 79 ♖h7 ♘e5+ 80 ♔b5 ♖b3+ 81 ♔c5 ♖d3 82 ♘d5+ 1-0

Game 63
Shirov-Topalov
Sarajevo 2000

---

1 d4 d5 2 ♘c3 ♘f6 3 ♗g5 e6 4 ♘f3 ♗e7 5 ♗xf6 gxf6 6 e4 dxe4 7 ♘xe4 a6

A relatively recent idea which is designed to push ...b7-b5 before fianchettoing the queen's bishop. The aim is to give Black more of a grip on the central light squares but it costs time and creates some weak-nesses.

8 c4

This move makes perfect sense. White cuts across his opponent's plans and fights for the same central light squares, now put-ting the onus on Black to demonstrate coun-terplay.

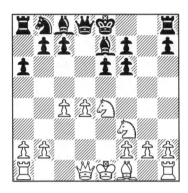

8...f5 9 ♘c3 ♗f6

After 9...c5 10 d5 ♗f6 White can place his queen more effectively: 11 ♕c2 e5 12 0-0-0 0-0 13 ♘d2 ♗g7 14 f3 ♕f6 15 ♗d3 b5 16 ♖df1! h6 17 ♔b1 b4 18 ♘a4 a5 and now 19 g4! undermined e4 and f5, thus securing White a clear advantage in Anand-Short, Dubai 2002.

10 ♕d2 c5 11 d5 0-0

White should probably meet the immediate 11...e5 with 12 h4, transposing back to the game after 12...0-0 13 0-0-0. Instead 12 ♕h6 e4 13 ♘d2 ♘d7 14 h4 ♕b6 gave Black good counterplay in Prasad-Barua, Raipur 2002.

12 0-0-0 e5

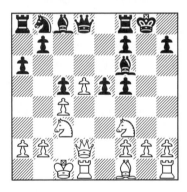

According to Ftacnik White is clearly better after 12...exd5 13 ♘xd5, yet Morozevich certainly felt that the capture on d5 had potential in order to bring his knight from b8 to

d4 via c6. Shirov-Morozevich, Astana 2001 went 12...♗g7 13 h4! exd5 14 ♘xd5 (14 cxd5 ♕d6 followed by ...b7-b5 looks complex) 14...♘c6 15 h5 h6 (preventing 16 h6) 16 ♖h3 and now Black has an interesting possibility in 16...b5!? (in the game Black lost a pawn after 16...f4? 17 ♖h4 ♘b4 18 ♘xb4 ♕xd2+ 19 ♖xd2 cxb4 20 ♖xf4 etc.). In Esplana-Kastanieda, Lima 2000, Black tried 12...♕a5 but after 13 ♔b1 ♗g7 14 h4 e5 15 ♖e1 ♘d7?! 16 ♗d3! White found a way to use the position of Black's queen, 16...e4? being refuted by 17 ♘xe4.

13 h4!?

Obtaining the g5-square for the knight whilst in some positions the rook might come into play via h3.

13...b5

After 13...e4 14 ♘g5 White is ready to challenge e4 with 15 f3.

14 d6

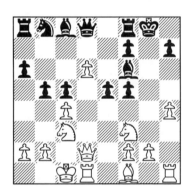

14...♘c6?!

Allowing the d-pawn to march on to d7 is probably a mistake, although after 14...♘d7 15 ♘d5 the position still looks very good for White.

15 d7! ♗b7 16 ♕d6 e4

After 16...♗e7 White has 17 ♕h6 (intending ♘f3-g5), and after 16...♕e7 there is 17 ♕c7, threatening the bishop on b7 and 18 ♘d5.

17 ♘d5 ♗g7

After 17...♗xb2+ 18 ♔xb2 exf3 19 gxf3

White also has the g-file for an attack.

18 ♘g5 ♘d4?!

The attempt to drive away the knight from g5 with 18...h6 is beautifully refuted by 19 cxb5 axb5 20 ♗xb5 ♘d4 21 ♘e7+ ♔h8 22 ♕g6!! fxg6 23 ♘xg6+ ♔g8 24 ♗c4+ etc.

19 ♘e7+! ♔h8 20 ♖h3!

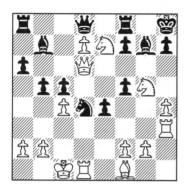

Threatening to bring the rook to g3. Black prevents this but at the same time weakens his pawn structure.

20...f4 21 ♔b1 b4 22 ♗e2!

White also wants his bishop in the attack, this piece being en route to h5.

22...f3

After 22...♘xe2 White plays 23 ♕xc5, threatening 24 ♕f5, while after 22...e3 or even 22...h6 there follows 23 ♗h5! – in short it seems that White has a winning attack.

23 gxf3 ♘xe2 24 ♕xc5 ♘f4 25 ♕f5 ♘g6 26 h5! ♕xe7 27 hxg6 1-0

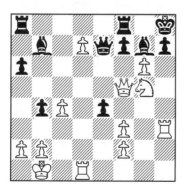

After 27...♕f6 (27...h6 28 gxf7) there follows 28 ♖xh7+ ♔g8 29 gxf7+ ♖xf7 30 d8♕+ ♖xd8 31 ♖xd8+ ♕xd8 32 ♕xf7 mate.

Game 64
Lobron-Murey
Randers Zonal 1982

---

1 d4 ♘f6 2 ♘c3 d5 3 ♗g5 e6 4 ♘f3 c5

A logical move, hitting White's d4-pawn. Unless White wants to play the solid but somewhat dull 5 e3 he has no choice but to play the next move.

5 e4 dxe4 6 ♘xe4 cxd4 7 ♗xf6?!

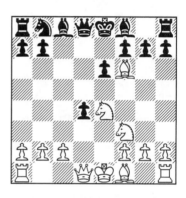

I don't think that White should make this exchange because Black now has nice centre pawns and the two bishops. Another interesting possibility is 7 ♗b5+, when 7...♘c6 8 ♘xd4 ♗d7 9 ♘xc6 bxc6 10 ♗e2 ♕a5+ 11 ♗d2 ♕e5 12 ♘xf6+ ♕xf6 13 ♗c3 ♕g5 14 0-0 left White with the superior pawn structure in Kotronias-Tseshkovsky, Niksic 1997. Alternatively 7...♗d7 8 ♗xd7+ ♘bxd7 9 ♕xd4 ♗e7 10 0-0-0 ♘xe4 11 ♗xe7 ♕xe7 12 ♕xe4 ♘c5 13 ♕e5 0-0 14 ♖d6 ♖fd8 15 ♖hd1 ♖xd6 16 ♕xd6 ♕xd6 17 ♖xd6 gave White a nagging edge in Janowski-Teichmann, Ostende 1905 thanks to the queenside pawn majority and more active pieces.

7...gxf6 8 ♕xd4

With White having exchanged on g6 already, 8 ♗b5+ seems to be quite well met by

8...♘c6 rather than 8...♗d7 9 ♗xd7+ ♘xd7 10 ♕xd4, which looked dangerous for Black in Landenbergue-Bouaziz, Cannes 1997. This probably explains why Bouaziz avoids repeating the second time around, for 8...♘c6 was played in Fontaine-Bouaziz, Cannes 1998, and this time, after 9 ♘xd4 ♗d7 10 ♘xc6 bxc6 11 ♗e2 ♕a5+ 12 c3 ♕e5 13 ♘g3 h5, Black had the initiative.

8...♕xd4 9 ♘xd4 f5 10 ♘f6+

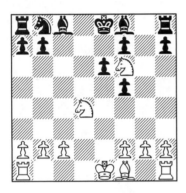

An adventurous continuation – will White's knight be well placed on h5 or not? It could be that the only way to justify 7 ♗xf6 is to indulge in such adventures. After the simple 10 ♘d2 Paavilainen-Kiltti, Finland 1998 continued 10...♗d7 11 ♘c4 ♘c6 12 0-0-0 ♘xd4 13 ♖xd4 ♗c5 with an excellent game for Black.

10...♔e7 11 ♘h5 ♗h6 12 f4 ♖d8

12...♘c6 looks much simpler to me, evicting the knight on d4 without further ado. If Black wants to keep his queenside pawns together then 12...♗d7 followed by ...♘c6 is a good idea.

13 0-0-0 ♘d7 14 g3 ♘f6

Black might have seen the following combination coming but assessed the resultant position as being satisfactory for him. However, by now it's rather too late to do much about it; 14...♘b6 is met by 15 ♗g2, with massive pressure.

15 ♘xf5+ exf5 16 ♖xd8 ♘xh5

16...♔xd8 17 ♘xf6 wins the h7-pawn.

17 ♖h8 ♘f6 18 ♗c4 ♗f8 19 ♖e1+ ♗e6 20 ♗d3 ♔d7 21 ♖e5 ♔c7 22 ♗xf5 ♘d7 23 ♗xe6 ♘xe5 24 ♖xh7 ♔b6 25 ♗d5! ♖d8 26 ♗e4

Having built up a large advantage, White plays indecisively. Both 26 ♗xf7 and 26 c4 seem to ensure the capture of the f7-pawn, when White should be winning.

26...♗c5 27 a3 ♘c4 28 ♗d3 ♗e3+ 29 ♔b1 ♘d6

Thus Black succeeds in protecting f7 and lives to tell the tale. White still has what chances are going, but the winning moment has passed.

30 ♖h5 ♔c6 31 c3 b5 32 ♔c2 ♗g1 33 ♖h6 ♔c7 34 ♖h5 ♖e8 35 ♗xb5 ♘xb5 36 ♖xb5 ♖e2+ 37 ♔b3 ♖xh2 38 ♖f5 ♖h7 39 g4 ♔d6 40 g5 ♗e3 41 ♔c2 ♖h4 42 ♖xf7 ♖xf4 43 ♖xf4 ♗xf4 44 g6 ♔e6 45 b4 ♔f6 46 ♔d3 ♔xg6 47 ♔c4 ♗e5 48 a4 ♔f6 49 b5 ♔e6 50 a5 ♔d7 51 ♔c5 ♗g3 52 ♔d5 ♗e1 53 c4 ½-½

53...♗xa5 54 c5 ♔c8 55 ♔c4 ♔b7 56 ♔b3 ♗d8 57 ♔a4 is a positional draw. White keeps his king on b4, c4 and a4, and if Black's king comes around towards d5 he exchanges the a-pawn with b5-b6.

Game 65
Hector-Berg
Solett Open, Skelleftea 2001

---

1 ♘c3 d5 2 d4 ♘f6

The move order in the game was actually 2...e6 3 ♘f3 ♘f6 4 ♗g5 ♗b4 etc. For the sake of clarity I am getting into a 'Veresov' position as quickly as possible.

3 ♗g5 e6 4 ♘f3 ♗b4

The 'MacCutcheon' move, against which I see only one interesting option for White... To complete the round-up of Black's possibilities, 4...h6 is possible, when 5 ♗xf6 ♕xf6 6 e4 ♗b4 transposes to Akopian-Antonio in Chapter 10.

5 ♕d3!?

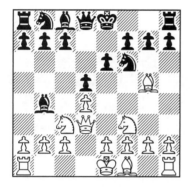

5...h6

This position has appeared in only a few games so it is difficult to know for sure what is best. Black has several very reasonable looking alternatives:

a) 5...c5 6 a3 (6 dxc5 ♘bd7 7 ♘d2 ♗xc5 8 e4? ♗xf2+ won a pawn for Black in Van der Lijn-Ward, Guernsey 1991) 6...♗xc3+ 7 ♕xc3 cxd4 8 ♕xd4 ♘c6 was played in Kivisto-Manninen, Espoo 1990, and now I like 9 ♕h4. In the game 9 ♕f4 ♕e7 10 ♘e5 h6 11 ♗xf6 gxf6 12 ♘xc6 bxc6 looked quite good for Black.

b) 5...♘bd7 6 ♘d2 (6 0-0-0 c5) 6...♗e7

was played in Huerta-Rodriguez Cespedes, Havana 1986, and now 7 0-0-0 looks preferable to 7 f4 (as played in the game), which seems rather exotic to me. Here 6...c5 can be met by 7 a3.

c) 5...0-0 6 a3 ♗xc3+ 7 ♕xc3 ♘bd7 was Opitz-Seifert, Dresden 1999, and now 8 ♘d2 looks interesting for White, who has a useful bishop pair, and an improvement on 8 e3 h6 9 ♗xf6 ♘xf6, which was utterly harmless.

6 ♗xf6

This looks quite nice for White so I'm not that bothered about finding an alternative. But perhaps White can also play 6 ♗h4 c5 7 a3 here. 7 dxc5 ♘bd7 favoured Black in Kagas-Mamedova, Chania 1997.

6...♕xf6 7 a3 ♗d6

After 7...♗xc3+ 8 ♕xc3 c6 9 e3, intending 10 ♗d3, White has more freedom.

8 e4 dxe4 9 ♘xe4 ♕e7 10 g3 0-0 11 ♗g2 ♘d7 12 c4 ½-½

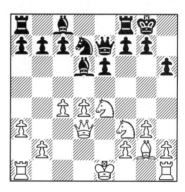

I don't know if there was any special reason why Hector agreed a draw here. Objectively speaking his position looks very attractive, with a nice space advantage and well placed forces.

Summary

After 3...e6 White really has to go e2-e4 if he wants any kind of initiative, and this inevitably means transposing to a French Defence. Yet by delaying this for a move with the cunning 4 ♘f3 White can cut out several of Black's options and keep the element of surprise on his side.

1 d4 ♘f6 2 ♘c3 d5 3 ♗g5 e6 4 ♘f3 *(D)* **♗e7**

> 4...c5 5 e4 - *Game 64*
> 4...♗b4 5 ♕d3 - *Game 65*

5 ♗xf6 ♗xf6

> 5...gxf6 6 e4 dxe4 7 ♘xe4 *(D)*
>> 7...b6 - *Game 62*; 7...a6 - *Game 63*

6 e4 *(D)*

> 6...b6 - *Game 59*
> 6...0-0 7 ♗d3 c5 - *Game 60*
> 6...dxe4 7 ♘xe4 0-0 - *Game 61*

4 ♘f3

7 ♘xe4

6 e4

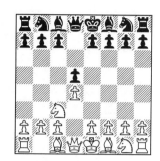

CHAPTER NINE

1...d5 2 ♘c3: 2...e6, 2...f5 and Others

1 d4 d5 2 ♘c3

After White plays 1 d4 d5 2 ♘c3 Black can attempt to steer the game onto his own turf with a variety of second moves apart from 2...♘f6. Thus 2...e6 and 2...c6 lead to the French and Caro-Kann respectively after 3 e4, while 2...f5 transposes directly to a Dutch Defence (normally this position is reached after 1 d4 f5 2 ♘c3 d5) and 2...♘c6 3 e4 is a Nimzowitsch. Fortunately White can cut down the amount of work involved by side-stepping most of these openings.

Veresov himself used to transpose to a French after 1 d4 d5 2 ♘c3 e6 3 e4, but White can also play 3 ♘f3, as in Taeger-Tessars. Should Black answer this with 3...♘f6 we'd get a transposition to Chapter 8 after 4 ♗g5. In the game he played 3...♗b4, when White surprised him with 4 ♕d3!? and soon obtained a nice two bishop advantage.

There's no way around the transposition to a Dutch after 1 d4 d5 2 ♘c3 f5, but White can stick to the Veresov pattern with 3 ♗g5. After the further 3...♘f6 my recommended line for White is the Veresovian 4 f3 (see Sokolov-Illescas and Macieja-Bartel) which offers interesting and dynamic play. My own view is that 3...♘f6 4 ♗xf6 is rather harmless for Black, yet many exponents of the Dutch choose to avoid these somewhat stodgy posi-

tions by selecting different third moves. Thus 3...g6 features in Khalifman-Lerner, 3...c6 in Sokolov-Nikolic (White should improve here with 4 e4!) whilst the very dodgy looking 3...♘c6 was played in Romero Holmes-Vallejo Pons.

Hort-Polgar illustrates how White can avoid transposition to a Caro-Kann by meeting 2...c6 with 3 ♗g5. This is also interesting news for Trompovsky specialists as after 1 d4 d5 2 ♗g5 they can meet the feared 2...c6 with 3 ♘c3 to reach the same position. White's development is somewhat easier and Black can soon find himself in trouble if he plays inaccurately.

Game 66
Taeger-Tessars
Bundesliga 1983/84

1 d4 d5 2 ♘c3 e6 3 ♘f3 ♗b4 4 ♕d3

A similar idea to the 2...♘f6 3 ♗g5 e6 4 ♘f3 ♗b4 5 ♕d3 variation which we saw in the Hector-Berg game from the previous chapter. White supports the knight on c3 and prepares both e2-e4 and queenside castling. In Ignatiev-Khavsky, St Petersburg 1996, White tried 4 ♗g5 f6 5 ♗d2 f5 6 e3 ♘f6 and now instead of 7 ♗d3 an interesting treatment is 7 ♘e2 ♗d6 8 ♘f4, achieving the ideal anti-Stonewall position for White's knights.

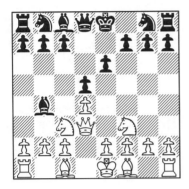

4...♘e7

The only other example of this position I could find was Kunath-Erpel, Weilburg 1998 in which Black played 4...♘c6, when 5 ♗f4 ♘f6 6 0-0-0 ♗xc3 7 ♕xc3 ♘e4 8 ♕e3 f6 9 ♘d2 ♘d6 10 g4 ♕e7 11 ♗g2 was promising for White. Black's most natural move seems to be 4...♘f6, transposing to Hector-Berg after 5 ♗g5.

5 a3 ♗xc3+ 6 ♕xc3 ♕d6 7 g3 ♘g6 8 h4 h5 9 ♗g2 ♘d7 10 0-0 c6 11 b3

White is clearly better here due to Black's weaknesses on the dark squares and awkward piece placements. Clearly it is far too soon to make any definitive assessment of 4 ♕d3, although it certainly looks interesting.

11...b5?!

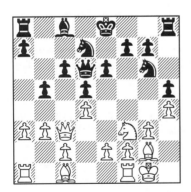

Yet another pawn goes to a light square.

White soon steps up a gear...

12 ♕a5 0-0 13 a4 ♕b8 14 ♕c3 ♗a6 15 axb5 ♗xb5 16 ♖e1 ♕b6 17 e4 ♖fe8 18 ♘g5 ♘f6 19 e5 ♘g4 20 ♗a3 a5 21 ♕f3 ♘h6 22 ♗c5 ♕c7 23 ♕xh5 a4 24 c4 dxc4 25 bxc4 ♗xc4 26 ♗e4 ♘f8 27 ♖e3 ♗d5 28 ♖f3 ♗xe4 29 ♘xe4 ♘g6 30 ♘d6 ♖f8 31 ♕g5 ♕d8 32 ♕d2 ♘e7 33 ♖fa3 ♘hf5 34 ♘xf5 exf5 35 ♖xa4 ♖xa4 36 ♖xa4 ♖e8 37 ♕g5 ♘g6 38 ♕xf5 ♕d5 39 ♖a7 ♕e6 40 ♕xe6 ♖xe6 41 f4 f5 42 h5 ♘h8 43 ♖a8+ ♔h7 1-0

Game 67
I.Sokolov-Illescas Cordoba
Hoogovens, Wijk aan Zee 1997

---

1 d4 d5 2 ♘c3 f5 3 ♗g5 ♘f6 4 f3!?

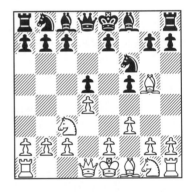

The move which is most in the spirit of the Veresov. White wants to play e2-e4.

4...♘c6

Trying to prevent e2-e4 by putting pressure on the d4-pawn. There are a number of alternatives:

a) 4...e6 5 e4 ♗e7 is a solid nut against which it is difficult for White to achieve very much. The best is probably 6 exf5 (6 e5 ♘fd7 7 ♗xe7 ♕xe7 looks like a super-solid version of the French) 6...exf5 7 ♕d2 0-0 8 0-0-0 c6 9 ♗d3 (the immediate 9 ♘h3!? is worth considering) 9...♘h5 10 ♗xe7 ♕xe7 11 ♖e1 ♕d6 12 ♘h3 ♘d7 13 ♕g5 g6 14 ♘e2 ♕f6 15 g4 fxg4 16 fxg4 ♕xg5+ 17

♘xg5 ♘g7 and Black maintained the balance in Sakaev-Malaniuk, Elista 1998.

b) 4...c5 is a sharper alternative, when there can follow 5 e4 (5 e3 e6 6 ♕d2 ♘c6 7 0-0-0 cxd4?! 8 exd4 ♗b4 9 a3 ♗a5 10 g4 was promising for White in Thorhallsson-Bern, Arnhem 1987) 5...♘c6 (5...dxe4 6 dxc5 ♕a5 7 ♕d2 ♕xc5 8 0-0-0 ♗e6 9 ♘h3 ♕c8 10 ♘f4 gave White a strong initiative in Ma-laniuk-Kamenets, Polanica Zdroj 2000, whilst 5...cxd4 is probably best met by 6 ♕xd4 ♘c6 7 ♗b5) 6 ♗b5 (6 ♗xf6 exf6 7 exd5 cxd4 8 dxc6 dxc3 9 ♗b5 bxc6 10 ♗xc6+ ♗d7 11 ♗xd7+ ♕xd7 12 ♕xd7+ ♔xd7 13 bxc3 ♗c5 was no worse for Black in Vaisman-Santo Roman, France 2000) 6...a6 7 ♗xc6+ bxc6 8 ♗xf6 gxf6 9 exd5 cxd5 10 dxc5 e6 11 ♕d4 ♕c7 12 ♘a4 ♔f7 13 b4, producing a complex and messy game in which Black had compensation for the pawn in Antonsen-Malaniuk, Lyngby Open 1991.

c) 4...♘bd7 5 ♕d3 e6 (5...g6 6 e4 ♘b6 7 e5 ♘h5 8 ♗e2 h6 9 ♗c1 c6 10 f4 ♘g7 11 ♕g3 put Black in all sorts of trouble in Klaric-Sinka, Caorle 1982) 6 0-0-0 ♗e7 7 ♘h3 0-0 8 e4 ♘b6 9 exf5 exf5 10 ♘f4 h6 11 ♗xf6 ♖xf6 12 h4 with an edge for White in Stefanova-Montell Lorenzo, Salou 2000.

For 4...c6 see Macieja-Bartel.

5 ♕d2

Preparing to castle long before proceeding with any central action. After the impetuous 5 e4?! Black plays 5...fxe4 6 fxe4 ♘xe4! 7 ♘xe4 dxe4 8 d5 ♘b4! 9 ♗c4 c6 with an excellent game.

5...g6

The alternative way for Black to develop is with 5...e6 6 0-0-0 ♗e7 7 e4 dxe4 (7...0-0!? is not unthinkable) 8 fxe4 fxe4 (8...♘xe4 9 ♘xe4 fxe4 10 h4 gives White compensation for the pawn) 9 ♗b5! ♗d7 10 ♗xf6 ♗xf6 11 ♘xe4, which favours White thanks to his superior development and the weak e6-pawn. Bronstein-Magergut, Moscow 1947 saw the interesting 6 e4!? dxe4 7 0-0-0 ♗b4 8 a3 ♗a5

9 ♗c4 0-0 10 ♘ge2 exf3 11 gxf3 and White had a promising initiative for the pawn.

6 0-0-0 ♗g7 7 ♗h6

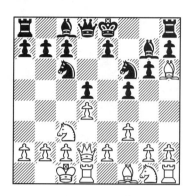

Not so much an attacking move as a positional one. The bishop on g7 is Black's 'good' bishop and without it his dark squares look rather weak.

7...0-0 8 ♘h3 a6 9 ♗xg7 ♔xg7 10 ♘f4 ♕d6 11 e3

After 11 h4? Black can equalise with 11...♘xd4! 12 ♘fxd5 (after 12 h5 or 12 ♕xd4 Black plays 12...e5) 12...♘xd5 13 ♕xd4+ ♘f6 etc.

11...♗e6 12 h4 ♗f7 13 h5 g5 14 h6+ ♔h8 15 ♘h3 g4

Not 15...♖g8? 16 e4.

16 ♘g5 ♗g6 17 ♘e2 e5 18 dxe5 ♕xe5 19 ♘f4 ♖ae8 20 ♗d3 ♕xe3 21 ♕xe3 ♖xe3 22 ♘fe6 ♖e8

If Black protects the c-pawn with 22...♖c8 White has 23 ♔d2 d4 (or 23...♖e5 24 f4) 24 ♘xd4 winning material.

23 fxg4?!

It might have been better to try 23 ♘g7 ♖8e7 (23...♖8e5 24 f4 ♖e7 25 ♗xf5) 24 ♗xf5 although 24...♖e2 continues to be un-comfortable for White.

23...♘xg4 24 ♘xc7 ♖8e5?!

According to Illescas Black should have played 24...♖c8 25 ♘xd5 ♖g3.

25 ♘f3! ♘f2 26 ♘xe5 ♖xe5 27 ♖he1 ♘xd1 28 ♔xd1 ♖xe1+?!

Probably the losing move. Black has to try

28...f4.

29 ♔xe1 ♘e7 30 ♔f2 ♘g8

Trying to keep White's king at bay with 30...d4 loses to 31 ♔g3 ♘g8 (or 31...♔g8 32 ♘e6) 32 ♔f4 ♘xh6 33 ♘e6, threatening both the pawn on d4 and 34 ♘c5.

31 ♘xd5 ♘xh6 32 ♔g3 ♗f7 33 ♘e3 ♗xa2

Or 33...♔g7 34 ♔f4 ♔f6 35 ♘xf5 etc.

34 b3 ♘g4 35 ♘d5 ♘e5 36 ♗xf5 ♘c6 37 ♘c3 ♘b4 38 ♔f4 ♔g7 39 ♔e3 h6 40 ♔d2 ♔f6 41 ♗c8 b5 42 ♔c1 1-0

Game 68
Macieja-Bartel
Polish Ch., Warsaw 2002

---

1 d4 d5 2 ♘c3 f5 3 ♗g5 ♘f6 4 f3 c6 5 ♕d2

White should seriously consider the immediate 5 e4, for example 5...♕b6 (5...fxe4 6 fxe4 ♘xe4 7 ♘xe4 dxe4 8 ♗c4 gives White excellent compensation for the pawn) 6 e5 ♘fd7 7 a3 e6 (7...♕xb2?? 8 ♘a4) 8 b4 a5 9 ♘a4 ♕c7 10 c3 b6 11 ♘h3 and Black was cramped in Doroshkievich-Rotshtein, Lvov 1986.

5...♗e6!?

Directed against 6 e4, although White can also delay this move. After 5...e6 6 0-0-0 ♗b4 7 e3 ♘e4 8 fxe4?! ♕xg5 Black had an edge in Nestorovic-Orlov, Belgrade 2001. With this in mind White should play 6 e4 while he still

can, for example 6...fxe4 (6...h6 might be met by 7 ♗xf6 ♕xf6 8 exf5 exf5 9 f4, intending ♘g1-f3-e5) 7 fxe4 ♗b4 8 e5 ♘e4 9 ♗xd8 ♘xd2 10 ♔xd2 ♔xd8 11 a3 ♗e7 12 ♘f3 c5 13 dxc5 ♗xc5 14 ♗d3 ♘c6 15 ♖hf1 gives White the initiative in the endgame.

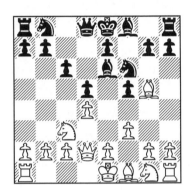

6 0-0-0

After 6 e4 dxe4 7 fxe4 fxe4 White can't bring his bishop to c4. If he recovers his pawn with 8 ♗xf6 exf6 9 ♘xe4 Black is at least equal after 9...♕b6 (followed by castling long). In Bukal-Beim, Austria 2002 White played the indecisive 6 ♘h3 ♘bd7 7 ♕d3?! (7 0-0-0 is better) with Black gradually assuming the initiative after 7...g6 8 0-0-0 ♗g7 9 ♕e3 ♗f7 10 ♗h6 0-0 11 ♗xg7 ♔xg7 12 ♘f4 ♕c7 13 ♘e6+ ♗xe6 14 ♕xe6 ♘g8 15 g3 ♖f6 16 ♕e3 e5 etc.

6...♘bd7 7 e3

Another possibility is 7 ♘h3, although after 7...h6 8 ♗xf6 ♘xf6 9 ♘f4 ♗f7 Black seems to be doing fine.

7...h6 8 ♗xf6

Here Tyomkin suggested 8 ♗f4!? and assessed the position as slightly better for White after 8...g5 9 ♗g3 ♗g7 10 h4. This may well be true, but 8...g5 certainly isn't forced. Black could, for example, consider 8...b5 which both commences queenside action and prepares to undermine the knight on c3, one of the main supporters of the crucial e3-e4 advance.

8...♘xf6 9 ♗d3 ♕d7 10 h3 0-0-0 11 g4

g5 12 h4

Had White tried 12 ♘ge2 (planning 13 ♘g3) Black could take the initiative on the kingside with 12...h5.

12...♗g7 13 gxf5 ♗xf5 14 hxg5 hxg5 15 ♘ge2 g4! 16 e4

In his notes Tyomkin suggested 16 ♗xf5 and assessed the position after 16...♕xf5 17 f4 ♖h3 18 ♖hg1 as equal. It seems to me that Black is better after 18...♖dh8 19 ♘g3 ♕d7 due to his domination of the h-file and passed pawn. Of course it's not easy to break through in this position.

16...♗e6 17 exd5? ♗xd5?

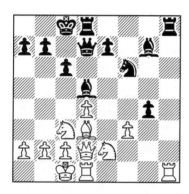

Missing the opportunity to win a pawn with 17...♖xh1 18 ♖xh1 ♗xd5 19 ♘xd5 ♕xd5, picking up f3. White could have avoided this by exchanging rooks on h8 before capturing on d5.

18 ♖xh8 ♖xh8 19 fxg4 ♘xg4 20 ♘xd5 ♕xd5 21 ♘c3 ♕f7?!

Around here Black's pieces start to lose their coordination. Instead 21...♕d7 22 ♔b1 ♗h6 is equal.

22 ♔b1 ♘h2?

Black could still hold the balance with the precise 22...♘f2, after which 23 ♖f1 ♗xd4 24 ♗f5+ ♕xf5 25 ♕xd4 e5 26 ♕xa7 ♖h1 simplifies the position and makes a draw likely.

23 ♕g5 ♕f6

The attempt to evacuate the knight with 23...♘f3 runs into 24 ♗f5+ e6 25 ♗xe6+

♕xe6 26 ♕xg7, winning a pawn.

24 ♗f5+

White could also play 24 ♕g3, when 24...♘f3 25 ♘e4 ♕f7 (25...♕xd4 26 c3 wins a piece) 26 ♖f1 leaves Black's knight in all sorts of trouble.

24...♔d8

24...e6 meets with 25 ♗xe6+, and after 24...♔b8 White has 25 ♕g3+ ♔a8 26 ♗e4, keeping Black's knight locked away in the corner.

25 ♕f4 ♕d6 26 ♕e3 ♗h6 27 ♕e2 ♖f8

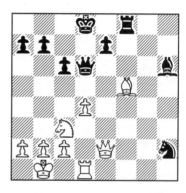

28 ♗e4?

White had an even stronger possibility in 28 ♘e4, when the knight heads for e6. The tactical point is that 28...♕f4 29 ♘c5 ♕xf5 30 ♘e6+ followed by ♘xf8 and ♕xh2 wins the exchange.

28...♕g3

After 28...e6 (to prevent 29 d5) White can choose between 29 ♘a4 (intending 30 ♘c5), 29 ♗h1 (intending 30 ♘e4 followed by ♘c5) and 29 ♕h5 followed by 30 ♕a5+, picking up the a7-pawn.

29 d5 c5 30 ♕b5

White also has the immediate 30 d6, after which 30...exd6 31 ♕b5 leaves Black defenceless.

30...♕c7

30...♕d6 would have been a more stubborn defence as the reply 31 ♕xb7 can be answered by 31...♕b6. Nevertheless, this looks very promising for White after 32

♕a8+ ♔d7 (32...♔c7 33 d6+) 33 ♕c6+ ♕xc6 34 dxc6+ as all his pieces are superbly placed and the passed pawn on c6 is particularly dangerous.

31 d6! exd6 32 ♕e2 ♗f4 33 ♘d5 ♕f7 34 ♘xf4?

Letting Black off the hook. White could conclude matters with 34 ♗g6!, when 34...♕g7 35 ♘xf4 ♖xf4 36 ♖xd6+ ♔c7 37 ♕xh2 wins a piece.

34...♕xf4 35 ♗xb7 ♘f1??

It looks as if both players were short of time. Black can force a draw with 35...♕f1! which forces the exchange of the major pieces after 36 ♕d2 ♕xd1+ 37 ♕xd1 ♖f1 etc. Now his king proves to be far too exposed.

36 a3 ♘e3 37 ♖e1 ♖e8 38 ♕a6 ♘c4 39 ♖xe8+ ♔xe8 40 ♗d5 ♘b6 41 ♕xa7! ♘xd5 42 ♕a8+ ♔d7 43 ♕xd5

The queen endgame is winning for White thanks largely to the superb position of his queen. She later comes to b3 to support the advance of the a-pawn.

43...♔c7 44 ♔a2 ♔b6 45 ♕b3+ ♔c7 46 c4 ♕e4 47 a4 ♕a8 48 ♕b5 ♕a7 49 a5 ♕a8 50 ♕b6+ ♔d7 51 a6 ♕c6 52 ♕a5 ♕a8 53 a7 ♔c6 54 ♕b5+ ♔c7 55 ♕a6 1-0

After 55...♔d7 56 ♔a3 ♔c7 (or 56...♕f3+ 57 ♔a4 ♕d1+ 58 ♔a5) the simplest is probably 57 b3 ♕h8 58 a8♘+ ♔b8 59 ♕xd6+ ♔xa8 60 ♕xc5 with an easy win.

Game 69
Khalifman-Lerner
Kujbyshev 1986

1 d4 d5 2 ♘c3 f5 3 ♗g5 g6

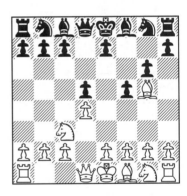

Black chooses not to commit his knight to f6 for the time being, avoiding the doubled pawns that result from 3...♘f6 4 ♗xf6 and, with ...♗g7 to now follow, ruling out plans based on ♕d2 and ♗h6. For 3...c6 see Sokolov-Nikolic, while 3...♘c6 is covered in Romero Holmes-Vallejo Pons.

4 e3 ♗g7 5 h4 ♗e6

Black has a major alternative in 5...c6, when 6 ♗f4!? (intending 7 h5) is quite promising (the immediate 6 h5 is answered by 6...h6 7 ♗f4 g5). After 6...♘d7 or 6...♘h6 White should open the h-file with 7 h5, so play might instead continue 6...♘f6 7 h5 .

⚘xh5 8 ☖xh5 gxh5 9 ♕xh5+ ♔f8 10 ♗d3 ♕e8 11 ♕h2, as in Gelfand-Kontic, European U20 Ch., Arnhem 1988, when White had good compensation for the exchange.

6 ⚘f3 c6 7 ♗f4

Once again the immediate 7 h5 is answered by 7...h6 8 ♗f4 g5 so (again) White first retreats the bishop.

7...⚘f6 8 h5 ⚘xh5?

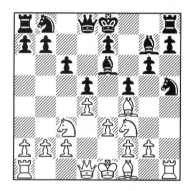

Allowing the following exchange sacrifice in the mistaken belief that he can weather the storm. But White's positional compensation will persist for a long time. Black should keep developing with 8...⚘bd7!?, when Ionov-Malaniuk, Budapest 1989 continued 9 hxg6 hxg6 10 ☖xh8+ ♗xh8 11 ⚘e5 (Kalinitschev-Legky, Tbilisi 1985 went 11 ♗d3 ⚘e4 12 ⚘g5!? and Black should have played the immediate 12...♗g8 rather than 12...⚘xc3 13 bxc3 ♗g8, allowing 14 ♗xf5!) 11...♗f7 12 ♗e2 ♕a5 13 ♕d2 ⚘xe5 14 ♗xe5 0-0-0 15 0-0-0 and White was marginally better. Black was fine in Khalifman-Legky, USSR 1987 after 9 h6 ♗f8 10 ♕d2 ♗f7 11 ⚘e5 e6 12 f3 ♗e7 13 g4 ⚘xe5 14 ♗xe5 fxg4 15 fxg4 0-0.

9 ☖xh5! gxh5 10 ⚘g5 ♗g8

After 10...♕d7 there follows 11 ♕xh5+ ♔d8 12 ♗d3 with considerable pressure for the sacrificed exchange.

11 ♕xh5+ ♔f8

If Black heads for the hills with 11...♔d7 there follows 12 ⚘f7 ♗xf7 (or 12...♕e8 13 ♕xf5+ e6 14 ⚘e5+) 13 ♕xf7 ♗f6 14 ♗d3

and White gets his first pawn for the exchange whilst maintaining a powerful bind.

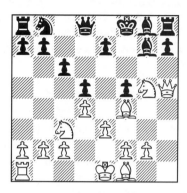

12 ♗d3 e6 13 g4 h6 14 ⚘f3 ♗f7 15 ♕h3 fxg4 16 ♕xg4 ⚘d7 17 ♗d6+ ♔g8 18 0-0-0 ⚘f6 19 ♕f4 ♗h5 20 ♗e5 ♗xf3 21 ♕xf3 ♕e7 22 ☖g1 ☖f8 23 ♕g3

White can also bring his knight into the attack with 23 ⚘e2, when 23...⚘d7 24 ⚘f4 ⚘xe5 25 dxe5 h5 26 ♕g2 is deadly.

23...h5 24 ♗d6 h4 25 ♕e5

Also possible are 25 ♕h2 and 25 ♕g5, both of which look very strong.

25...♕d7 26 ♗xf8 ♔xf8 27 ⚘e2 ⚘h5 28 ♕b8+ ♔f7

After 28...♔e7? there is 29 ☖xg7+ ⚘xg7 30 ♕xh8 and White emerges a piece up.

29 ♗g6+ ♔e7 30 ♗xh5 ☖xb8 31 ☖xg7+ ♔d6 32 ☖xd7+ ♔xd7

The endgame is winning for White but he needs to make sure that Black's h-pawn is firmly blockaded. Khalifman handles any technical difficulties very well.

33 ♗g4 ♔d6 34 ♔d2 ♖g8 35 f3 e5 36 dxe5+ ♔xe5 37 ♔e1 ♖h8 38 ♗h3 c5 39 ♔f2 b5 40 ♘f4 ♖h6 41 ♘d3+ ♔d6 42 f4 b4 43 f5 c4 44 ♘f4 ♔e5 45 ♔f3 ♖d6 46 ♘h5

White also has 46 ♘e6 as after 46...♖a6 there follows 47 ♘c5 ♖xa2 48 ♘d7+ ♔d6 49 f6 etc.

46...d4 47 exd4+ ♖xd4 48 f6 ♖d8 49 ♗f1 ♔f5 50 ♗xc4 ♔g5 51 ♘f4 ♔xf6 52 ♘d5+ ♔g5 53 ♘xb4 ♖d2 54 ♔e3 ♖d1 55 ♘d3 h3 56 ♘f2 h2 57 b3 h1♕ 58 ♘xh1 ♖xh1 59 ♔d4 ♖h4+?

Black's last chance was 59...♔f6, when 60 ♔c5 ♔e7 61 ♔c6 ♖h2 62 ♗d3 ♔d8 63 ♔b7 a5 offers some practical chances.

60 ♔e5 ♔g4 61 ♗e6+ ♔f3 62 c4 ♖h2 63 c5 ♖xa2 64 c6 1-0

Game 70
I.Sokolov-Pr.Nikolic
Dutch Ch., Rotterdam 1998

---

1 d4 d5 2 ♘c3 f5 3 ♗g5 c6 4 e3

This quiet approach may not be White's best. Very sharp is 4 e4!

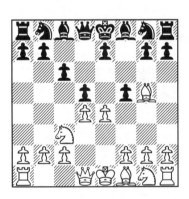

This looks far more dangerous for Black. 4...dxe4 5 f3 ♕b6 6 ♕d2 ♕xb2 7 ♖b1 e3!? 8 ♕xe3 ♕a3 9 ♗c4 presented White with excellent compensation for the pawn in Poluliakhov-Glek, USSR 1990, which leaves

4...fxe4: 5 f3 ♘f6 6 fxe4 dxe4 7 ♗c4 ♗g4!? 8 ♕d2 ♘bd7 9 h3 ♘b6 10 ♗b3 ♗h5 11 ♘ge2 h6 was Litus-Malaniuk, Katowice Open 1991, and now, instead of 12 ♗e3? ♘bd5 13 ♘g3 ♗g6, which was good for Black, 12 ♗xf6 exf6 13 ♘xe4 would have favoured White. White also maintains a strong initiative after either 7...♗f5 8 ♘ge2 ♘bd7 9 0-0 ♘b6 10 ♗b3 ♕d7 11 ♘g3, as in Bauer-M.Tseitlin, Bad Zwesten Open 1997, or 7...♘bd7 8 ♕e2 ♕a5 9 ♗d2 ♕f5 10 ♘h3 ♘b6 11 ♗b3, Popchev-Panbukchian, Bulgarian Ch., 1994.

Another interesting possibility is 4 ♕d3!?, when Glek-Fishbein, Philadelphia 1990 continued 4...♘a6 5 f3 ♕a5 6 ♕d2 ♘f6 7 a3 (the immediate 7 e4?! allows Black to equalise with 7...fxe4 8 ♘xe4 ♕xd2+ 9 ♘xd2 ♘b4) 7...b5 8 e4 fxe4 9 ♘xe4 ♕xd2+ 10 ♘xd2 ♗d7 11 ♘b3 e6 12 a4! ♘b4 13 ♔d1 bxa4 14 ♘c5 ♗xc5 15 dxc5 and White had slightly the better endgame. Perhaps 8...b4 should be tried, matters being far from clear after 9 ♘a2 fxe4 10 ♗xa6 ♗xa6 11 axb4 ♕b6.

Less good for White is 4 ♕d2 h6 5 ♗f4 ♘f6 6 f3 e6 because 7 e4?! here is dubious due to 7...fxe4 8 fxe4 ♗b4 etc.

4...♕b6 5 ♖b1 ♘d7 6 ♗d3 g6 7 h4

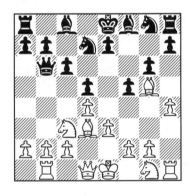

With White being unable to castle queenside I don't think this is the right plan. He might be well advised to choose a different move here:

a) After 7 ♘h3!? Black should find an alternative to 7...e5?! as White can then gain the advantage with 8 ♗xf5! ♗g7 9 ♗d3 exd4 10 exd4 ♗xd4 11 0-0 as in Loeffler-Videki, Kecskemet 1991.

b) 7 f4 is a heavyweight positional move used in Crouch-Galdunts, Krumbach Open 1991, when 7...♘gf6 8 ♘f3 ♘e4 9 ♗xe4 dxe4 10 ♘d2 ♛a6 11 g4 e6 gave rise to a complex positional battle.

c) As White's rook is already on b1, ready to support a queenside pawn advance, 7 ♘f3 ♗g7 8 ♘e2 ♘gf6 9 0-0 made a lot of sense in Dokhoian-Kisnev, Copenhagen Open 1991 as White is going to advance his queenside pawns. The game continued 9...♘e4 10 c4 h6 11 ♗h4 ♘df6 12 ♗xf6 ♘xf6 13 ♘e5 g5 14 ♘g3 e6 15 cxd5 cxd5 16 ♘h5 0-0 17 ♘xg7 ♔xg7 18 ♛a4 with a clear advantage.

7...♗g7 8 h5 h6 9 ♗f4 g5 10 ♗h2 e5!

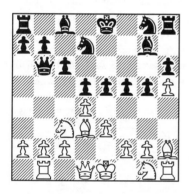

A strong move which solves Black's opening problems. After 10...e6 White can apply pressure to Black's kingside pawn structure with 11 g4!.

11 ♗xf5 exd4 12 exd4 ♘e7!

12...♗xd4 13 ♗g6+ ♔d8 14 ♛d2 leaves Black's king displaced.

13 ♛e2

Attempting to hold the pawn with 13 ♗xd7+ ♗xd7 14 ♘ge2 gives Black excellent counterplay after 14...♘f5 15 ♗e5 ♗xe5 16 dxe5 ♛c7 or 16...0-0-0. After either 14 ♘ce2 or 14 ♘f3?! Black can play 14...♗g4, while 14 ♗e5 is well met by 14...♗xe5 15 dxe5 ♖f8 or

15...0-0-0.

13...♛xd4?!

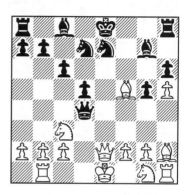

It might be even better to play 13...♗xd4!, when 14 ♗xd7+ ♗xd7 15 ♗e5 ♗xe5 16 ♛xe5 0-0-0 is very unpleasant for White. Alternatively 14 ♘d1 ♔d8! 15 ♗xd7 (or 15 ♗e6 ♖e8 16 c3 ♘f5 when White's king is getting caught in the centre) 15...♗xd7 and Black has a clear advantage due to his bishop pair and well centralised forces.

14 ♘f3 ♛f6 15 ♗e6

White is left with an unpleasant position after 15 ♗xd7+ ♗xd7 16 ♗e5 ♛f7 followed by castling long. At least Black cannot castle queenside when the bishops are exchanged on c8.

15...♘b6 16 ♗xc8 ♖xc8 17 0-0 0-0 18 ♘e5

There is a strong case for 18 ♗e5 to trade off Black's strong dark-squared bishop.

18...♖ce8 19 ♖be1 ♘f5

Preferable to 19...d4?! because after 20 ♘e4 ♛e6 21 ♘g4 White's knights take up threatening posts.

20 ♛g4 ♘h4 21 ♘d1 ♛e6 22 ♛b4 ♛c8 ½-½

Game 71
Romero Holmes-Vallejo Pons
Elgoibar 1997

1 d4 d5 2 ♘c3 f5 3 ♗g5 ♘c6

A somewhat strange looking move which does have certain points to it. Black develops a piece, covers the e5-square and gets himself a move closer to castling long. On the other hand the knight might be pinned by a bishop coming to b5, thus renewing the problem with the e5-square.

4 e3 g6

Dinstuhl-Hoffmann, Germany 1992 featured the weird 4...♕d7?!, when 5 ♘f3 seems the most sensible, threatening 6 ♗b5 followed by 7 ♘e5. In the game White played some strange moves himself, starting out with 5 ♕f3, and 5...e6 6 h3 ♗d6 7 a3 ♘ge7 8 ♗d3 0-0 9 ♗xe7 ♕xe7 10 ♘ge2 brought about a fairly equal game.

5 ♗b5

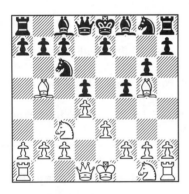

5...♘h6

Another odd move by Black. The simple 5...♘f6 looks better, 6 ♗xf6 exf6 7 ♕f3 a6 8

♗a4 ♗b4 9 ♘ge2 b5 10 ♗b3 ♘e7 giving Black a solid game in Vesely-Florian, Kosice 1961.

6 ♘f3 ♘f7 7 ♗f4 ♕d7?!

This move is completely beyond me. I would play simply 7...♗g7 in order to complete development.

8 ♘a4 e6

After 8...b6 9 c4 Black would be in all sorts of trouble, so he has to give up his dark-squared bishop, leading to other problems.

9 ♘c5 ♗xc5 10 dxc5 b6?

Black should probably play 10...♕e7, not that this is pleasant after 11 ♗xc6+ bxc6 12 ♕d4, clamping down on the e5-square. Now White seizes the opportunity to open things up.

11 c4! bxc5?

Black's last chance was to play 11...a6, when 12 ♗xc6 ♕xc6 13 cxd5 ♕xc5 14 0-0 ♕xd5 15 ♕xd5 exd5 16 ♗xc7 b5 is still excellent for White.

12 cxd5 exd5 13 ♖c1 c4 14 b3! ♖b8 15 bxc4 dxc4 16 ♕a4 ♖b6 17 ♕xc4!

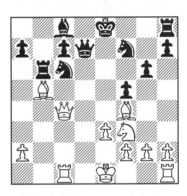

After 17 ♖d1 a6 18 ♖xd7 axb5 Black has some fighting chances. Now it's just a question of time.

17...♗b7 18 0-0 ♔d8

It can't have been easy to play this move but 18...0-0 runs into 19 ♘d4 etc.

19 ♖fd1 ♘d6 20 ♗xd6

White can also play 20 ♘e5 ♘xc4

(20...♘xe5 21 ♗g5+ wins the queen with check) 21 ♖xd7+ ♔c8 22 ♗xc4 with an extra piece.

20...cxd6 21 ♘d4 ♔c7 22 ♗a4

Another powerful move is 22 ♕a4, threatening – amongst other things – to double on the c-file.

22...♖c8 23 ♘b5+ ♔b8 24 ♘xd6 ♖d8 25 ♘f7

Also good is 25 ♘b5 ♕e7 26 ♕f4+ ♔a8 27 ♖xd8+ etc.

25...♕xd1+ 26 ♗xd1 ♖d7 27 ♗f3 ♖c7 28 ♘d6 ♗a6 29 ♕g8+ 1-0

1 d4 d5 2 ♘c3 c6

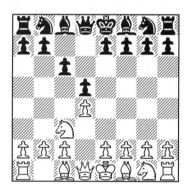

Naturally this could transpose to a Caro-Kann should White play 3 e4, but here we will look at an independent try for White which keeps the play along Veresov lines.

2...♘c6 is a peculiar response which leads to the Nimzowitsch Defence after 3 e4. Again an independent try is 3 ♗g5, when H.Myers-Sage, Chicago 1984 staggered along with the moves 3...h6 4 ♗h4 g5 5 ♗g3 ♗g4 6 f3 ♗h5 7 e3 ♗g7 8 ♗b5 ♕d7 9 ♘a4 e6 10 ♘c5 ♕c8 11 c3 ♘ge7 12 h4, with White clearly better. Not that this proves very much!

After 2...c5 we get a Chigorin Defence

with colours reversed and an extra tempo for White. Perhaps White can best exploit this with 3 e4 cxd4 (3...dxe4 4 d5 ♘f6 5 f3 exf3 6 ♘xf3 puts Black in a quite dangerous line of the Blackmar-Diemer Gambit as the inclusion of the moves ...c7-c5 and d4-d5 give White a lot of central space) 4 ♕xd4 dxe4 5 ♕xd8+ ♔xd8 6 ♘xe4 ♘f6 was played in Richter-Mieses, Swinemuende 1931, and now 7 ♘xf6 would have weakened Black's structure and left him with a permanent disadvantage. Richter's 7 ♘g5, on the other hand, earned only a temporary initiative.

2...♗f5 3 ♗g5 c6 transposes to the main game.

3 ♗g5 ♗f5

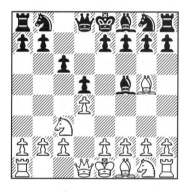

A preliminary 3...h6 doesn't help that much, but Black should certainly aim to castle kingside in this position. Hort-Hanley, Wijk aan Zee 2002 went 4 ♗h4 ♗f5 5 e3 ♘d7 6 ♗d3 ♗xd3 7 ♕xd3 ♘gf6 8 ♘f3 e6 9 e4 dxe4 10 ♘xe4 ♗e7 11 ♗g3 ♘xe4 12 ♕xe4 ♘f6 13 ♕e2 0-0 14 0-0 with only a slight space advantage for White to work with.

After the immediate 3...♕b6 White should play the sensible 4 ♖b1, e.g. 4...g6 5 e3 ♗g7 6 ♘f3 (6 ♗d3 ♘f6 7 f4 is well worth considering) 6...♘f6 7 ♗d3 ♗g4 8 h3 ♗xf3 9 gxf3!? ♘bd7 10 f4 e6 11 b4 which led to a heavyweight positional battle in Hoi-Rasmussen, Tonder 1993. However, in Khachian-Doroshenko, Bucharest 1993 White offered the b-pawn with 4 ♕d2, which turned out to be a good move when Black didn't take it and played 4...♗f5 instead!

4 e3 ♘d7

After 4...♕b6 the move 5 ♖b1 can come in handy in lines such as 5...♘d7 6 ♗d3 ♗xd3 7 cxd3 thanks to the possibility of a minority attack (b2-b4-b5).

5 ♗d3 ♗xd3 6 ♕xd3 ♕b6

Black should play simply 6...♘gf6 and aim to castle kingside.

7 0-0-0 0-0-0 8 ♘f3 g6 9 e4 dxe4 10 ♘xe4 h6 11 ♗e3 ♕a5 12 ♔b1

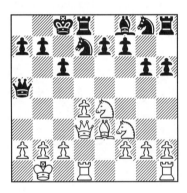

White's extra space gives him a clear edge. Black's version of the Caro-Kann looks distinctly dubious..

12...♗g7 13 c4 ♘gf6 14 ♘xf6 ♗xf6 15 ♖he1 ♔b8 16 ♗d2 ♕a6?!

Black's queen is awkwardly placed on this

square if White later moves one of his rooks along the third rank. Exchanging queens with 16...♕f5 is also bad after 17 ♕xf5 gxf5 18 ♗f4+ ♔c8 19 d5, so the modest 16...♕c7 is probably the right move.

17 ♕c2 e6 18 ♗f4+ ♔a8 19 c5 b6

Black must have been loathe to play this move, but she no doubt saw 20 ♖e3 coming.

20 ♗c7 ♖c8 21 ♗d6 ♖he8 22 ♖e3 ♕b7 23 ♖b3 ♗e7 24 ♗xe7 ♖xe7 25 ♘d2

The knight is heading for d6, which induces some additional desperation.

25...♕c7 26 g3 e5 27 cxb6 axb6 28 ♖e3 ♖ce8 29 d5 ♘b8 30 ♖a3+ ♔b7 31 d6! ♕xd6 32 ♘e4 ♕e6 33 ♘d6+ ♔c7 34 ♖a7+ ♔d8 35 ♘xf7+ ♔c8 36 ♘d6+ ♔d8 37 ♘b7+ ♔c8 38 ♘d6+ ♔d8 39 ♘xe8+ ♔xe8 40 ♖a8 1-0

A classy performance by Hort.

Summary

Despite Black's best efforts White can keep the game along Veresov lines by using subtle move orders. White is not obliged to transpose to the French, Caro-Kann or Nimzowitsch Defences, and can insist on the Veresov treatment should Black go for a Dutch with 2...f5.

1 d4 d5 2 ♘c3 f5

2...e6 3 ♘f3 ♗b4 *(D) - Game 66*

2...c6 3 ♗g5 *- Game 72*

3 ♗g5 *(D)* **♘f6**

3...g6 *- Game 69*; 3...c6 *- Game 70*; 3...♘c6 *- Game 71*

4 f3 *(D)*

4...♘c6 *- Game 67*; 4...c6 *- Game 68*

3...♗b4

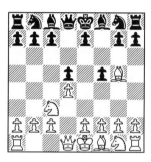

3 ♗g5

4 f3

CHAPTER TEN

1...♘f6 2 ♘c3: 2...c5, 2...d6, 2...g6 and Others

1 d4 ♘f6 2 ♘c3

By refusing to meet 1 d4 ♘f6 2 ♘c3 with 2...d5 Black announces his intention to try to unbalance the position. With 2...c5 he invites transposition to a Schmid Benoni (with 3 d5), 2...d6 and 2...g6 would lead to a Czech or Pirc Defence after 3 e4 and 2...e6 prepares to play a French after 3 e4 d5. To avoid playing in your opponent's back garden we need some more 'Veresov' moves and ideas.

There aren't too many players who enjoy the Schmid Benoni after 2...c5 3 d5 but this can occasionally crop up and White must have a plan of action. I think that the move which is most in the spirit of the Veresov is 3 ♗g5, which officially transposes to a line of the Trompovsky (1 d4 ♘f6 2 ♗g5 c5 3 ♘c3) and leads to very sharp play. The main line occurs after 3...cxd4 4 ♕xd4 ♘c6 5 ♕h4 e6 when White will hoist the pirate flag by castling long (see Miladinovic-Gustafsson). Varying with 5...b5 worked out alright for Black in Grimm-Tseitlin but White played very passively in this game and he can improve by castling long on move 7 or 8. Black's other options are to play 3...♕a5 and 3...♕b6, which are covered in De la Villa-Glavina Rossi.

If White wants a somewhat quieter life he might well consider 3 dxc5, as in Mestrovic-

Medic. This takes the game right off the beaten track and results in positions in which Black has to be careful. In theory Black may be able to equalise but in practice he has experienced some difficulties.

As far as the 'attempted Pirc' is concerned, White can meet 2...g6 with 3 ♗g5, after which 3...d6 can be met with 4 ♗xf6 (Klinger-Maxion). Generally speaking I'm not very fond of this exchange on f6 but here Black is several moves further away from his best set up (one with pawns on d5 and f5). If he protects the knight with 3...♗g7, then White can prepare to exchange this bishop and castle long with 4 ♕d2.

If Black plays 2...d6 a transposition is possible after 3 ♗g5 g6 4 ♗xf6, but there is another option in 3...♘bd7. In Fahnenschmidt-Eis the game transposed to a line of the Philidor in which White's bishop is supposed to be poorly placed on g5. However, I'm not so sure this is the case.

In the event of 2...e6 White would normally play 3 e4, when 3...d5 is a Classical French. But we can avoid transposing directly to a French by playing 3 ♗g5. If Black then plays 3...d5 we would be in Chapter 8. 3...h6 4 ♗xf6 ♕xf6 5 e4 leads to a line of the Trompovsky and is covered in Anand-Karpov and Hall-De Firmian.

Game 73
Miladinovic-Gustafsson
Germany-Greece Match, Fuerth 2002

1 d4 ♘f6 2 ♘c3 c5 3 ♗g5!?

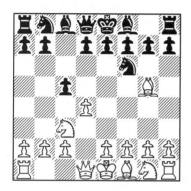

The 'Veresov' move, though this position usually arises via a Trompovsky move order (1 d4 ♘f6 2 ♗g5 c5 3 ♘c3). White's 'best' move may well be 3 d5 which transposes into a Schmid Benoni, but here we'll concern ourselves with the move which is most in the spirit of the Veresov.

3...cxd4

3...d5 transposes to Chapter 4, and 3...♕a5 is examined in the game De la Villa-Glavina Rossi. One other possibility for Black is 3...♕b6, when Gufeld and Stetsko consider only 4 d5 ♕xb2 5 ♗d2 with a Trompovsky. White has an interesting alternative in 4 ♘f3, when Nataf-Levacic, Cannes 1996 continued 4...cxd4 (after 4...♕xb2 White can play 5 ♘a4 ♕b4+ 6 c3 ♕a5 7 ♘xc5 d6 8 ♘b3 ♕xc3+ 9 ♘fd2 ♘c6 10 ♗xf6 gxf6 11 e3 with compensation for the pawn) 5 ♕xd4 ♕xd4 6 ♘xd4 ♘c6 7 ♘db5 ♖b8 8 0-0-0 a6 9 ♘c7+ ♔d8 10 ♘7d5 and White had strong pressure. Also worth consideration is 4 ♗xf6 gxf6 5 ♘d5.

4 ♕xd4 ♘c6 5 ♕h4

This position is very interesting for both sides. White intends to castle queenside, push e2-e4 and f2-f4. Black, on the other hand,

can develop a strong attack on the queenside in case White castles immediately.

5...e6

The most common move, but not the only one. In De la Villa-Miezis, Elgoibar 1995 Black played 5...d6, although after 6 e4 ♗e6 7 ♗d3 ♖c8 8 ♘ge2 ♘e5 9 f4 ♘xd3+ 10 cxd3 ♕b6 11 f5 White had more space, a lead in development and active pieces. For 5...b5 see Grimm-Tseitlin.

6 e4

White has also played the immediate 6 0-0-0, transposing after 7 e4.

6...♗e7

After 6...h6 White should probably play 7 0-0-0 with similar play to the main line, while in reply to 7 f4 Black has 7...♕b6, when 8 0-0-0? is bad in view of 8...♘h7!.

7 f4

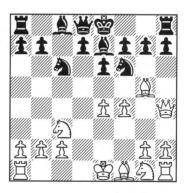

It may well be that 7 0-0-0 is a more accurate move order. This can also lead to the position after White's 9th move but with different divergences being possible en route. For example 7...♕a5 8 f4 d6 9 ♘f3 leads back to the game, 7...a6 8 f4 b5 9 e5 b4 10 exf6 gxf6 11 ♘e4 fxg5 12 fxg5 ♕a5 13 ♔b1 b3 14 axb3 ♘b4 15 ♘f6+ ♔d8!? 16 ♕d4 ♕a2+ 17 ♔c1 ♕a1+ 18 ♔d2 produced a wild situation in Vaganian-Knaak, Tallinn 1979 which White went on to win, 7...0-0 8 f4 h6 9 ♘f3 hxg5 10 ♘xg5 ♕c7! 11 e5! ♘xe5 12 ♘d5! exd5 13 fxe5 ♕xe5 14 ♖e1 ♕f5! 15 ♖xe7 ♕g4! 16 ♖xg4 ♘xg4 17 ♗b5! gave White the better endgame in Krasenkow-Degraeve, Cappelle la Grande 1990 and 7...h6 8 f4 ♖g8 9 ♗xf6 ♗xf6 10 ♕g3 ♗xc3 11 ♕xc3 ♕a5 12 ♕xa5 ♘xa5 13 e5 g5! gave Black quite a good endgame in Dorfanis-Atalik, Katarini 1993. In this last variation one should note that 9 ♘f3 hxg5 10 fxg5 leaves Black's knight on f6 without a move, and I wonder if White can use this to develop his initiative.

Besides the ultra-violent lines based on castling long, White can also consider going the other way. Conquest-S.Garcia, Havana 1996 went 7 ♘f3 ♕a5 8 ♗b5 d6 9 0-0 ♗d7 10 ♖fe1 a6?! (10...0-0 is probably better) 11 ♗xc6 ♗xc6 12 e5 dxe5 13 ♘xe5 ♖c8 14 ♖ad1 0-0?! (14...♕b4) 15 ♖d3! when, suddenly, White had a very potent attack. The game concluded 15...♕b4 16 f4 ♕b6+ 17 ♔h1 ♕xb2 18 ♖g3 ♔h8 19 ♗h6 g6 (19...gxh6? 20 ♕xh6 ♘e8 allows 21 ♕xf8+ ♗xf8 22 ♘xf7 mate) 20 ♗g5 ♔g7 21 ♕h6+ ♔g8 22 ♗xf6 1-0, since 22...♗xf6 23 ♖h3 leads to forced mate.

7...d6

The main argument against 7 f4 is that Black can use the fact that White hasn't castled to play an immediate 7...b5!?, Nei-Taimanov, USSR 1981 continuing 8 e5 b4!? 9 ♘b5 (9 exf6 gxf6 is better for Black) 9...a6 10 ♘d6+ (10 exf6 gxf6 11 ♘d6+ ♗xd6 12 ♗xf6 ♗e7 13 ♗xe7 ♕xe7 also leaves Black with the more compact structure) 10...♗xd6 11

exd6 ♘d4!? and now, according to Taimanov, White should play 12 ♗d3 when 12...♗b7 13 ♕f2 h6 14 ♗h4 ♘b5 15 ♗xb5 axb5 16 ♘f3 is complex. In the game 12 0-0-0 ♘f5 13 ♗xf6 ♘xh4 14 ♗xd8 ♖xd8 15 ♘e2 ♗b7 16 ♖g1 f6!? gave Black the better endgame due to the pressure against White's kingside. Note that here (7...b5) 8 ♘xb5 ♕a5+ 9 ♘c3 ♘xe4 is just bad for White, and 8 ♗xb5 ♕b6 gives Black compensation for the pawn.

Another attempt to reveal the dark side of 7 f4 is with 7...♕b6, when Ochoa-Browne, New York 1989 went 8 0-0-0 ♕e3+ 9 ♔b1 ♘xe4 10 ♘xe4 ♕xe4 11 ♗d3 ♕xg5 12 ♕xg5 ♕d4 13 ♘f3 ♕f6 14 ♕h5 ♕xf4 15 ♘g5 ♘e5 16 ♖hf1 ♕g4 17 ♕xg4 ♘xg4 18 ♘xf7 ♖f8 19 ♘d6+ ♔e7 20 ♖xf8 ♔xf8 21 ♗xh7 ♔e7 22 h3 ♘e3 23 ♖d2 ♘d5 24 ♘xc8+ ♖xc8 25 ♗e4 and White had the better endgame, though it's not clear what was happening en route.

8 0-0-0 ♕a5 9 ♘f3

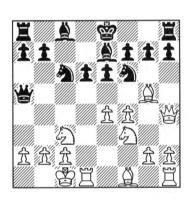

9...h6

This has been applauded as being Black's best option, although it seems that there are other possibilities:

a) 9...♗d7 looks like a natural developing move, when 10 ♕e1, 10 ♗b5 and 10 ♗d3 all seem reasonable for Black after 10...h6. However, 10 ♘d2 with the idea of 11 ♘c4 is problematic for Black, Sell-Berger, Germany 1999 continuing 10...♖c8 11 ♘c4 ♕c5 12

♘a4 ♛b4, and now 13 a3 ♛xa4 14 b3 ♛a6 15 ♘xd6+ wins Black's queen for what appears to be inadequate compensation.

b) 9...a6 protects b5 (when 10 ♘d2 can be met by 10...b5) but Black needs a good answer to 10 ♛e1, as 10...b5 11 e5 b4 12 exf6 gxf6 13 ♗xf6 ♗xf6 14 ♘e4 was good for White in Mensch-Nicoara, France 1999.

c) 9...0-0 seems to 'castle into it' but I don't see any concrete objection.

10 e5

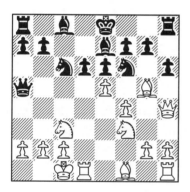

This seems to be most in the spirit of the opening, but White has also played a preliminary 10 ♗b5. Rabinovich-Gershon, Israel 1996 went 10...♗d7 11 e5 dxe5 12 ♘xe5 ♘xe5 13 fxe5 ♗xb5 14 ♘xb5 (14 exf6 ♗c6 was good for Black in Sjodahl-Akesson, Sundsvall 1989) 14...♛xb5 15 exf6 ♛xg5+ and Black had a large advantage in the endgame. According to Serper White should play 12 ♗xc6! ♗xc6 13 ♘xe5, after which 13...♖c8 is equal in his view but nice for Black in mine. White should avoid 12 fxe5? ♘xe5.

10...dxe5 11 fxe5 ♘xe5 12 ♘xe5

In Iuldachev-Serper, Tashkent 1993 White played 12 ♗b5+ ♗d7 13 ♘xe5 ♗xb5 14 ♘xf7!? but after 14...♔xf7 15 ♗xf6 ♗xf6 16 ♛h5+ ♔g8 17 ♛xb5 ♗xc3 18 ♛xb7 ♗xb2+! 19 ♛xb2 (19 ♔xb2? ♛e5+!) 19...♔h7 White's king was the more exposed.

12...♛xe5 13 ♗b5+ ♔f8 14 ♗f4

This position is very complicated and dif-

ficult to assess. White clearly has compensation for the pawn thanks to his superior development and Black's loss of castling rights. But is it enough?

14...♛c5 15 ♛e1 a6 16 ♗d3

Probably the best square for the bishop as after 16 ♗a4 b5 17 ♗b3 ♗b7 Black gains time for development.

16...♗d7 17 ♖f1

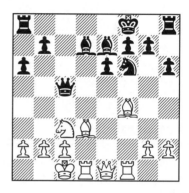

A logical move, eyeing Black's king down the f-file. In San Emeterio-Lalic, Madrid 2001, White allowed exchanges before playing this move, but after 17 ♘e4 ♘xe4 18 ♗xe4 ♗c6 19 ♖f1 ♖c8 20 ♗g6 ♗e8 21 ♗d6 ♛g5+ 22 ♔b1 ♛xg6 23 ♗xe7+ ♔g8 his compensation disappeared. Kalinitschew-Gustafsson, Dresden 2002 varied with 17 ♖g1 ♗c6 18 g4 ♖d8 19 h4 ♗f3 20 g5 hxg5 21 hxg5 ♘d5 22 ♘xd5 ♛xd5 but here White saw nothing better than going into an endgame a pawn down after 23 ♗e2 ♛xd1+ 24 ♗xd1 ♖xd1+ etc.

17...♗c6 18 g4 ♖d8

Can Black get away with 18...♘xg4 here? It is certainly not for the faint-hearted, but I don't see a clear attacking line for White. Practical trials would be helpful...

19 ♗e3 ♛e5 20 ♛f2 ♗b4!? 21 ♘e2 ♖d7! 22 h3 ♔e8 23 ♗d4

White could also consider safeguarding his king with 23 ♔b1 before undertaking positive action.

23...♛d5

23...♕g5+ 24 ♔b1 ♘e4 25 ♗xe4 ♗xe4 26 ♘f4 is quite promising for White, who threatens 27 ♘h5, while 26...e5 can be answered with 27 ♕e2.

24 ♗xf6 gxf6 25 ♔b1

Snatching back the pawn with 25 ♕xf6? leaves Black with much the better endgame after 25...♕g5+ 26 ♔b1 ♕xf6 27 ♖xf6 ♗e7 and 28...h5.

25...♗e7 26 ♘f4 ♕c5!

Offering to return the pawn in order to exchange queens. Stubbornly hanging on to the booty with 26...♕g5 puts Black under considerable pressure after 27 ♖de1 (or perhaps 27 ♘h5!?).

27 ♕xc5 ½-½

Black might have considered playing on as after 27...♗xc5 28 ♘h5 ♗e7 29 ♘xf6+ ♗xf6 30 ♖xf6 ♔f8 his passed e-pawn might become dangerous.

Game 74
Grimm-Mi.Tseitlin
Passau 1998

---

1 d4 ♘f6 2 ♘c3 c5 3 ♗g5 cxd4 4 ♕xd4 ♘c6 5 ♕h4 b5!? 6 e4

Not 6 ♘xb5? in view of 6...♕b6!, when the b2-pawn falls. White has an alternative in 6 0-0-0, after which 6...b4 7 ♘d5 ♕a5 8 e4 ♕xa2 9 ♘c7+ ♔d8 10 ♘xa8 ♕a1+ 11 ♔d2 ♕xb2 produces a wild position which is difficult to assess with any accuracy, while 6...e6

7 ♗xf6 gxf6 8 ♘e4 ♗e7 9 ♘d6+ ♗xd6 10 ♖xd6 ♔e7 11 ♖d1 was quite good for White in Puranen-Shishkov, Paide 1999.

6...a6 7 ♘f3?!

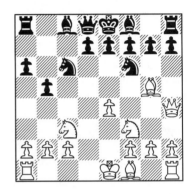

The critical line seems to be 7 0-0-0 ♕a5 (7...h6 8 ♘d5 ♗b7 9 ♗xf6 gxf6 10 ♘e2 ♕a5 11 ♔b1 was good for White in Nei-Diesen, Helsinki 1990) 8 ♔b1 d6 9 ♘ge2 ♗e6 (9...b4 10 ♗xf6 gxf6 11 ♘d5 looks better for White), and now instead of 10 ♘c1, as in A.Jackson-Gladyszev, Isle of Man 2000, 10 ♗xf6 gxf6 11 ♘f4 looks better for White.

7...d6 8 ♗e2?!

White's plan of castling kingside is quite out of the spirit of the position. Here too I prefer 8 0-0-0; White's king seems safe enough on the queenside.

8...e6 9 ♗xf6?! ♕xf6 10 ♕xf6 gxf6 11 0-0-0 ♗b7 12 ♘d4 ♖c8

This endgame is better for Black's two bishops.

13 ♘xc6 ♗xc6 14 a4 ♖g8 15 ♖hg1 bxa4 16 ♗xa6 ♖b8 17 ♖d4? ♖g5

Missing an opportunity presented by White's last move. Black can play even more strongly with 17...♗h6+ 18 ♔b1 ♗f4, when the bishop is coming to e5 with great effect.

18 ♗d3?

White should play 18 g3 in order to meet 18...♖c5 19 ♖c4 ♖xc4 20 ♗xc4 ♗h6+ with 21 f4. The entry of Black's dark-squared bishop will decide matters.

18...♖c5 19 ♖c4?!

19 ♘a2 is more tenacious.

19...♗h6+ 20 ♔b1 ♖xc4 21 ♗xc4 ♗d2 22 ♔a2 ♗xc3 23 bxc3 ♗xe4 24 ♗d3 ♗xd3 25 cxd3 ♖b3 26 ♖c1 d5 27 d4 f5 28 g3 h5 29 h4 ♔e7 30 c4 dxc4 31 ♖xc4 ♖f3 0-1

A bit of a lame performance from White.

Game 75
De la Villa-Glavina Rossi
Zaragoza Open 1995

---

1 d4 ♘f6 2 ♘c3 c5 3 ♗g5 ♕a5 4 ♗xf6 gxf6 5 e3

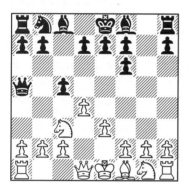

White can also gain space with 5 d5, though 5...f5 clears a nice diagonal for Black's dark-squared bishop and gives him greater potential for counterplay. Plachetka-Ftacnik, Frenstat 1982 continued 6 e3 ♗g7 7 ♕d2 d6 8 ♘ge2 ♘d7 9 ♘f4 ♘b6 10 ♗b5+ ♔f8 11 ♗e2 ♕b4 12 ♘d3 ♕a5 13 ♘f4 ♗d7 and White's queenside came under fire.

5...d6?!

This natural looking move has surprisingly serious consequences due to the weakening of Black's light squares. In this position 5...f5 has nothing like the same effect as the a1–h8 diagonal is blocked by the pawn on d4. Shereshevsky-Veremeichik, Minsk 1978 continued 6 ♕h5 cxd4 7 exd4 ♕b6 8 0-0-0 ♕h6+ 9 ♕xh6 ♗xh6+ 10 ♔b1 d6 11 g3 ♗d7 12 ♗g2 ♗c6 13 d5 ♗d7 14 f4 and White had a significant space advantage and poten-

tial pressure on the e-file.

After 5...e6 White played 6 ♕h5 in Llobel Cortell-Zapata, Andorra 2002, and after 6...d5 7 0-0-0 cxd4 8 exd4 ♘c6 9 ♔b1 ♗d7 10 ♘ge2 ♖c8 he should have played 11 f4, intending f4-f5 with promising play. In the game 11 ♕f3 was rather pointless. 6 d5 ♗g7 7 ♘ge2 ♘a6 8 g3 ♘c7 9 ♗g2 ♘b5 10 0-0 ♘xc3 11 ♘xc3 f5 wasn't clear in De la Villa-Wiersma, Berlin 1997.

If Black plays a preliminary 5...cxd4 6 exd4 and then 6...e6 White can't put his queen on h5. 7 d5 ♗a3 8 ♕c1 ♕b4 9 ♖b1 ♕xc3+ 10 bxc3 ♗xc1 11 ♖xc1 b6 was fine for Black in Mi.Tseitlin-Pokojowczyk, Slupsk 1978, but 7 ♕f3 f5 8 0-0-0 looks quite good to me. 6...d6 7 ♗b5+ ♗d7 8 ♗xd7+ ♘xd7 9 ♕f3 e6 10 ♘ge2 was good for White in De la Villa-Glavina Rossi, Aceimar 1995.

6 ♕h5 ♘c6 7 ♗c4 e6

The only other way to defend f7 is with 7...♘d8 but then 8 ♗b5+ is very unpleasant.

8 d5!

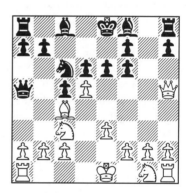

8...♘e5

8...éxd5 9 ♗xd5 is horrible for Black in view of his pawn weaknesses, but the text is not much better.

9 dxe6 ♔d8 10 e7+ ♗xe7 11 ♗e2 b5 12 ♘f3 ♗b7 13 ♘xe5 fxe5 14 0-0-0 f6

Ugly, but by now there is little choice. After 14...b4 there follows 15 ♕xe5 ♖g8 16 ♖xd6+ ♗xd6 17 ♕xd6+ ♔c8 18 ♘d5 etc.

15 ♗xb5 a6 16 ♗a4 ♕c7 17 ♘d5 ♗xd5

18 ⦰xd5

The opposite coloured bishops favour White in this position due to Black's appalling weaknesses on the light squares. There's little he can do to repair the damage.

18...⦰b8 19 ⦰hd1 ⦰b6 20 ⦰f7 ⦰c8 21 ⦰5d3 ⦰b7 22 ⦰b3 ⦰a7 23 ⦰d5 a5 24 ⦰a3 ⦰b5 25 ⦰c4 ⦰b7 26 ⦰dd3 ⦰hb8 27 ⦰db3 ⦰b4 28 c3 d5

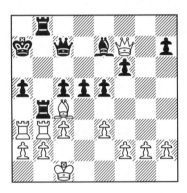

A final attempt to complicate matters which White could probably have negotiated more effectively. 28...⦰xb3 29 axb3 leaves Black with no counterplay whatsoever.

29 cxb4 cxb4 30 ⦰xa5+

I prefer 30 ⦰xd5, when 30...bxa3 31 ⦰xb8 ⦰xb8 32 b3 should be winning for White.

30...⦰xa5 31 ⦰xd5 ⦰c7 32 ⦰f7?

32 ⦰b1 is better, now Black gets right back into it.

32...⦰c8 33 ⦰d2 ⦰xc4?

Returning the favour. 33...e4! poses White unexpectedly difficult problems as it takes escape squares from the king and leaves the rook stuck on b3.

34 ⦰xe7+ ⦰c7 35 ⦰d6 f5 36 ⦰xb4 ⦰c1+ 37 ⦰e2 ⦰c2+ 38 ⦰d2 ⦰c6 39 f3 f4 40 exf4 ⦰a6+ 41 ⦰f2 1-0

Game 76
Mestrovic-Medic
Pula Open 1996

---

1 d4 ⦰f6 2 ⦰c3 c5 3 dxc5

Mestrovic has shown a preference for capture, which leads to Sicilian type structures.

3...e6

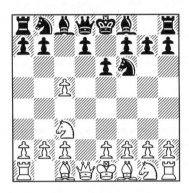

After 3...⦰a5 Mestrovic has most recently played 4 a3!?, when 4...⦰xc5 5 e4 d6 6 ⦰e3 ⦰a5 7 ⦰d3 g6 8 ⦰d2 ⦰c6 9 ⦰b5!? ⦰d8 10 0-0-0 a6 11 ⦰c3 b5 12 ⦰d5 ⦰xd5 13 exd5 left him with a significant space advantage in Mestrovic-Termeulen, Gent 1999. This is an improvement on 4 ⦰f3 e6 5 ⦰d2 ⦰xc5 6 e4 d5 7 ⦰b3 ⦰c7 8 exd5 ⦰b4 9 ⦰b5+ ⦰d7 10 ⦰xd7+ ⦰xd7 11 0-0 ⦰xc3 12 bxc3 ⦰xd5, which left him with the inferior position in Mestrovic-Fercec, Zadar 1997.

4 e4 ⦰c6 5 ⦰e3

Making Black agree to the exchange of dark-squared bishops before returning the pawn. In Mestrovic-G.Horvath, Keszthely 1981 White played 5 ⦰f3 but after 5...⦰xc5 6 ⦰d3 ⦰c7 7 0-0 a6 8 ⦰e2 ⦰g4 Black had a thoroughly satisfactory position.

5...⦰a5 6 ⦰d3 ⦰xc5 7 ⦰xc5 ⦰xc5 8 ⦰f3 0-0 9 0-0 a6

This position contains just a dash of poison. In order to cover his dark squares Black should put a pawn on d6 but this pawn can then become a target. A sample is 9...d6 10 a3 e5 11 h3 ⦰e6 12 ⦰a4 ⦰a5 13 c4 with the better game for White. Mestrovic-Tomasic, Opatija 1995 varied with 9...h6, when 10 a3 d5 11 ⦰e2 a6 12 ⦰ad1 b5 13 ⦰fe1 b4 14 axb4 ⦰xb4 15 ⦰b1 ⦰b7 16 exd5 exd5 gave White an edge thanks to the isolated d-pawn.

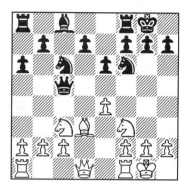

10 a3 ♘g4 11 ♘a4 ♛a7

This allows a clever reply, but in any case White has something. 11...♛a5 12 c4 gives White a space advantage.

12 e5! f5

The point behind White's last move is that 12...♘cxe5 is answered by 13 ♘xe5 ♘xe5 14 ♗xh7+ ♔xh7 15 ♛h5+ followed by 16 ♛xe5, when Black has serious weaknesses on the dark squares. In the game Black is also left with pawn weaknesses.

13 exf6 ♘xf6 14 c4 d5 15 ♛e2 ♗d7 16 b4 ♖ae8 17 ♘c5 ♗c8 18 ♛c2 dxc4 19 ♛xc4 ♔h8 20 ♘e4 e5 21 ♘fg5

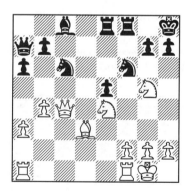

Switching from positional play to a direct attack. The threat is 22 ♘f7+.

21...♘xe4 22 ♗xe4 ♖f4

After 22...g6 there follows 23 ♗xg6 hxg6 24 ♛h4+ ♔g7 25 ♛h7+ ♔f6 26 ♘e4+ with a winning attack.

23 g3 ♖f6 24 ♘f7+ ♔g8 25 ♘g5+ ♔h8 26 ♗g6?

Spectacular but quite wrong – the players could have been in time-trouble around here. The obvious 26 ♘xh7 is winning.

26...♖e7?

Missing a chance to get back into the game with 26...♖ef8! when Black is suddenly threatening the f2-pawn.

27 ♖ad1 ♛b6 28 ♗xh7 ♗e6 29 ♘xe6 ♔xh7 30 ♖d6 ♔h8 31 ♛h4+ ♔g8 32 ♘g5 ♖h6 33 ♛c4+ ♔f8 34 ♖fd1 ♛c7 35 ♖xh6 gxh6 36 ♘e6+ ♖xe6 37 ♛xe6 ♘d4 38 ♛xh6+ ♔g8 39 ♛g6+ ♔h8 40 ♛e4 ♔g8 41 ♛d5+ 1-0

Game 77
Klinger-Maxion
Bad Wörishofen 1990

---

1 d4 ♘f6 2 ♘c3 g6 3 ♗g5 d6

If Black plays 3...♗g7 in this position it makes sense for White to set about exchanging his dark-squared bishop with 4 ♛d2. Chubenko-Babaev, Baku 2000 continued 4...d6 (4...d5 transposes to Reprintsev-Kachar from Chapter 7) 5 0-0-0 0-0 6 h4!? c6 and now rather than the wild 7 g4!? (which, admittedly, gives White compensation after 7...♗xg4 8 f3 ♗e6 and now 9 h5!) White could have played 7 h5!, opening the h-file.

4 ♗xf6 exf6 5 g3

White has established slightly the better

pawn structure. The problem for Black is that the only effective arrangement for his pawns is to play ...d6-d5 and ...f6-f5 followed by bringing his knight to f6 via d7. But in the current position this takes time.

5...♗g7 6 ♗g2 0-0 7 ♘h3 ♖e8

Had Black tried the immediate 7...f5 White could play 8 0-0 ♘d7 9 e3 ♘f6 10 ♘f4 ♖e8 11 ♘ce2 d5 12 b3 intending 13 c4.

8 0-0 c6 9 e3 ♘d7 10 ♘e4 ♘f8 11 ♘f4 d5 12 ♘d2 ♘e6 13 ♘d3 ♘g5 14 c4

White could also prepare this thrust with 14 b3.

14...dxc4 15 ♘xc4 ♗e6 16 ♖c1 ♗d5 17 ♘f4 ♗xg2 18 ♔xg2 ♘e6 19 ♘xe6 ♕d5+?!

I don't understand why Black wanted to recapture on e6 with the queen rather than rectifying some of the damage to his pawn structure. After 19...fxe6 20 b4 White has a small but clear advantage, with extra space and a queenside bind.

20 ♕f3 ♕xe6 21 b4 ♖ad8 22 ♘a5 ♕e7 23 b5 ♖d5

Allowing White a decisive positional sacrifice of a piece. In any case Black's position is very difficult; after 23...cxb5 24 ♘xb7 White's control of the c5-square secures control of the c-file.

24 ♘xb7! ♕xb7 25 bxc6 ♕b5 26 c7 ♖c8 27 ♖b1 ♕d7 28 ♖b8 ♖h5

White wins material after 28...♖b5 29 ♕a8.

29 ♖c1! ♗f8

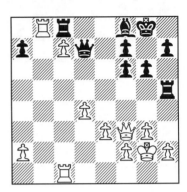

If Black first grabs the h2-pawn with 29...♕h3+ 30 ♔g1 ♕xh2+ (30...♗f8 31 ♕g2) 31 ♔f1 and then plays 31...♗f8 there follows 32 ♔e2! ♖xc7 33 ♖xc7 ♖f5 34 ♕xf5! gxf5 35 ♖cc8 with a winning position for White.

30 h4 ♖xc7 31 ♕a8 ♖a5

31...♖xc1 introduces a mate: 32 ♖xf8+ ♔g7 33 ♖g8+ ♔h6 34 ♕f8.

32 ♖xc7 ♕xc7 33 ♖xf8+ ♔g7 34 ♖g8+ ♔h6 35 ♕f3 f5 36 e4 ♕c1 37 g4 fxg4 38 ♕xf7 ♖a3 39 ♕g7+ ♔h5 40 ♕xh7+ ♕h6 41 ♖h8 1-0

Game 78
Fahnenschmidt-Eis
Rheda-Wiedenbrueck 2001

---

1 d4 ♘f6 2 ♘c3 d6 3 ♗g5 ♘bd7

Besides 3...g6 (as in Klinger-Maxion)

Black can try 3...c6, when I suggest waiting for a move with 4 ♘f3. Then 4...b5 (4...♘bd7 5 e4 e5 6 ♗c4 transposes to the note to Black's 5th move, below) 5 ♗xf6 exf6 6 e3 favours White due to Black's compromised pawn structure.

4 e4 e5 5 ♘f3 ♗e7

After 5...c6 6 ♗c4 b5 7 ♗b3 a6 8 a4 b4 (8...♗b7 9 d5 b4 10 dxc6 ♗xc6 11 ♘d5 also looks like an edge for White) 9 ♘e2 h6 10 ♗xf6 ♕xf6 11 0-0 Black's weak pawns on the queenside are a target. White can also play 6 a4, when 6...h6 7 ♗e3 ♘g4 8 ♗c1 exd4 9 ♕xd4 ♘de5 10 ♗e2 ♗e7 11 0-0 ♗f6 12 ♕d1 ♘xf3+ 13 ♗xf3 ♘e5 14 ♗e2 0-0 15 f4 ♘g6 16 ♕d3 was slightly better for White in Vaganian-Kasparov, USSR Ch., Minsk 1979.

6 ♗c4 0-0 7 0-0 c6 8 a4 ♕c7

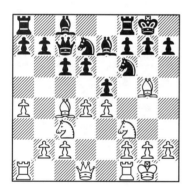

We have reached a Philidor Defence in which conventional wisdom states that White's bishop is not too effectively placed on g5. I'm not at all sure about this, as you shall see. In Bronstein-Summerscale, Hastings 1995, Black varied with 8...b6, when 9 ♖e1 a6 10 ♕d3 ♗b7 11 ♖ad1 ♕c7 12 ♘h4 g6 would have left White with a pull after 13 ♘f3, intending ♗h6 and ♘g5. In the game Bronstein played 13 ♘e2, but then 13...exd4 14 ♘xd4 ♘e5 15 ♕b3 ♘xc4 16 ♕xc4 ♘xe4! 17 ♘e6! fxe6 18 ♕xe6+ ♖f7 19 ♗xe7 d5 20 ♗a3 ♕c8 21 ♕xc8+ ♖xc8 left him slightly worse in the endgame.

9 h3

I prefer this calm waiting move to the 9 ♕e2 of Rausis-Areklett, Pelaro 2002, though there too White had a little something after 9...♖e8 10 ♗h4 ♘b6 11 dxe5 dxe5 12 ♗b3 ♗g4 13 h3 ♗xf3 14 ♕xf3 ♖ad8 15 ♘e2 ♘c8 16 ♘g3 thanks to the latent pressure against f7.

9...♖e8 10 ♖e1 ♘f8

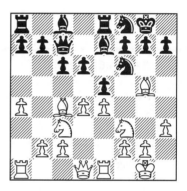

The most typical 'Philidor' move is 10...b6, but here the position of White's bishop on g5 has an interesting effect. After 11 d5 ♗b7 (11...c5 12 a5 leaves Black very cramped) 12 ♗xf6! ♘xf6 13 dxc6 ♗xc6 14 ♕d3 White has control over the d5-square.

11 ♕d2 a6?!

Allowing White to mark the b6-square down as a weakness. A more consistent follow-up to Black's previous move would have been 11...♘g6 but then 12 a5 still leaves White with a slight plus.

12 a5 ♗e6 13 ♗f1 ♖ad8 14 ♗e3 c5?!

White was menacing the b6-square but the cure is worse than the disease. Black should probably hang tough with 14...♕b8.

15 dxe5 dxe5 16 ♕c1 ♗d7

It looks wrong to retreat the bishop like this – 16...h6 must surely be a better move. However, White would have an edge after 17 ♘d2 followed by 18 ♘c4 with insidious pressure mounting due to Black's weak squares.

17 ♗c4 ♗e6 18 ♖a4 ♗d7? 19 ♘g5! ♘e6

20 ♘xe6 ♗xe6 21 ♗xe6 fxe6 22 ♕a1 ♗d6 23 ♖c4 ♕e7 24 ♘a4

Concentrating further on the c5-pawn. Black's position goes rapidly downhill.

24...♖c8 25 ♕a3 ♘d7 26 ♖d1 ♖c6 27 ♕d3 b5 28 axb6 ♘xb6 29 ♘xb6 ♖xb6 30 b4 ♖c8 31 bxc5 ♗xc5 32 ♖xc5 1-0

32...♖xc5 33 ♕d8+ wins a piece.

Game 79
Anand-Karpov
FIDE World Ch., Lausanne 1998

1 d4 ♘f6 2 ♘c3 e6 3 ♗g5 h6

Black has another independent try in 3...c5, when 4 d5 ♕b6 5 ♗xf6 gxf6 6 ♖b1 f5 7 e3 ♗g7 8 ♘ge2 d6 9 g3 ♘d7 was the continuation of Riedel-Ksieski, Germany 1998, and now 10 ♗g2 would have left White with an attractive position due to the difficulties Black will have in resolving the pawn position in the centre (in the game White solved the problem for Black with 10 dxe6?!). White can meet 4...h6 quite effectively with 5 ♗xf6 ♕xf6 6 e4, when his permanent space advantage and better development more than compensate for Black's possession of the bishop pair.

3...♗b4 4 ♕d3 d5 5 ♘f3 transposes to Hector-Berg in Chapter 8, and 3...d5 is also covered in Chapter 8.

4 ♗xf6 ♕xf6 5 e4

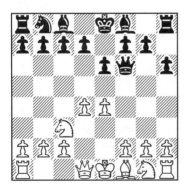

Reaching a position which is well known

from the Trompovsky.

5...d6

Black can also play 5...g6, although this gives up the option of an extended fianchetto with ...g7-g5, which prevents White's dangerous and expansive plan based on ♕d2 and f2-f4. After 6 ♕d2 ♗g7 7 0-0-0 0-0 8 f4 d6 9 ♘f3 b6 10 h4 h5 11 e5 ♕e7 12 ♗d3 ♗b7 13 ♘e4 ♘d7 14 ♘fg5 dxe5 15 fxe5 c5 16 c3 cxd4 17 cxd4 ♖ad8 18 ♔b1 ♘b8 19 ♘d6 White was more comfortable in Gelfand-Rozentalis, Tilburg (rapid) 1992, while he was also better in Benjamin-Yermolinsky, US Ch. Playoff 1994 after 6...d6 7 f4 ♕e7 8 ♘f3 ♗g7 9 0-0-0 a6 10 ♗d3 ♘d7 11 f5 e5 12 ♘d5 ♕d8 13 dxe5 ♘xe5 14 ♖hf1 c6 15 ♘e3 0-0 16 ♘xe5 ♗xe5 17 ♘g4.

6 ♕d2 g5

Preventing White's f2-f4 idea. 6...g6 7 f4 transposes to the 5...g6 lines above.

7 ♗c4!?

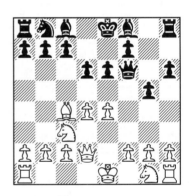

An interesting and quite dangerous idea. White intends to put his knight on e2, castle kingside and then possibly open up the f-file with f2-f4. Another idea is to bring his knight to h5 via g3. Several other moves have been tried, for example:

a) 7 0-0-0 ♗g7 8 g3 ♘c6 9 ♗b5 (9 ♘b5 ♕d8 10 ♘e2 a6 11 ♘bc3 b5!? gave Black counterplay in Adams-Topalov, Madrid 1996) 9...♗d7 10 ♘ge2 a6 11 ♗xc6 ♗xc6 12 f4 0-0-0 13 ♖hf1 1-0 was Hodgson-Gabriel, Horgen 1995. Alternatively 8 e5 dxe5 9 dxe5

♕e7 10 f4 ♘c6 11 ♘f3 ♗d7 12 h4 gxf4 13 ♕xf4 0-0-0 14 ♘e4 ♘b8!, intending ....♗c6 and ...♘d7, gave Black a good game in Adams-Karpov, Las Palmas 1994, while 8 ♔b1 ♘c6 9 ♗b5 ♗d7 10 e5?! dxe5 11 d5 exd5 12 ♘xd5 ♕d6 left White with inadequate compensation in Gunter-Britton, Hastings 1995.

b) 7 h4!? ♗g7 (7...g4!? 8 f4 gxf3 9 gxf3 h5 10 f4 ♗h6 11 ♘ge2 ♘c6 12 0-0-0 ♗d7 13 ♔b1 0-0-0 14 ♕e3 e5 was double-edged in Forchert-Brenke, Bundesliga, Germany 1996) 8 hxg5 hxg5 9 ♖xh8+ ♗xh8 10 0-0-0 ♘c6 11 ♘f3 ♕f4 (according to Tsesarsky 11...g4 would have been good for White after 12 ♘b5 ♔d8 13 e5! ♕g7 14 ♘g1) 12 ♕xf4 gxf4 13 ♗b5 ♗d7 14 ♘e2! e5 15 ♖h1 and White had the better endgame in Tyomkin-Tsesarsky, Ramat Aviv 2000.

7...♘c6 8 ♘ge2 ♗g7 9 ♖d1 ♗d7 10 0-0 0-0-0

According to Anand White would meet 10...0-0 with 11 ♕e3, intending f2-f4.

11 ♘b5!

The immediate 11 b4 is less effective due to 11...g4 12 b5 ♘a5, when the knight does a good job in holding up White's attack.

11...a6 12 ♘a3

Threatening to launch a queenside pawn storm with 13 c3 and 14 b4. Black must react quickly before his position becomes critical.

12...g4! 13 f4 gxf3 14 ♖xf3 ♕e7 15 c3 h5 16 ♖df1 ♖df8 17 b4 ♘a7 18 ♘c2 ♗h6 19 ♕e1 ♔b8 20 ♗d3 ♗c6! 21 ♘f4

♖fg8 22 d5

22 ♘xh5 is strongly met with 22...f5.

22...♗e8

After 22...♗xf4 White plays 23 dxc6! e5 24 cxb7 in order to weaken Black's queenside.

23 ♕f2

23 ♘xh5? is still a dubious proposition after 23...♕g5! 24 ♘g3 ♕h4 with dangerous threats.

23...♗g7 24 ♘d4! ♗d7 25 dxe6 ♗xd4 26 cxd4 fxe6 27 e5 ♗c6 28 ♘g6 ♕d8??

An oversight which costs Black the game. He should play 28...♖xg6, when 29 ♗xg6 (29 ♖f8+ ♖xf8 30 ♕xf8+ ♘c8 31 ♗xg6 ♕g5 wins for Black) 29...♗xf3 30 ♕xf3 dxe5 31 dxe5 ♘c6 (or 31...♕xb4 32 ♕f6) 32 ♕f6 offers White slightly preferable prospects.

29 ♘xh8 ♗xf3 30 ♘f7 ♕h4

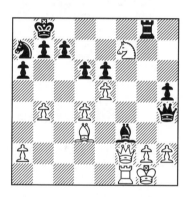

Forcing White to be careful. After 30...♗xg2 White wins with 31 ♘xd8 ♗e4+ 32 ♕g3 ♖xg3+ 33 hxg3 ♗xd3 34 ♖f8! etc.

31 ♕xf3

Not 31 ♕xh4?? ♖xg2+ 32 ♔h1 ♖f2+ with a draw.

31...♕xd4+ 32 ♔h1 d5 33 ♖d1! ♕xb4 34 ♖b1 ♕a4 35 ♕xh5 ♘c6 36 ♕e2 ♗a7 37 ♕f2+ b6 38 ♖c1! ♔b7 39 h3! ♖c8 40 ♕f6

Having secured his defences White can finally go after the e6-pawn.

40...♘d4 41 ♘d8+!

Anand pointed out that White could also

play 41 ♘d6+, when 41...cxd6 42 ♕e7+ ♚b8 43 ♖xc8+ ♚xc8 44 exd6 ♕c6 45 ♕f8+ (45 ♗xa6+ is probably also good) 45...♚d7 46 ♕g7+ ♚xd6 47 ♕xd4 wins without too much trouble.

41...♚b8 42 ♘xe6 1-0

After 42...♕a3 43 ♖d1 White is simply a piece up.

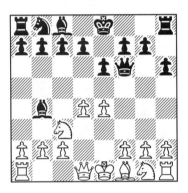

Game 80
Hall-De Firmian
Malmo 1999

1 d4 ♘f6 2 ♘c3 e6 3 ♗g5 h6 4 ♗xf6 ♕xf6 5 e4 ♗b4

According to Trompovsky guru Julian Hodgson this is the most testing continuation. Black proceeds with his development and after exchanging his dark-squared bishop will put his central pawns on dark squares.

6 ♕d2

The sharpest continuation, but not the only one. White has also tried simple development with 6 ♘f3, when 6...d5 7 e5 ♕d8 8 a3 ♗e7 9 ♗d3 c5 10 dxc5 ♗xc5 11 0-0 ♘c6 12 b4 ♗e7 13 ♘b5 a6 14 ♘bd4 ♕b6 15 c3 ♗d7 16 ♕d2 ♖c8 17 ♖ac1 gave White a clear advantage in the form of his nicely centralised pieces in Akopian-Antonio, Las Vegas 1999. Igor Stohl's suggestion of 6...♗xc3+ 7 bxc3 d6 should be met with 8 e5 before Black plays that move himself and fixes the central pawns on dark squares.

Tchoubar-Solozhenkin, New York 1994 continued 8...dxe5 9 ♘xe5 ♘d7 10 ♗b5 c6 11 ♘xd7 ♗xd7 12 ♗d3 0-0 13 ♕g4 ♖ac8 14 ♖b1 b6 15 0-0 c5 16 ♗a6 ♖c7 17 ♕g3 ♕d8 18 ♖fd1 and White had the initiative. Another possibility is 6...d6 but after 7 ♕d2 ♘d7 8 a3 ♗a5 I think that 9 b4 ♗b6 10 ♘a4 followed by 11 c4 gives White a space advantage that will not be easy to combat.

6...c5

Black's main alternative is the solid 6...d6. Gallagher has suggested the immediate 7 f4 but this seems to be well answered by 7...e5. Instead there is 7 a3, e.g. 7...♗xc3 (7...♗a5 8 ♘ge2 c6?! 9 b4 ♗c7 10 a4 0-0?! 11 a5 left Black very cramped in Knaak-Enders, Bundesliga 1998) 8 ♕xc3 ♘c6 (Black has also tried 8...0-0 9 ♘f3 ♕e7 but then 10 ♗d3 b6 11 0-0 ♗b7 12 ♖ae1 c5 13 d5 still leaves White with a useful space advantage) 9 ♘f3 0-0 10 ♗d3 ♕e7 11 e5 (White has to do this before Black equalises with his own ...e6-e5) 11...f6 (11...♖d8 12 0-0 ♗d7 13 ♖fe1 dxe5 14 dxe5 left Black with little breathing space in Szymanski-Balogh, Artek 1999) 12 exd6 cxd6 13 0-0 f5 14 ♖ae1 ♕f6 15 b4 a6 16 a4 ♖d8 17 b5 axb5 18 axb5 ♘e7 19 ♖a1 ♘d5 20 ♕b3 ♗d7 21 ♖fe1 and the tension was building in White's favour in Gelfand-Rozentalis, Tilburg 1994.

7 a3 ♗xc3 8 bxc3 d6 9 f4!?

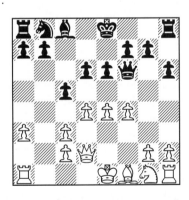

This enterprising continuation is the most dangerous for Black, and it might also be dangerous for White. After his brilliant win against Yudasin (see below), Hodgson curiously switched to 9 ♘f3, when Hodgson-Rowson, York 2000 continued 9...0-0 10 ♗e2 ♘c6 11 0-0 e5 12 dxc5 dxc5 13 ♕e3 ♗g4 (13...b6 14 ♗c4 ♗g4 was equal in Hodgson-De Firmian, Amsterdam 1996) 14 ♕xc5 ♖fc8 15 ♕e3 ♕f4 16 ♕xf4 exf4 17 ♖ab1 ♗xf3 18 gxf3 b6 when White's extra pawn was quite immaterial. The suspicion must be that he does not like 9 f4 e5!?, although the consequences do not seem terribly clear.

9...e5!?

Taking some dark squares before White gets in 10 e5. In Hodgson-Yudasin, New York 1994 White stood better after 9...0-0 10 ♘f3 ♘c6 11 ♗b5 ♘a5 12 ♗d3 b6 13 0-0 ♗b7 14 ♖ae1 ♖ac8 15 e5 ♕e7 16 f5 etc.

10 ♗b5+ ♗d7 11 ♖b1!

Maintaining the initiative. 11 ♗xd7+ ♘xd7 leaves Black excellently placed.

11...exf4?

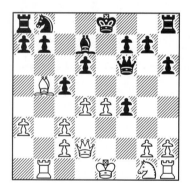

After this the position resembles a King's Gambit – in fact quite a good one because White soon recovers his pawn. It seems preferable to play 11...cxd4 12 cxd4 exd4, when 13 ♘f3 (13 ♗xd7+ ♘xd7 14 ♖xb7 meets with 14...♘c5) 13...♘c6 14 0-0 0-0 15 ♘xd4

♖fe8 is about equal.

12 ♘e2 g5 13 ♗xd7+ ♘xd7 14 ♖xb7

Now Black has serious problems because the powerful posting of White's rook on the seventh rank causes a certain amount of inconvenience; Black must lose time castling.

14...♘b6 15 ♕d3 ♕e6

White meets 15...0-0 with 16 h4, when all his pieces are converging on Black's king.

16 h4 ♕c8

Black could win the exchange with 16...c4 17 ♕f3 ♕c8 but after 18 ♖xb6 axb6 19 hxg5 ♖xa3 20 ♔d2 White threatens both 21 hxg6 and 21 ♘f4 and gets excellent positional compensation.

17 ♕a6 0-0 18 hxg5 hxg5 19 e5!

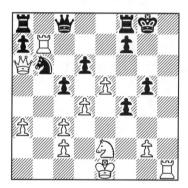

McShane gave 19 ♕d3 as winning for White after 19...♕xb7 20 ♕h3 f6 21 ♕h8+ ♔f7 22 ♕h7+ but Black can improve on this with 19...♖d8.

19...♖e8?

Losing. McShane recommended 19...c4 but after 20 exd6 ♖e8 White can win with 21 d7 ♘xd7 22 ♕h6 etc. Black's only chance is 19...♘c4, although after 20 exd6 it is probably good for White in any case.

20 ♕d3! 1-0

20...♕xb7 21 ♕h7+ ♔f8 22 ♕h6 ♔e7 (22...♔g8 23 ♕h8 mate) 23 ♕xd6 is mate.

Summary

Conventional wisdom states that Black doesn't need to worry about the Veresov if he plays the Pirc or Schmid Benoni. I don't think this is the case, White can keep the game in Veresov channels, which are very dangerous for Black.

Once again the attempt to transpose to the French (this time with 1...♞f6 and 2...e6) can be side-stepped by White quite effectively.

1 d4 ♞f6 2 ♞c3 c5 *(D)*

    2...g6 3 ♗g5 - *Game 77*

    2...d6 3 ♗g5 - *Game 78*

    2...e6 3 ♗g5 h6 4 ♗xf6 ♛xf6 5 e4 *(D)*

        5...d6 - *Game 79*; 5...♗b4 - *Game 80*

3 ♗g5

    3 dxc5 - *Game 76*

3...cxd4

    3...♛a5 - *Game 75*

4 ♛xd4 ♞c6 5 ♛h4 *(D)*

    5...e6 - *Game 73*; 5...b5 - *Game 74*

    2 c5   *5 e4*   *5 ♛h4*

INDEX OF COMPLETE GAMES